HOW TO SAVE OR MAKE THOUSANDS
WHEN YOU BUY OR SELL YOUR HOUSE

HOW TO SAVE OR MAKE THOUSANDS WHEN YOU BUY OR SELL YOUR HOUSE

By Jens and Jackie Nielsen

ILLUSTRATED BY RON DUCKWITZ
EDITED BY MARY LYON

DOLPHIN BOOKS
DOUBLEDAY & COMPANY, INC., GARDEN CITY, NEW YORK

Originally published by Doubleday & Company in 1971.
DOLPHIN BOOKS editions 1974, revised 1979

ISBN: 0-385-13522-X
Library of Congress Catalog Card Number 78–62635

PREFACE

Under what conditions do you owe the broker commission?

Under what conditions will your earnest money be returned to you?

How much less than your listing price will you receive from the sale of the property?

What prorating method will be used?

Who owns the fixtures?

These are just a few of the questions answered in this book. A wrong answer can cost you thousands of dollars just as a correct answer can save you thousands of dollars.

Our objective is to acquaint you with a typical real estate transaction: to investigate what a buyer should expect from a seller, what a seller should expect from a buyer, and what each can expect from the real estate broker.

This book is not intended to be a substitute for a real estate broker or attorney. Real estate laws differ by states, so it is impossible to handle in one book a discussion of real estate law as it applies to all situations.

Your real estate broker and your attorney are essential to an equitable and harmonious real estate transaction.

We hope that our interpretation of the laws surrounding the typical real estate transaction will stimulate you to ask questions and to make inquiries and will persuade you to complete the worksheets in this book before entering upon a real estate transaction.

CONTENTS

PART II. BE A WISE BUYER

PART III. LEGAL AND FINANCIAL ASPECTS OF REAL ESTATE TRANSACTIONS

PART I

Be a Wise Seller

Chapter One

THE COST OF SELLING A HOUSE

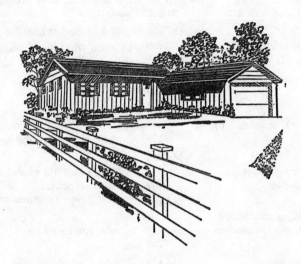

THE SORRY TALE OF WOEFUL BILL

Three weeks ago Bill Nordeen was optimistic, even enthusiastic. Bill had been given a substantial promotion with a raise to match it.

One of the provisions of Bill's promotion was that he move. Bill would have to move his family, his wife and four children, to another community over five hundred miles away.

At first Bill's family didn't like the idea of moving and leaving their friends. However, after spending two weekends in the other community looking for a house, exploring the church and school systems, and the facilities for entertainment and recreation, they changed their minds.

Next Bill found a year-old house which his wife adored. Even the children were beginning to look forward to moving; two acres went with the property so at last Bill would be able to buy his children the pony they wanted.

To excite Bill even more, the property, he learned, could be bought for only $70,000. Three years before, Bill had paid $70,000 for the property he now owned, but since then the neighborhood had blossomed with new shopping centers and handsome new houses. Land values had soared.

Bill listed his property for sale at $70,000, confident that he could find a buyer at that price. During the first week after he had listed his property, he received offers of $65,000 and $67,000 which he refused. Then ten days after he had listed the property, Bill's broker brought him a buyer who was willing to pay the full $70,000 for the property.

Bill was proud of this maneuver, for he had originally paid $70,000 for the property, had lived in it for three years, and had then been able to sell it for $70,000. Now he could sell his property and buy the new property without any money lost. Bill had made a "good deal."

Today Bill is still bewildered about what happened. Instead of receiving $70,000—the selling price agreed upon—Bill ended up with only $64,130 from the sale of his property. What had happened?

Bill simply hadn't stopped congratulating himself on what a good deal he had made long enough to consider what it would cost him to sell his property. Let's look at what happened to poor Bill, who sold his property for $70,000 but ended up with only $64,130.

How Bill Sold for $70,000 yet Received Only $64,130

Price paid by the buyer:	$70,000
Subtract: Broker's commission of 6%	$4,200
	$65,800
Subtract: Attorney's fee at closing	$400
	$65,400
Subtract: Cost of title policy demanded by the buyers	$220
	$65,180
Subtract: Cost of survey demanded by the buyers	$250
	$64,930
Subtract: Cost of real estate taxes prorated at time of closing	$600
	$64,330
Subtract: Cost of paying a contractor's lien for work done during the previous year	$200
Amount received by Bill	$64,130

The buyer actually paid Bill $70,000 for the property, but Bill's selling costs were $5,870, hence he only had $64,130 left after paying these costs; $5,870 went toward paying the costs of closing the real estate transaction.

Today Bill is dissatisfied, unhappy with his broker, and not nearly as enthusiastic about his move into the new community and the new house as he was when he agreed to sell for $70,000. He thinks that somehow he lost $5,870 when he sold his house.

Bill wasn't cheated. He was just careless. If he had wanted actually to receive $70,000 from the sale of his property, he should have taken the time and made the effort to learn what his closing costs would be. This would have involved making some telephone calls and asking some questions, but it would have prevented Bill's big disappointment.

If Bill had taken the time and made the effort to learn what his closing costs would be, he could then have arrived at his selling price in the following manner:

How Bill Could Have Received $70,000 from That Sale

Dollars that Bill wanted to receive from the sale of his property:	$70,000
Add: Broker's commission at 6%	$4,200
	$74,200
Add: Attorney's fees	$400
	$74,600
Add: Cost of title policy	$220
	$74,820
Add: Cost of survey	$250
	$75,070
Add: Prorated real estate taxes	$600
	$75,670
Add: Cost of having a contractor's lien removed	$200
Selling price if Bill wanted to actually receive $70,000	$75,870

THE COST OF SELLING

Usually a seller decides on a selling price through some sort of mental gymnastics. If he doesn't get his asking price, he rationalizes the fact by telling himself that his original asking price was too high.

Seldom is a property originally offered at a fair market value: a price that an able buyer is willing to pay, a price that a seller is willing to sell for.

Instead, the final selling price results from bar-gaining and negotiating between the seller and buyer. As a seller, be prepared to make concessions to your buyer. But be aware also of what your selling costs may be.

The Appraisal (a must)

The appraisal is a professional's opinion of the true market value of the property.

Don't be surprised if your prospective buyer in his offer to purchase your property requests that you supply an appraisal of the property. He may even make the other conditions of his offer dependent upon the appraisal. With an appraisal the buyer is assured that he is not offering more for the property than it is worth.

What assurance have you that you aren't selling the property for less than its true market value? Can you afford to lose $1,000 or $5,000 because you underprice your property?

Have an appraisal made of your property before you decide on a selling price. (Refer to pages 21–22 for appraisals.) Are you content to sell for the appraised value? Even though the buyer agrees to pay your asking price, based on the appraised value, you will end up with less because of your selling costs.

For example, the appraiser decides that your property is worth $65,000, so you list and sell it for $65,000. After the deal is closed, you have $62,000 or perhaps only $60,000, depending upon what it cost you to sell the property.

Selling costs fall into two groups—those you have as a matter of course and those which result from negotiating with the buyer.

Broker's Commission (always)

In the listing contract you agree to pay the broker a commission when he produces a buyer for you at a price and on terms acceptable to you. His commission may be 5% or even 10% of the selling price, depending upon the sort of property and local practices.

Anticipate this expense and add it to the net dollars you want to receive from the sale of your property. (Refer to pages 17–19 on when you owe commission.)

Attorney's Fee (always)

You are expected to supply the buyer with an abstract of title and a deed to the property. (The abstract continuation costs—the charge by the abstract company for bringing your abstract up to date—is usually paid by the attorney, who then collects from you.)

You will also owe the attorney for drafting your deed, for checking your sales contract, and for representing you at the closing.

Attorneys usually base their fees on a schedule recommended by the local bar association. Depending upon the local practices, this could be anywhere from 1% to 2% of the selling price. Usually when the selling price is more than $30,-000 a percentage isn't used; the rate is negotiated between the seller and his attorney.

Ask your attorney what his fee will be and add this amount to the net dollars you want to receive from the sale of the property.

Proration of Real Estate Taxes (always)

Whoever holds title to the property at the end of the tax year is expected to pay the real estate tax on the property for that year.

For example, you sell the property on June 30. You held title for the first six months of the year and the buyer owns the property for the last six months of the year. The buyer will receive the tax bill for the entire year.

You owned the property for the first six months of the year so you owe the taxes for that period. At the closing you pay the buyer an amount equal to six months' taxes on the property. When the tax is due, the buyer pays the entire amount. (Refer to pages 117–119 for prorating.)

State Real Estate Transfer Taxes or Fees (possible)

Some states impose a tax or fee upon the seller when he transfers his property title to another. Most state laws, where real estate transfer taxes are imposed, require that the tax be paid before the local recorders will record the instrument by which the title is transferred.

Does your state impose a real estate transfer tax or fee on the sale of real estate? Some examples are:

State	Amount	What is taxed
New York	.05% of the net when the sale exceeds $25,000	Assumed mortgages are excluded from the tax base.
Illinois	50¢ for each $500 or fraction thereof.	If the property is sold subject to a mortgage, amount of the mortgage is excluded from the tax base.
Pennsylvania	1%	Pennsylvania has authorized local governmental units to levy this tax. (Check with your local officials.) Assumed mortgages are excluded from the tax base.
Massachusetts	$1 for each $500 or fraction thereof.	Assumed mortgages are excluded from the tax base.

Income Tax from Profitable Sale of Your House (possibly)

Buy a house with a small down payment and with monthly payments less than rent. Keep it in good repair and make a few improvements. Sell it wisely and realize a handsome profit.

But how handsome is your profit—the return on the dollars you invested—when you have to pay an income tax on it?

Will you have to pay an income tax on your sale? How much? Study the chapters which explore the requirement to pay an income tax on the profitable sale of your house.

Special Assessments (possibly)

Special assessments are charges against a property for improvements which benefit the property. These charges are usually made payable over several years. (Refer to page 99 for special assessments.)

For example, last year your street was widened at a cost to you of $500 payable over a five-year period. You still owe $400 on the assessment. The buyer probably will ask that this entire balance be paid before he accepts title to the property.

Have you any unpaid special assessments?

Survey (possibly)

The survey is a diagram of the property showing lot lines and all encroachments. A wise buyer will want a survey of the property and usually will ask the seller to supply it and pay for it. Anticipate this selling cost.

Liens (possibly)

A contractor may place a lien on your property for the cost of labor, services, and materials he supplied for the improvement of your property. (Refer to pages 125–127 for liens.)

Have you any unpaid bills for work done on the property? Possibly a lien has been placed on your property. The buyer will ask that liens be removed before he accepts title to the property.

Owner's Policy of Title Insurance (possibly)

This is a commitment by a title insurance company declaring that the title to the property is merchantable. Under the conditions written into the contract, they agree to defend the policyholder if there are any attacks against the title. (Refer to pages 90–91 for owner's policy of title insurance.)

The buyer may pay for this insurance but usually he makes it a part of his offer to purchase contract that the seller provide the owner's policy of title insurance.

Costs depend upon the value of the property and the number of problems the insurance company anticipates if they have to defend the title. Usually there is a minimum fee for the first $1,000 of value and a sliding scale of fees for values over $1,000. On a $55,000 house, anticipate a fee of around $200.

Points (possibly)

With an FHA (Federal Housing Administration) insured loan or a VA (Veteran's Administration) guaranteed loan, there are usually "points" charged. (Refer to page 138.)

The interest rates on FHA-insured and VA-guaranteed loans are controlled by the Government and usually these interest rates are lower than the rates on other types of mortgage loans. The lender makes up the difference by charging points, with each point being 1% of the mortgage.

For example, the FHA can insure loans made at not more than 8½% plus ½% for the mortgage insurance. Lending agencies are charging 9½% on first mortgage loans. The lending agency agrees to the loan at 9% but only if it is allowed to charge 8 points. The mortgage is for $40,000, so the charge for 8 points is $3,200. The Government requires that the borrower not pay these points directly, so it frequently becomes an added cost to the seller.

If your buyer will use FHA-insured or VA-guaranteed financing, who will pay the points charge?

Closing Costs When Buying Another House (possibly)

When you sell your house and buy another, in addition to paying the costs of selling, you have to pay the costs of buying another house. This is not a direct cost of selling but it should be remembered since it will account for some of the dollars which seem to disappear when you sell a house and rebuy.

Probably you will hire professionals to move your personal possessions, at least your furniture and appliances. Will you have to refinance when you buy your next house? Probably the interest is now higher than it was when you financed your present house. Again you will need the services of an attorney to check the marketability of the title, to check that zoning regulations are complied with, and possibly to prepare a new mortgage for you.

If instead of buying another house, you plan to rent, possibly you will have to pay a tax on the profit you realized through the sale of your house. Your selling costs will vary according to how many concessions you make to the buyer. For example, will you agree to furnish him with a survey of the property at your expense or will you refuse because you already have your selling price at a minimum?

When you deduct selling costs from the net dollars you want to receive for the property, you lose. When you originally price your property at a minimum, every concession you make to a buyer will be just one more disappointment to you.

Estimate what your total selling costs will be. To arrive at a selling price, add this total to the actual dollars you want to receive from the sale of the property. You can always negotiate and agree to a lower price if you escape some of your anticipated selling costs.

WORKSHEET FOR COMPUTING PRICE AT WHICH TO LIST YOUR PROPERTY TO RECEIVE THE DOLLARS YOU WANT

Actual net dollars you want to receive from the sale of your
property $_____

    Add cost of an appraisal $_____

    Add broker's commission $_____

    Add attorney's fees $_____

    Add your share of the real estate taxes (prorated) $_____

    Possibly add state real estate transfer taxes or fees $_____

    Possibly add income tax from the profitable sale of your
        house $_____

    Possibly add unpaid balances on special assessments $_____

    Possibly add the cost of a survey $_____

    Possibly add the cost of having liens removed $_____

    Possibly add cost of an owner's policy of title insurance $_____

    Possibly add a charge for points if the buyer will use FHA-
        insured or VA-guaranteed mortgage financing $_____
    Price at which you should list your property $_____

Delay completing this worksheet until after you have read the other chapters under "Be a Wise Seller," but DO complete this worksheet before determining a price at which to list your property for sale.

Chapter Two

RELATIONSHIP OF SELLER AND BROKER: LISTINGS

RELATIONSHIP CREATED WHEN YOU SIGN A LISTING

When you list your property for sale with a real estate broker, the signed listing is your employment contract with the broker.

You create an agency relationship—you are the principal and the broker is your agent—in which the broker agrees to work for you, on your behalf, and under your direction in exchange for your agreement to pay him a commission if he performs certain functions for you.

The broker has a fiduciary duty to you to make a continuous, bona fide effort to find a buyer for your property at the price and on the terms you have outlined in your listing contract, or at a price and on such terms as are otherwise acceptable to you.

You employ the broker to find a purchaser for you—not to sell your property. What if your broker finds a purchaser at the price and on the terms outlined in your listing contract and then you decide you don't want to sell? Has he fulfilled his employment contract and is he entitled to his commission even though the property isn't sold? (Refer to pages 17–19, dealing with situations in which you must pay commission.)

As your employee or agent, your broker's duty is to represent the property honestly to all prospective buyers. Do not expect your broker to misrepresent your property or to fail to disclose pertinent facts to prospective buyers solely be-

cause you, as the broker's employer, would prefer that certain things remain undisclosed.

The doctrine of *caveat emptor,* which means "let the buyer beware" and under which a purchaser buys at his own risk, does not apply to real estate transactions.

Your real estate broker operates under the doctrine of elementary fair conduct, which dictates that he must honestly represent properties to all prospective buyers.

The doctrine of elementary fair conduct dictates that the broker be liable when:

The broker intentionally misrepresents property to a buyer, or

The broker through carelessness makes a misrepresentation to the buyer, and the buyer believes this misrepresentation, acts upon it, and is damaged because he believed it and acted upon it, or

The broker remains silent, failing to mention to the buyer something about the property which could influence the buyer's opinion as to the value of the property.

Expect your broker to make a professional, continuous, bona fide effort to find a purchaser for your property. Do not expect your broker to misrepresent your property to any prospective purchaser.

LISTINGS

A listing contract is the creation of an agency whereby the broker agrees to work for you and on your behalf in exchange for a commission if he is able to find a purchaser ready, willing, and able to purchase your property at the price and

on the terms outlined in your listing or at any other price and terms acceptable to you.

A listing contract is simply a form of employment contract.

Most listing contracts are of the exclusive type.

They are preferred by brokers, and when employed through an exclusive listing contract, brokers work harder and spend more time than with other types of listing.

Exclusive Listings

You should use an exclusive listing contract since it is the type most likely to produce a buyer for you. Exclusive listings differ as to when you owe commission.

The broker receives commission regardless of who finds the buyer:

With this type of contract, the broker is entitled to commission when the property is sold or a purchaser is found, whether or not the purchaser was found by him, by another broker, or by anybody else.

If you sign this contract and personally sell the property during the term of the contract, you probably will still owe commission.

With another type of exclusive listing, the broker does not receive commission if the seller makes a private sale.

With this type of contract, you are not required to pay commission if you personally locate the buyer and make the sale.

If the broker locates the buyer or has negotiated with him, you may not make a private sale to escape paying commission.

It will be up to the court to decide who actually found the purchaser. In most cases if the broker aggressively advertises the property, it will be difficult to deny his role in bringing the purchaser to you.

Joint Exclusive Listing Contract

With a joint exclusive listing contract you list your property with two brokers who work together to sell your property. They split the commission according to their own agreement.

This differs from an open listing in that you agree to pay commission to these two brokers only if they procure a purchaser for you during the life of the listing. In an open listing you make no guarantee as to how many brokers have been given the opportunity to find a buyer for you.

The joint exclusive listing contract may provide that the broker receive his commission regardless of who procures the purchaser. You pay commission even though you personally sell the property.

Or the joint listing may provide that you are not required to pay commission if you personally sell the property.

REVOCATION OF EXCLUSIVE LISTINGS

With the listing contract you enter into an agreement whereby you agree to pay a broker commission if he finds a buyer for you at the price and on the terms outlined in your listing or any price and terms acceptable to you. You give the broker the exclusive right to find a buyer for you during a given period of time—the listing period.

After you give the broker this right, why should you wish to break the contract and terminate the listing?

While employed by the contract the broker is duty-bound to make a continuous, bona fide effort to find a buyer for you. Perhaps you think he is not making an adequate effort. May you then cancel the listing contract?

Yes, in some cases, but be prepared to prove that the broker has not made a continuous, bona fide effort and to prove that you wish to cancel the listing in good faith.

No, if at the time you wish to terminate the contract the broker has a signed offer from a purchaser who is ready, willing, and able to purchase the property.

No, if the broker can prove that he has made and is making a continuous, bona fide effort to sell the property.

Even though you are able to prove to a court's satisfaction that you are operating in good faith, when you want to terminate an exclusive listing, in some cases the broker will be reimbursed for expenses incurred while trying to find a buyer for you.

ADVANTAGES OF EXCLUSIVE LISTINGS

1. Readily accepted by all brokers, and
2. Brokers make a maximum effort to fulfill terms of the contract, and
3. Fairest to the broker.

DISADVANTAGES OF EXCLUSIVE LISTINGS

1. Except for joint listings, the listing is restricted to the efforts of one broker, and
2. There can be misunderstandings as to when the seller owes commission.

WARNINGS

When you enter into an exclusive listing, be sure it is clearly understood whether you have to pay commission if you personally sell the property.

Do not list your property for long periods. It varies in different areas, but six months is usually considered reasonable for the sale of urban property and one year for rural property. It is wiser to list for a shorter period with the option of renewing the listing than it is to tie up the property for an unreasonable length of time through an exclusive listing.

Know whether your listing contract contains a "standard negotiation clause" and, if it does, understand the implications of this clause.

Usually this clause provides that you may owe your broker a commission even though he is unable to procure a purchaser for you during the listing period if:

1. The broker negotiated with a likely purchaser during the term of the listing, and
2. If the broker submitted this likely purchaser's name to you in writing prior to the expiration of the listing, and
3. If this named person actually buys the property within six months after the termination of the listing.

Open Listings

With an open listing contract, even though you may list the property with several brokers, you agree to pay commission only to the broker who actually sells the property on the terms outlined in the listing or at any other price and terms acceptable to you.

You may list the property with many brokers at the same time. You create employment contracts in which you agree to pay commission only to the broker who actually finds a buyer for you.

REVOCATION OF OPEN LISTINGS

Provided your contracts do not specify otherwise, you may cancel the listings at any time before a broker produces a buyer agreeable to purchasing the property at your price and on your terms. All listings are automatically terminated when the property is sold.

Any cancellation of the listing contracts prior to the sale of the property must be in good faith and not to escape paying commission.

For example, a broker receives an offer at a price lower than your listing price. You refuse the offer and cancel your listings. Then you make a private sale to the buyer at the lower price. You intentionally canceled the listing to escape paying commission. A court would probably require you to pay commission, as the broker fulfilled his employment contract (listing contract) with you when he produced a buyer ready, willing, and able to buy on terms acceptable to you.

ADVANTAGES OF OPEN LISTINGS

1. It is possible to have many brokers working for you—trying to find a buyer for you, and
2. Usually you can personally sell the property and not have to pay commission.

DISADVANTAGES OF OPEN LISTINGS

1. Brokers will not work as hard under an open listing contract (using their time and money) as they will under an exclusive listing contract, and
2. Many outstanding brokers won't accept open listings.

WARNINGS

Have it clearly understood, and in writing, whether you will be required to pay commission if you personally sell the property.

Have it clearly understood whether or not you are required to reimburse the brokers for expenditures they've made in their efforts to sell your property if you cancel your listing contracts.

For example, with an open listing, you may have many brokers working for you. If you want to cancel all the listings, will you have to reimburse each broker for his advertising costs?

Have it clearly understood at what price and under what terms you agree to sell the property. If you sell at a lower price and then, a day later, one of the listing brokers produces a buyer ready, willing, and able to pay your original price, will you owe the broker commission?

Oral Listings

In most states a real estate broker may not bring a court action against his principal (the seller) to collect commission due him on an oral listing.

Usually, before a contract for the sale of real estate is legally binding and commission has to be paid, the contract must:

1. Be in writing, and
2. Describe the real estate listed, and
3. State the price, and
4. State the terms of the sale, and
5. List the commission to be paid, and
6. Must be signed by the person who agrees to pay the commission.

Why should a broker make any effort to sell a property when all he has is an oral listing? If he accepts your oral listing and makes an effort to sell the property, be complimented because he is showing faith in your integrity. If he refuses your oral listing, don't be insulted, as it isn't good business to spend time and money working under a contract which can't be enforced.

If a broker does spend his time and money in an effort to find a purchaser for you under an oral listing, you have a moral obligation to pay him the orally agreed upon commission if he locates a buyer for you.

ADVANTAGES OF ORAL LISTINGS

1. None

DISADVANTAGES OF ORAL LISTINGS

1. Usually not legally binding, and
2. Brokers are reluctant to spend time and money working under oral contracts, and

3. Most brokers will make little effort to sell the property for you if you are not sincere enough to give them a written listing.

WARNINGS

In some cases even with oral listings the courts have decided that the seller has accepted the commission as a debt and has a legal obligation to pay the debt. For example, when you pay the broker cash toward his commission, it can be held that you recognized and accepted the debt and have an obligation to pay it.

Also, if as payment toward his commission you give the broker a promissory note, you give money to a third person to hold for the broker, or you give the broker a written promise to pay him, you declare that you owe the debt and assume the legal obligation to pay the commission.

Net Listings

A net listing contract provides that the commission you owe the broker when he finds a buyer for you will be the difference between your listing price and the actual amount the broker receives from the sale of the property.

For example, you enter into a net listing contract with a broker agreeing to sell your home for $45,000 and agreeing to allow the broker any money he receives from the sale of your house in excess of $45,000. He sells your house for $55,000 and, in this case, he receives as his commission $55,000 less your listing price of $45,000 or $10,000.

This is why net listings are undesirable and very rarely used. Wouldn't you feel cheated if a broker earned $10,000 on the sale of your $45,000 house?

When you sign a listing contract, you create an agency relationship. The broker as your agent is duty-bound to get the best possible deal for you. Can he be working 100% on your behalf when he is trying to earn a maximum profit for himself?

Most brokers wouldn't even consider working under net listing contracts.

Multiple Listing Services

A multiple listing service is a service through which the listing you give one broker is distributed to other brokers so that they may all have a chance to find a buyer for your property.

Usually you deal only with the broker who took your listing and when the property is sold you pay the entire commission directly to him. The listing broker then distributes the commission according to the rules of the multiple listing service.

ADVANTAGES OF MULTIPLE LISTING SERVICES

Many brokers have exposure to your listing and the opportunity to find a buyer for you. This greatly increases your chances of finding a buyer.

DISADVANTAGES OF MULTIPLE LISTING SERVICES

If you do not wish it to be widely known that you want to sell your property, avoid multiple listing services.

BROKER'S DUTIES TO THE SELLER—WHAT HE IS REQUIRED TO DO

Continuous Bona Fide Effort

Your broker should during the entire life of the listing make a continuous, bona fide effort to sell your property at the price and on the terms you have outlined in your listing. He should do more than just put up a "for sale" sign and hope for prospects. He should actively advertise your property, talk to prospects about your property, and show your property to these prospects.

Your broker is duty-bound voluntarily to cancel any exclusive listing if he is unwilling to incur the expense and take the time to make a continuous, bona fide effort to sell the property. (Refer to pages 10–11, 24–25 for exclusive listings.)

If you are dissatisfied with the effort your broker is making to sell your property, possibly you can have the exclusive listing canceled. Check with your attorney. You may cancel the exclusive listing if you can prove that the broker is not making a continuous, bona fide effort to sell the property.

With an open listing in which you agree to pay commission only to the broker who actually sells your property, the broker who doesn't make a continuous, bona fide effort is only depriving himself of a possible commission and hurting his reputation.

If you are dissatisfied with the effort your broker is making under an open listing, simply list your property with another broker. (Refer to pages 11–12 for open listings.)

Undivided Loyalty

Your broker should put your interests above his own and above those of anybody else. When you sign a listing, you put the broker in your employment. As your employee or agent, his loyalties belong to you.

For example, after listing your property, your broker learns that a new highway which will greatly increase the value of your property is being planned. By relaying this information to a prospective buyer, your broker greatly enhances his chances of a sale and of earning his commission. He can present the property as underpriced and as a good investment with the new highway coming in.

However, your broker owes his loyalty to you. In this situation, he is duty-bound to inform you of the impending highway so that you can adjust your selling price.

Confidential Relationship

You are allowed a confidential relationship with your broker. He is not to use information told him in confidence to his own advantage. For example, suppose when you listed your property you confided to your broker that the reason for selling was that you were being transferred and you needed to complete the sale within thirty days.

By telling this to a prospective buyer, your broker would tempt the buyer to make a lower offer on the basis that he knew you wanted and needed to sell within thirty days. Your broker is duty-bound to not disclose information given him in confidence.

BROKER BUYING FOR HIMSELF

Suppose you list your property with a broker at a price which he knows is too low. Or, when the broker takes your listing, he already knows of a prospective buyer who is willing to pay much more than the price at which you have listed it.

The broker could easily make a profit greater than his commission by personally buying your property and then reselling it. Your broker may buy the property you have listed with him only if he informs you that he is buying it for himself and has your consent.

What is to prevent him from having his wife, another member of his family, or one of his employees buy it and then resell it to him at a later date? Without your knowledge and consent, your broker may not buy the listed property outright, through his wife, his relatives, or his employees.

EXTRA PROFITS

Your broker should inform you of all profits which result from the listing.

Perhaps a prospective buyer needs financing and your broker is able to arrange mortgage financing for him. Your broker receives a commission for directing the buyer to the source of financing. Your broker is duty-bound to inform you of this profit, which resulted solely from your listing.

When your broker enters into the listing contract to find a buyer for you, he agrees to work for you and on your behalf for the commission as stated in the listing. Your broker is duty-bound to inform you of all profits other than his commission that result from that listing.

Honest Representation

Your broker is required at all times honestly and fairly to present to prospective buyers the facts about the property you are selling. Perhaps there is a large supermarket within walking distance of the house you are selling. While showing your property to a prospect, your broker learns that one of the things that appeal to the prospect is the accessibility of the supermarket.

You have told your broker that the supermarket will soon be closed and converted into a warehouse. Your broker is required to pass this information on to the prospective buyer even though it will decrease his chances of making a sale and earning his commission.

When you sign the listing contract, you create an agency relationship under which you are responsible for the acts of your agent, the broker.

If your broker misrepresents facts you give him or fails to inform a prospective buyer of pertinent facts, you can be held responsible. This can result in a lost sale for you plus possible court actions and damages.

Keeping of Funds

Your broker is required to deposit all funds belonging to others in his real estate trust account. This includes all money paid by the buyer toward the purchase price of the property.

If personal property other than money is given by the buyer as payment toward the purchase price of the property, your broker is responsible for the safekeeping of this property.

When you accept a buyer's offer to purchase your property and your acceptance is personally delivered or mailed to the buyer, you create a firm contract for the sale of your property.

If the buyer wishes to withdraw from this contract, the broker should not return to the buyer, without your written consent, any earnest money payments the buyer has made toward the purchase price of the property.

Copies of Forms

Listing form. Your broker is required to give you a copy of your signed listing contract. Usually a broker is required to keep a copy of this contract on file for three years.

Offer to purchase form. Your broker should submit to you every offer to purchase he receives from prospective buyers regardless of whether the offers conform to your listing.

Offer to purchase with acceptance contract or sales contract. This is the form on which the buyers outline under what conditions they will buy your property and you, by signing the acceptance, agree to sell your property to them on their terms.

You should receive a copy of this form signed by both you and the buyers. Usually a broker is required to keep a copy of this contract on file for three years.

BROKER'S DUTIES TO THE SELLER—THINGS HE MAY NOT DO

Act as Your Attorney

Your broker may do nothing more than fill in the blank spaces on the forms necessary to execute your real estate transaction. He may not make changes in these forms or draft instruments which he is not authorized to complete.

Your broker may not fill out forms involved in any real estate transaction in which he is not acting as the broker. For example, if you have not listed your property with a certain broker, do not ask that broker as a favor to complete for you forms involved in that transaction.

If your broker is not also an attorney, do not ask him to give you his opinion as to:

1. Your legal rights in a transaction, or
2. The legality of any instrument or form, or
3. The validity of a real estate title.

Your broker may not make provisions in your estate to create a life estate. For example, you may wish for your mother to have the use of your property for her lifetime and then upon her death for the property to be sold, with the money to be distributed among your children. This is a life estate for your mother; drafting it is an attorney's job.

Your broker may not make provisions in your estate to create a remainder estate. For example, you wish for the ownership of your property to be transferred to your son upon your death. Again, this type of estate should be set up by an attorney.

Take a Lien to Collect Commission

Your broker may not put a lien on your property to collect his commission. (Refer to pages 125–127 for liens.)

Someone with whom you have contracted to supply labor or materials for the improvement of your property may put a lien on your property to collect the amount you owe him. If you don't pay him, he may have the property sold to collect the amount due him.

A broker is not allowed to put such a lien on your property to collect his commission. The easiest way for a broker to collect his commission is for him to find a buyer for you on your terms and at your price. Under these conditions there is no question as to whether he has fulfilled his employment contract with you. You should be glad to pay the commission.

Pay Commission to an Unauthorized Person

Your broker may split his commission only with another broker or brokers. (Refer to page 13 for multiple listings.)

For example, as a result of advertising your property, your broker has found another broker who has a buyer for the property. Your broker has the listing but another broker has located the buyer. They are allowed to split the commission.

Your broker is not allowed to pay any part of his commission to any person other than a licensed real estate broker.

Why is this? For example, you list your property and your broker locates a prospect. While visiting with this prospect your broker learns that the prospect intends to question your neighbors about the value of your property and about the quality of the environment.

Before the prospect has a chance to get in touch with your neighbors, your broker approaches them and agrees to pay them $50 each for any help they can give him in selling your property. The $50 could distort your neighbors' opinion as to the real value of your property. It could result in their giving other than a completely honest opinion.

Your broker is duty-bound to present your property honestly to all prospective buyers. He violates this obligation if he in any way distorts the opinion of any other person by paying such person any part of his commission.

Representing More Than One Party

Perhaps your broker has been commissioned by a prospective buyer to locate a particular type of house for him. If the broker locates this property for the buyer, he will collect a finder's fee from him.

Your property perfectly fits the kind of house your broker's buyer wants. The broker stands a good chance of collecting two fees—a finder's fee from the buyer for having found the property for him and a commission from you for having found a buyer for your property.

Is it possible for your broker to be loyal to both buyer and seller? Your broker is duty-bound to try to get the best deal possible for you. In this situation he is also duty-bound to get the best possible deal for the buyer. Is this possible?

Your broker is allowed to represent both you, the seller, and the buyer, but only with your knowledge and consent. In the above example, your broker is duty-bound to inform you of his position with the buyer.

Give Directed Appraisals

Your broker may not give an appraisal of real estate to be listed if his acquiring of the listing is dependent upon the appraisal.

For example, through experience in selling other houses, you know the value of an appraisal in convincing prospective buyers that you are pricing your property fairly. You approach a broker and indicate to him that you would like to list your property with him but only if he will give you an appraisal of your real estate which matches or exceeds the price at which you would like to sell.

It doesn't have to be all that blunt. You could simply indicate that if he thought, as shown by his appraisal, that your property was not worth the price at which you wanted to list it, you would be better off listing with another broker.

To be fair, do not ask your broker to give you an appraisal of property you wish to list with him. This will prevent any future hard feelings or friction in your working relationship caused by his giving an appraisal higher or lower than you expect or want.

Appraisals of Property in Which the Broker Has an Interest

Your broker may not give an appraisal on property to be bought or sold if he has an interest in the real estate unless he outlines in the appraisal exactly what his interests are in that real estate.

An appraisal is supposed to be the honest, unbiased opinion of property value by a qualified but disinterested person. Such a person cannot be disinterested if he has a personal interest in the property which he is appraising.

WHAT IS A REASONABLE COMMISSION?

In most cases there is no set rate at which real estate brokers are expected to charge commission.

Exceptions to this occur in that many brokers belong to state and national associations and organizations which have established commission rates. Also many brokers engage in co-broking with state and national organizations which require that they charge an established commission rate. Brokers in other communities themselves establish policy as to what commission rates they charge.

Still, unfortunately, many brokers are free to charge any commission they choose. This is un-

fortunate because it gives you, the seller, an easy opportunity to cheat yourself.

A friend of ours, because of a problem with his digestion, made a weekly visit to his doctor. The office call, plus the weekly prescription, cost him $9. This continued for two years and the problem remained unsolved. Finally I convinced my friend that he should go to a clinic and be checked by specialists. This cost him $174 but he has not been bothered with the problem since. Specialists usually cost a little more, but are almost always worth it.

Nobody knows better than your broker what

his services are worth. Should you shop around to find the broker who will take your listing at the lowest commission rate? Do you shop around for a doctor who will charge the lowest fees or do you select your doctor on the basis that you consider him to be the one who can best satisfy your medical needs?

Do you want a broker to bring you prospective purchasers whose offers are less than you expect for your property or do you want a broker who is able to bring you a purchaser who is willing to buy your property at your price and on your terms?

Any broker whom you are able to talk into lowering his commission is willing to do so only because:

1. The broker needs the listing. If he is really successful at finding buyers, he shouldn't have to lower his fee to get new listings. Listings should come to him automatically because of his reputation.

2. The broker intends to spend less money on advertising your property and intends to spend less time trying to find you a buyer than he ordinarily would when he is working toward payment of his normal commission.

Your broker knows what his services are worth. Don't ask him to work for less. You will only be cheating yourself.

CONDITIONS UNDER WHICH YOU OWE COMMISSION

Whether or not you owe commission depends upon the type of listing contract you sign and the provisions it contains. (Refer to pages 9–13 for listings.)

The court always makes the final decision, but, as laymen, we are allowed to explore different situations and predict the outcomes.

Although You List the Property with a Broker, During the Listing Period You Personally Sell the Property

Usually an exclusive listing contract provides that the broker is entitled to commission if he sells the property, another broker sells it, or it is sold by anybody else. The broker receives his commission regardless of who sells the property.

To break an exclusive listing you need to prove that the broker has not, and is not, making a continuous, bona fide effort to sell the property. After breaking the listing, you can personally sell the property and not owe a commission, but you will be asked to reimburse the broker for expenses he incurred while advertising and trying to sell the property.

Open listings usually allow you to sell the property personally without paying commission; however, it can be difficult to prove the buyer did not come to you because of the broker's efforts. When you list your property and then personally sell it, be prepared to pay commission. Usually you owe it.

The Broker Finds a Buyer for You and Then You Decide Not to Sell

The listing contract is an employment contract between you and the broker in which you agree to pay the broker a commission if he produces a buyer ready, willing, and able to buy your property at your price or at any other price and terms acceptable to you.

Technically, you do not employ the broker to sell the property. He enters into the listing contract solely to find you an acceptable buyer. When the broker produces the acceptable buyer, and whether or not the property is sold, whoever signed the listing owes the broker commission.

Although You Have a Buyer, You Are Unable to Sell Because Your Wife Refuses to Sign the Title Transfer Papers

You could get into an argument with your wife and, to prove you are the head of your household, list your house for sale.

Theoretically, when the broker produces a buyer ready, willing, and able to buy your house, regardless of whether your wife signs the title transfer papers, you owe commission.

The listing contract is an employment contract and when the broker produces an acceptable buyer, he fulfills his role in the contract and you owe commission.

The Broker Finds a Buyer for You
After the Listing Expires

Listing contracts may contain a "standard negotiation clause" which provides that you owe commission when the broker produces a buyer after the listing expires if:

1. The broker negotiated with the prospective buyer to the point that this person was considered a likely purchaser, and this negotiation took place during the life of the listing, and

2. The broker submitted this likely purchaser's name to you in writing prior to the expiration of the listing, and

3. If the likely purchaser actually buys the property within six months after the expiration of the listing.

There is a sound reason why brokers like to have this clause a part of the listing contract.

For example, the broker makes a strenuous, expensive, and continuous, bona fide effort to sell your property during the life of the listing. One week before the listing expires, the broker finds a likely purchaser. The broker isn't able to get an offer signed that week but is certain that the likely purchaser will eventually buy the property. The broker is entitled to commission if he can turn the prospect into a buyer.

If the "standard negotiation clause" is not a part of the listing contract, or if the broker fails to satisfy the requirements of this clause, ordinarily your obligations to the broker cease when the listing expires.

You Accept the Buyer's Offer and
Then the Buyer Backs Out of the Deal

The broker fulfills his contract with you when he produces a buyer ready, willing, and able to purchase the property. Surely a buyer who signs an offer to purchase is a ready, willing, and able purchaser. You owe the broker commission.

The broker fulfilled his contract with you. The buyer is breaking his contract with you. Your case is against the buyer. When he signs the offer and you accept it, a firm contract for the sale of the property is concluded.

You may bring an action of specific performance against the buyer to force him to go ahead with the contract, you may sue him for damages, or you may ask for the buyer's earnest money as liquidated damages.

The Broker Is Unable to Find a Buyer
at Your Price So You Accept an Offer
at a Lower Price

Usually the listing contract provides that you owe commission when the broker produces a buyer ready, willing, and able to buy at your price or at any other price and terms acceptable to you.

When you accept a buyer's offer, for no matter how much less than your original asking price, the broker fulfills his employment contract with you and you owe commission.

Remember the broker's commission is based on percentage, so when the property sells for less than the original asking price, the broker receives less. The broker, of course, wanted to find a buyer for you at your price.

The Broker Personally Buys the Property
You List with Him

A broker may buy property listed with him, but only with the seller's knowledge and consent. For example, you list your property for $45,000. The broker knows that it can be sold for at least $55,000. Instead of telling you this, the broker buys the property from you for $45,000 and resells it for $55,000. When this occurs the broker has violated his fiduciary duty to get you the best possible deal.

If the broker tells you that he himself wants to buy your property and tells you why, and you accept his offer to purchase, has he not thus produced a buyer ready, willing, and able to purchase the property on terms acceptable to you?

He has fulfilled his employment contract with you and usually you owe commission.

The Broker Represents Both You and the Buyer

When you sign a listing, you create an agency relationship with the broker. All fruits of an agency belong to the principal, in this situation, you.

When the broker receives a finder's fee from the buyer for locating the property for him and a commission from you for locating the buyer, can he make the best possible deal for you?

A broker may only represent two parties to any one transaction when both parties are aware of it and consent to it.

Usually when the broker represents both parties and they are aware of it and consent to it, even though the broker receives a finder's fee from the buyer, you owe commission.

Oral Listings with the Broker

In most states, a broker may not bring a court action to collect commission for work done under an oral contract, even though he is bound to the same rules of conduct with an oral listing as he is with the formal written listing.

Usually before the broker may sue for commission, there must be a written listing which includes:

1. The price of the property, and

2. The terms on which you will sell, and

3. A description of the property, and

4. The period during which the listing is valid, and

5. The signature of whoever agrees to pay the commission.

The surest way for a broker to earn his commission is for him to produce a buyer ready, willing, and able to buy your property. There should be no question whether the broker is entitled to commission when the property is sold at a price agreeable to you.

When you find yourself in a situation in which you question whether the broker has fulfilled his employment contract—the listing contract—and deserves the commission, check with your attorney.

Chapter Three

SET A FAIR MARKET VALUE ON THE PROPERTY AND SELL IT AT A PROFIT

WHAT IS YOUR PROPERTY WORTH?

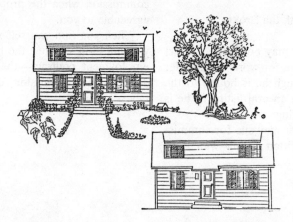

A prospective buyer sees your property only as a piece of real estate—land and buildings, plus location. He places no sentimental or emotional value on the property. He may picture mentally what the property will be worth after he makes some changes, but the price he is willing to pay will be based on the value to him of the land and buildings plus the location.

Unlike the prospective buyer, you no doubt have a strong sentimental attachment to your property. Possibly you have lived there many years, several of your children have grown up there.

You have a photo album of snapshots showing your children during their childhood, playing in the back yard under the shade of that beautiful willow tree. Some of the color snapshots show your magnificent rosebushes planted along the garage. You spent many pleasant hours tending those roses. And one of the things you will miss after you have moved is the relaxing time you spent visiting with your favorite neighbor.

A prospective buyer may think your beautiful willow tree actually detracts from the value of your property, and that it is aging and soon will have to be removed. To a buyer, the rosebushes might represent nothing more than an investment of $1.98 each. Certainly a prospective buyer cannot yet place a value on any friendships in the neighborhood that he might possibly develop sometime in the future.

In many cases, the owner, because of sentimental or emotional attachments to the property, or to the neighborhood, is not able to arrive at a realistic, fair market value price on his property.

When a property owner arrives at a sale price without recourse to outside evaluations, too often the property is overpriced because the owner has included in his selling price the value he puts on the property for emotional or sentimental reasons.

Properties which are overpriced tend to stay on the market too long. Like any commodity offered for sale, the longer it is offered and not sold, the more wary buyers become.

Remember that usually a buyer will ask the broker how long the property has been listed for sale. If the buyer learns that the property has been listed for six months, the question may pop into the buyer's mind as to why it hasn't been sold. Surely others have looked at the property. If they didn't consider it worth the listed price, why should the would-be buyer pay the listed price? If the price were a "good deal" surely the property would have been sold long ago.

On the other hand, when a property owner sets his own selling price—again without reference to outside sources—it is possible for him to lose potential profits by selling at too low a price.

Possibly you, the owner, have not enjoyed the neighborhood. Instead of making friends you have developed a strong dislike for the neighborhood. Living there has become a continuous chore of making necessary repairs and maintaining the property.

Under these or similar circumstances the tendency is for you to put too low a selling price on the property. Underpriced properties are quickly bought by buyers who recognize a bargain. You enjoy a quick sale, but you forfeit profits because you underprice your property.

Putting a fair market value price on your property—not underpriced or overpriced—requires consultation with experienced persons who are completely devoid of any emotional or sentimental attitudes toward the property.

Seek the advice of an appraiser.

Appraisals

An appraiser is acquainted with current real estate values. Have property values gone up or down, and to what extent? The appraiser knows.

Commonly a property owner, knowing that real estate values have gone up, puts a selling price on his property equal to what he paid for it plus what he considers a reasonable profit.

For example, he paid $50,000 for the property. Knowing that real estate prices have gone up, he adds $10,000 to his original purchase price and sells the property for $60,000. He is satisfied that he has been shrewd, as he has recovered all of his original investment and has made a profit of $10,000.

In this age of soaring real estate prices, he may have lost an additional profit by having underpriced his property. An appraiser might have determined that it was actually worth $65,000 instead of $60,000.

The tendency is for a seller to be content with a profit no matter how small the profit is. The result is that many properties in areas where real estate prices are soaring are being sold at less than fair market values. An appraisal can result in an owner's selling his property at profits much greater than he would have made in determining his own selling price.

Following the advice of an appraiser can also prevent overpricing the property—adding sentimental or emotional values—which can result in the property's not being sold.

Having an appraisal made is no guarantee that the property will sell at that price, but the appraisal is certainly a weighty selling tool. Show it to a prospective buyer as evidence that the price you are asking is merely the value put on the property by an appraiser.

If you do not know any appraisers in your area, simply telephone the county courthouse and ask for the probate secretary to the county judge. She has the list of people appointed as appraisers within the county plus their fee schedule. (The cost of an appraisal is tax-deductible.)

FHA APPRAISALS

For a mere $75 you can get an FHA (Federal Housing Administration) appraisal of your property. FHA appraisal application forms are available from any FHA office, from most banks, and from most savings and loan associations.

Costing only $75, they are an inexpensive selling tool. You are able to tell and show a prospective buyer that "the price we are asking is the amount at which the property has been appraised by the FHA."

An FHA appraisal is doubly effective in situations in which the buyer is going to need an FHA-guaranteed loan to finance part of the purchase price of the property.

REAL ESTATE BROKERS

Realizing that real estate brokers are involved in the buying and selling of real estate, the temptation exists to ask a broker's opinion "off the cuff" as to what a property is worth.

BEWARE! A broker may not give an appraisal

of real estate to be listed with him if his getting the listing is dependent upon the appraisal. The entire area of seeking the opinion of a broker when the broker is likely to be involved in the transaction is a sensitive one. (See pages 65–68 for broker's duties to the buyer.)

Remember that a broker earns his commissions by procuring buyers for sellers of real estate. If a broker were assured that you intended to list your property with him, wouldn't it be to the broker's advantage to have an attractive price on the property?

Wouldn't the broker prefer that you have a selling price on the property low enough so that he could be reasonably sure of finding a buyer and earning his commission?

If the broker is not assured that you will list your property with him, wouldn't he at least be inclined to enhance the possibility of your listing the property with him by indicating to you "off the cuff" that he could sell the property for you at an attractive price?

The rules are:

1. A real estate broker who is not involved in the transaction can usually give you an excellent appraisal.

2. Do not rely on just "off the cuff" opinions regardless of their source.

3. Avoid opinions as to the value of the property when the person who gives the opinion can gain from the sale of the property.

Considering the small cost involved, it is a wise seller who uses an appraisal:

1. As a selling tool. "Mr. Buyer, my price is precisely the appraised value of the property."

2. As a check that he as seller is not underpricing the property and hence losing possible profits.

3. As a check that he is not overpricing the property and therefore not getting the property sold at his price.

This is the age of the "do-it-yourself" people. Rather than use the services of an appraiser, some people elect to use a do-it-yourself method of arriving at a selling price. Let's explore some of the methods used and reveal their shortcomings.

Evidence of Tax Records

By checking your tax records you can see the trend in the assessed evaluation of your property. Has the assessed evaluation remained the same? Has it gone down or up?

What does the tax assessor consider to be the true value of your property?

Telephone the city clerk's or county treasurer's office and ask at what per cent of recommended full value your property was assessed. The assessed valuation of your property is also on record in these offices.

Divide the percentage into the assessed valuation and the answer is your property's true value as determined by the assessor.

$$\frac{\$ \quad \text{true value as determined by the assessor}}{\text{assessed valuation}}$$

Percentage of recommended full value

$$50\% \quad \frac{\$60,000 \text{ true value}}{\$30,000}$$

Fluctuations in the assessed valuation of a property do not usually show an accurate trend in the rate at which the property is appreciating or depreciating.

For example, the assessed valuation on your property has gone up $1,000 each year for the three years you have owned it. Would a fair market value price on your property be your purchase price plus the $3,000?

Not only is this not necessarily true but it is very unlikely. Increased assessed valuations reflect only an increase in the cost of supporting the community and do not necessarily reflect any increase in the value of any individual properties within the community.

Reference to tax rolls is of value only as a basis for forecasting trends, such as possible future tax rates. It is sometimes useful in comparing the assessed valuation of one property as compared to the assessed valuation of another property.

Checking the Selling Price of a Similar Property

You know a property in town which has recently been sold and which you have always considered to be comparable in value to your property. Check the price for which the other property was sold and ask yourself whether you shouldn't be able to get as much for yours.

The fallacy in this approach is that *you* are the one who considers the properties similar. Can *you* make a valid comparison? Probably not, since the value you put on your property is affected by sentimental and emotional values added to the actual value of the land and buildings.

Do the two houses have the same number of rooms? Do they have equal floor space? Would it cost the same to duplicate each property? Are the lot sizes and shapes similar?

Do the two properties have the same assessed valuation? Check at the city clerk's or county treasurer's office.

Usually there will be differences between the two properties and you consider them similar only because (and the reasons usually are many and varied) you always thought that you would be able to enjoy life in about the same manner as the owner of the other property.

Purchase Price plus Cost of Improvements

Doesn't it seem logical that you should be able to arrive at a fair selling price by adding the cost of the improvements you made on a property to your original purchase price and then adjusting this final figure for appreciation or depreciation of the property?

What factor are you going to use to adjust your final figure for appreciation or depreciation? Properties in some communities are rapidly appreciating while similar properties in other communities are depreciating.

Have you entered the cost of your improvements into the price at a fair value? Are you confident that you didn't pay more for some of the improvements than they were worth?

When you bought the property was the price you paid more or less than the property was actually worth?

There are too many uncertainties in this approach for it to be anything better than a complicated guess as to what could be considered a fair market value price for the property.

Relying on Neighbors' Opinions

Ask your neighbor what he thinks you will be able to get for your property. He probably will enjoy playing "appraiser" and will give you a serious and honest opinion. Regardless of how much respect you have for his opinion, is he qualified to give you an appraisal?

Just as people buy stocks on hot tips from friends and neighbors, some people insist upon relying on the opinion of friends and neighbors when arriving at a selling price for their property.

Before you ask your neighbor for his opinion, ask yourself, "Is he an appraiser?"

Many other methods have been tried by do-it-yourselfers. It is doubtful if these methods ever result in their selling their properties for more than they are actually worth. They may have listed their properties for more than they are worth only to be forced at a later date to lower their prices to get the properties sold.

Many do-it-yourselfers have listed and sold their properties for less than they were actually worth.

The Answer

Have an appraisal made of your property before you decide on a selling price.

INFORMATION TO GATHER, DECISIONS TO MAKE BEFORE MEETING WITH YOUR BROKER TO LIST YOUR PROPERTY

To prevent misunderstandings between you and your broker, and possibly later between you and your buyer, it is important that your broker have certain information.

One function of the listing contract is to make a record of this information. Remember you will receive a copy of your signed listing. This is your employment contract with the broker and your record of exactly what you are offering to sell.

Before meeting with your broker, have the following definite information available and the following decisions made:

Exact Description of the Property You Want to Sell

The description should be more detailed and inclusive than just a simple statement as:

"My house at 1114 John Street, Dodgeville, Wis."

It is better to have the exact description of the property. For example:

"Part of the Northeast Quarter of the Northwest Quarter (NE½ NW¼) of Section numbered Twenty-seven (S-27), Township numbered Six North (T-6N), Range numbered Three East (R-3E), commencing at the Southwest corner of said 40 acre tract, thence East 416½ feet, thence North 1320 feet, thence West 416½ feet, thence South 1320 feet to the place of beginning, containing 12.62 acres of land, all in Iowa County, Wis."

This tells a prospective buyer exactly what you are offering for sale. There is such a description of your property available to you. Check your warranty deed, your land contract, your abstract of title, your owner's policy of title insurance, or your tax bill.

The description of the real estate I wish to sell is _____
_____

Price at Which You Are Willing to Sell

In arriving at a price, refer to your worksheet on pages 30–31 to determine at what price you have to sell to receive the net dollars you want from the sale of your property.

The price at which I will sell is $_____

Terms on Which You Will Sell

Do you want all cash, and if so, when do you want it paid? Are you willing to offer financing?

Offering terms can produce buyers who can't handle an all-cash purchase. Offering terms often makes it possible to sell at a higher price. Some buyers expect to pay less when they can offer all cash and provide their own financing.

Possibly you have a mortgage against the property which contains a prepayment penalty clause. Perhaps you will be wise to ask that the buyer assume and agree to pay this mortgage rather than pay it off yourself and have to pay extra because of the prepayment penalty clause. (Refer to pages 128–139 for mortgages.)

Will you sell on a land contract? Because of the modest down payment usually required on a land contract, many consider this type of financing the quickest way to sell real estate. (Refer to pages 142–148 for land contracts.)

Are you willing to accept a first or second purchase money mortgage as partial payment toward the selling price?

Possibly you have not yet located the type of property you want to buy and can make a trade as part of your transaction.

The more options you give a buyer, the better are your chances of realizing a sale.

The terms on which I will sell are ___
_____

Period for Which You Wish to List Your Property

Remember when you sign the listing you agree to pay the broker a commission if he procures a buyer ready, willing, and able to purchase the property on the terms you outlined in your listing contract or on any other terms acceptable to you.

For how long do you want to give your broker

this opportunity? Be fair to the broker. Remember he will be spending his time and money advertising the property and showing it to prospects. He is repaid for his time and expenses only if he is eventually paid a commission.

Although this varies, urban listings are commonly for six months and rural listings for one year. In some areas, through mutual consent, brokers establish set periods for which they accept listings. In most cases it is wiser to list for a short period of time with the option of renewing the listing than it is to list for a longer term.

If at the expiration of the listing, the property isn't sold and you think the broker is making a satisfactory effort to sell it, be fair and renew the listing contract with him.

The period for which I want to list my property is _____

_____

How Do You Want Prorating Handled?

(Refer to pages 117–121 for prorating.)

What portion are you willing to pay and what portion do you expect the buyer to pay of the real estate taxes for the year in which the property changes hands? How about utility bills for the month of closing, the rents, premiums on prepaid insurance policies which the buyer has assigned to him, and interest on any mortgages which you allow the buyer to assume and agree to pay?

A lot of friendships are never made because of a failure to have prorating methods clearly understood by both seller and buyer before the settling of these items comes due.

Usually such items are prorated using one of two methods:

Prorated to the day you close your transaction—the day the buyer pays you and you transfer ownership of the property to him. Or

Prorated to the month of closing on the basis that if the closing takes place after the fifteenth of the month, the seller is considered the owner and owes for that month.

If the closing takes place on or before the fifteenth of the month, the buyer is considered the owner for that month and owes for that month.

The prorating method I want used is ____

_____

Which Will You Furnish to the Buyer, Abstract of Title or Owner's Policy of Title Insurance?

In most cases, the buyer's wishes will dictate whether you supply him with an abstract of title or an owner's policy of title insurance.

Possibly, though, the buyer will have no preference. State in the listing contract which you prefer to supply him. Base your choice on what it costs to supply either one.

Check which one you currently have and then check with an abstract company and a title insurance company as to what the cost would be to you to supply either an abstract or an owner's policy of title insurance.

(Refer to pages 88–91 for a discussion of these items.)

I prefer to supply a buyer with (choose either abstract of title or owner's policy of title insurance) _____

_____

How Money Forfeited by the Buyer Will Be Distributed

For example, your broker found a buyer willing to buy the property on your terms. The buyer gave your broker $5,000 earnest money to be applied toward the purchase price of the property. You accept the buyer's offer, which results in a firm contract of sale between you and your buyer.

Then the buyer decides that he doesn't want to go ahead with the purchase. During this period, at your request and on your behalf, your broker paid to have a lien removed from your property and for having your abstract brought up to date.

In addition, your broker spent considerable time and money showing your property to prospective buyers, advertising your property, and in finally locating this buyer for you.

You too have an investment. During this period

—since your buyer made his offer—the property was no longer advertised for sale. You lost possible contact with other prospective buyers.

When your buyer fails to go ahead with the purchase as agreed, he forfeits the $5,000 earnest money. It should be clearly understood between you and your broker who is to receive what portion of any forfeited money when such a situation arises.

Usually the forfeited money will first be used to repay the broker for any cash advances he made on your behalf. In this example, the broker is reimbursed for the money he spent to have the lien removed and for having your abstract brought up to date.

One half of the remaining money goes to the broker. This amount should not be in excess of the commission he would have earned if the sale had been consummated. The remaining half goes to you as the seller.

Any money forfeited by the buyer will be

_____

_____

of misunderstanding, outline clearly in your listing exactly what is to be included in your selling price.

The following items will be included in the selling price:

(circle either "yes" or "no")

Attached antennas	yes	no
Water conditioner	yes	no
Draperies	yes	no
Curtains and rods	yes	no
Venetian blinds	yes	no
Window shades	yes	no
Awnings	yes	no
Carpeting	yes	no
Hot water heater	yes	no
Heating unit	yes	no
Linoleum	yes	no
Lighting fixtures	yes	no
Bathroom accessories	yes	no
Screen doors and windows	yes	no
Storm doors and windows	yes	no
Others _____	yes	no
_____	yes	no
_____	yes	no

What Will Be Included in the Listing Price?

(Refer to pages 121–123 for explanation of fixtures.)

Your broker just telephoned to let you know he has a prospective out-of-state buyer who wants to look at your property this afternoon. You have to be away but agree to let the broker show the prospect your house. Later the prospect makes an offer to buy your property at your price and on your terms.

All goes well until it is time to close the transaction. Then the buyer claims he thought your draperies and carpeting were included in the selling price. You had not intended that these items be included, but finally, so that the buyer will go ahead with the deal, you include your draperies and carpeting in your selling price.

Personally, though, you still think that somehow you were cheated out of your draperies and carpeting, as it never was your intention that they be included in your selling price. To avoid this kind

How Will Special Assessments Against the Property Be Handled?

(Refer to page 99 for special assessments.)

Do you now have or do you know of any planned improvements which will result in special assessments against your property?

These are assessments levied against properties by a city or village for improvements made for the benefit of the properties, such as street paving, curb, gutter, or sidewalk installation, and the installation of water and/or sewage systems.

Special assessments usually are made payable over several years so that at any one time there may be payments remaining due on an assessment for work completed years before or there may be future payments for work planned but not yet started.

For example, if the work was completed three years ago and is to be paid for in ten yearly installments, are you or the buyer responsible for the remaining seven payments?

Special assessments for work started before the

buyer makes his offer usually are paid for by the seller.

Special assessments for work to be started after the buyer makes his offer are paid for by the buyer.

To avoid conflicts on the basis that the buyer claims "you should pay for this since you didn't tell me about it when I agreed to buy your property," include in your listing complete information about all present and planned special assessments against your property.

The special assessment is for _____
The amount and number of payments still due are _____
The special assessment is to be paid by
_____

How Will Required Repairs on the Property Be Handled?

For example, the city fire inspector gave you notice to have your basement fireproofed within sixty days. Or possibly you were ordered to have some electrical wiring repaired or to have some plumbing updated.

If your house is sold before the work is completed, are you or the buyer to pay for the job?

Include in your listing detailed information about any notices which have been served upon you requiring repairs, alterations, or corrections of any existing conditions about your property and specify who is to pay for these repairs.

Work required on the property is _____
_____
The work is to be completed by _____
_____
Estimated cost of the required repairs is $_____
This estimate was given to me by _____
_____
Cost of the repairs will be paid by _____
_____

Complete Information About Your Insurance

Usually insurance policies on residential real estate are written for three-year periods and are prepaid. Depending upon what your policy allows, you have several choices as to what happens to your coverage when you sell your property:

1. You may cancel your policy as of the date the buyer legally becomes the new owner, or

2. You may transfer your policy and coverage to a different property, or

3. You may have your policy and coverage assigned to the buyer.

Your buyer will be interested in the cost of insuring the property. Possibly the buyer considers your coverage at the price you are paying a "good deal" and your allowing the policy to be assigned to him can be helpful in selling him your property.

Obviously it is good salesmanship to make it easy for a buyer to buy. When you allow your policy to be assigned to the buyer, you make it easy for him, especially if this is the first property insurance he has needed, as in the case with a new property owner.

Include in your listing complete information about the insurance you carry on your property.

The name, address, and telephone number of my insurance agent is _____
The expiration date of my policy is _____
The amount of my coverage is $_____
The cost of my coverage is $_____
The type of policy I have is _____

Complete Information About the Real Estate Taxes on the Property

As a prospective buyer of your property, I expect you to tell me what the taxes were on your property for the previous four years.

Why not just for the previous year? I am interested in the trend. Are the taxes escalating because of new or improved schools or expansion of public utilities or services?

Also I want to know if you made any improvements before listing your property simply to make it more attractive to me, but which will result in increased property taxes next year. Do not scare away a prospective buyer because he thinks you are reluctant to tell the true and complete story behind the taxes on your property.

If you haven't your tax bills handy, see your assessor. This information is on record and available to you.

Year   assessed valuation×*mill rate*=*taxes*
19____
19____
19____
19____

Recent improvements on the property which can result in increased taxes next year are _____

_____

Complete Information About
Any Liens on the Property

(Refer to pages 125–127 for liens.)

Anybody who supplies labor or materials for the improvement of your real estate may file a lien on your property for the amount due him.

The contractor or subcontractor is given a limited time from the last date he supplied labor or materials in which to file his lien. The lien is then good for a period of time set by your state's statutes.

In some cases the one who supplied labor or materials and filed the lien may have your property sold through a foreclosure action to collect the amount due him, provided you don't otherwise pay him. The lien is against the property and not against the person who requested the labor or materials.

If there is a lien against the property while you still own the property, you owe it. If you do not remove the lien before selling the property, when your buyer becomes the new owner, he will owe the amount represented by the lien.

If you recently had any work done on your property, check to learn if there has been a lien filed against it for labor or materials. In your listing, include information about all liens so that your buyer will be fully aware of them.

Liens against the property are _____

_____

Complete Information About
Any Easements on the Property

(Refer to pages 123–125 for easements.)

An easement is the right of a person or persons to go upon the land of another for a particular purpose.

For example, possibly you gave a neighbor the right to cross over your property to reach a portion of his property. Or you gave another neighbor the right to park his automobile on your property.

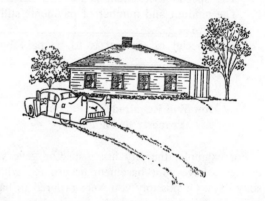

Don't let easements you have granted come as a surprise to your buyer. In your listing describe the easements on your property.

Easements against the property are ____

_____

Complete Information About
Any Mortgages on the Property

A mortgage is a lien against the property as security for a debt, and if the debt isn't paid voluntarily, the property can be sold through a foreclosure by sale action to raise enough money to pay the debt.

A buyer will be interested in knowing about any mortgages against the property. He will request that the mortgages be paid off, or in some cases that he be allowed to assume and to pay the mortgages.

Possibly you have a mortgage against your property which contains a prepayment penalty clause which stipulates that you have to pay extra if you make payments ahead of their due dates.

Provided the mortgage doesn't have a non-assignment clause, in some cases it is wise to allow the buyer to assume and to pay this type of mortgage as part of the purchase price. Possibly because of a lower interest rate, allowing the buyer to assume and to pay your mortgage will be helpful in convincing him that he should buy your property.

Your buyer is entitled to know about all mortgages existing against the property. Make this information available to him through your listing.

Mortgages which I plan to pay off before the closing are_____

_____

Mortgages which I will allow the buyer to assume and to pay are _____

_____

The type of mortgage is _____
The balance owing on the mortgage is $___
The interest rate on the mortgage is ___%
The name, address, and telephone number of the mortgagee is _____

_____

Complete Information About Maintenance Costs

Your buyer will want to know what it costs to maintain the property. For example, what does it cost to heat the house, what do water and sewage cost, and what has your electricity bill been?

The fixtures and basic design of the house can make a big difference in the portion of the electricity bill which goes toward lighting.

The buyer will probably inquire about what you originally paid for the property. Are you selling it for more or less? Surely you have spent something on improving the property. Find your receipts. Take credit for your improvements.

Include in your listing what the maintenance costs have been and itemize the cost of improvements you have made on the property.

The average cost of heating the building is $_____

The monthly cost for electricity has averaged $_____

Yearly costs for water and sewage have been $_____

Since buying the property, I have made the following improvements:

Improvement	Cost
_____	$_____
_____	$_____
_____	$_____

Who Will Sign the Listing Contract?

If the broker produces a buyer ready, willing, and able to purchase the property at the price and on the terms specified in the listing or at any other acceptable price and terms, whoever signed the listing contract has to pay commission.

There does not have to be a sale of the property for the broker to earn his commission. The listing contract is an employment contract and the broker fulfills his role when he produces a buyer whose offer is at a price and on terms acceptable to whoever signed the listing contract.

For example, a husband signs a listing contract for the sale of his house. His wife doesn't sign the listing contract. The broker produces a buyer whose offer is accepted by the husband. At the closing the wife refuses to sign the deed, so the sale never takes place.

The husband owes the broker commission. The broker fulfilled the employment contract when he produced a buyer acceptable to the husband, who signed the listing. When you sign a listing contract expect to pay commission.

The listing contract will be signed by ____

_____

WORKSHEET TO COMPLETE BEFORE MEETING WITH YOUR BROKER TO LIST YOUR PROPERTY

1. The description of the real estate I want to sell is _____
_____

2. The price at which I will sell is $_____

3. The terms on which I will sell are _____
_____

4. The period for which I want to list my property is _____
_____

5. The prorating method I want used is _____
_____

6. I prefer to supply a buyer with (choose either abstract of title or owner's policy of title insurance) _____

7. Any money forfeited by the buyer will be _____
_____

8. The following items will be included in the selling price (circle either "yes" or "no")

Attached antennas	yes	no		Hot water heater	yes	no
Water conditioner	yes	no		Heating unit	yes	no
Draperies	yes	no		Linoleum	yes	no
Curtains and rods	yes	no		Lighting fixtures	yes	no
Venetian blinds	yes	no		Bathroom accessories	yes	no
Window shades	yes	no		Screen doors and windows	yes	no
Awnings	yes	no		Storm doors and windows	yes	no
Carpeting	yes	no				

Others _____ yes   no

_____ yes   no

_____ yes   no

_____ yes   no

9. There are special assessments against the property for _____
_____

10. The amount and number of payments still due on these assessments are _____
_____

11. The special assessments are to be paid by _____
_____

12. Work I have been ordered to have done on the property is _____
_____

13. I have been ordered to have this work completed by _____

14. Estimated cost of the required repairs is $_____

15. This estimate was given to me by _____

16. Cost of the repairs will be paid by _____

17. The name, address, and telephone number of my insurance agent is

_____

18. The expiration date of my policy is _____

19. The amount of my coverage is $_____

20. The cost of my coverage is $_____

21. The type of policy I have is _____

22. Real estate taxes on the property have been

$$Year \quad assessed\ valuation \times mill\ rate = taxes$$

19____

19____

19____

19____

23. Recent improvements on the property which can result in increased
taxes next year are _____

24. Liens against the property are _____

_____

25. Easements against the property are _____

_____

26. Mortgages which I plan to pay off before the closing are _____

_____

27. Mortgages which I wish the buyer to assume and agree to pay are ____

_____

The type of mortgage is _____

The balance owing on the mortgage is $_____

The interest rate on the mortgage is _____%

The name, address, and telephone number of the mortgagee is _____

_____

28. The average cost of heating the building is $_____

29. The monthly cost for electricity has averaged $_____

30. Yearly costs for water and sewage have been $_____

31. Since buying the property, I have made the following improvements:

Improvement	Cost
_____	$_____
_____	$_____
_____	$_____

32. The listing contract will be signed by _____

HAVE THE PROPERTY LOOKING SHIPSHAPE—
FIX UP, PAINT UP TO SHOW IT

The shade on our vestibule light fixture has been broken for several years. The light fixture still operates, only the shade is broken. It isn't repaired because we no longer notice that it is broken.

Probably, though, most people entering our house do notice it.

But isn't this typical? Aren't most householders blind to little defects and disfigurements? They grow accustomed to them and no longer see them.

When you or your broker shows your house to prospective purchasers, you ought to show it to greatest advantage. The prospective buyer expects this. Before your house is shown is the time to fix up, paint up, and make minor repairs. It is time to put the property in the very best of shape.

What could possibly be overlooked by you as being unimportant could be very important to a buyer, so important that you get a "no sale" instead of a "sale." Because you may be partially blind to what needs fixing, you would be wise to have a stranger inspect your property, to make a list of things which he thinks need to be done to dress up the place.

The stranger will see things you have overlooked for years. Because he is a stranger his list will be complete, not cushioned to spare your feelings.

An excellent person to inspect your house would be someone from a local hardware store or lumberyard. Not only can such a person be very critical, he also can recommend materials and give you estimates on costs.

The list might include such things as replacing switch plates, door mat, or shower curtains. These are small, inexpensive items which can radically affect first impressions of a would-be buyer.

Why not prune the trees and shrubs? This certainly makes a property more attractive. And it creates the impression that the owner is conscientious about the appearance of his place and has taken extra pains to keep the property in good shape.

Clean the house thoroughly. Usually it is wise to have an outsider do the house cleaning. Professional cleaners, although costly, will do a more thorough job than you could possibly do even if you had the time with your busy schedule.

Rearrange the contents of closets so that the closets look more spacious. Would a room or rooms be more attractive if they were freshly painted? Why not patch that crack in the plaster and then paper that wall?

If some major remodeling or redecorating is needed and you think you can't afford it, at least have a professional estimate made of what the cost would be. If additional rooms could easily be added, have estimates made of the cost of these additions.

Be honest. Your prospective buyer may suspect that you have made repairs and done some last minute fix-up jobs just to make the property more salable. The question may be in his mind—how long will that fresh coat of paint on the kitchen wall last? Did the seller use the cheapest possible paint? What does that wallpaper cover?

An excellent way of convincing a buyer of the quality of the materials used on your property is to show him a scrapbook of samples of the materials you've used plus an index showing where you bought the materials.

The scrapbook should contain paint can labels, plus a record of where you bought the paint, as well as wallpaper samples and a record of where you bought the wallpaper.

If you have extra floor tile or carpeting or leftover paint, extra wallpaper or pieces of wall paneling, tell your buyer about these and show them to him. It will be comforting to him to know that he has extra materials on hand for making future repairs.

Sell a home and not just a house.

Did you originally buy the house because of the basic soundness of its structure? Probably not. Probably one of the reasons which swayed you in buying the house was that your wife was attracted by some of its features, possibly the comfortable kitchen or a spareroom that she could use as a storage and sewing room.

Your prospective buyer and his wife know what they want. They are trying to visualize how the house will look after they have moved in their furniture and appliances. They are looking for a home, not a house.

Show them that your house is a comfortable home, a nice place to live in. Have potted plants or freshly cut flowers in the house. Maybe a gay, colored tablecloth will brighten up the entire kitchen. Have enough lights on so that the rooms will seem large and airy. Does somebody in your family smoke heavily? Spray the house with a scented disinfectant.

The prospective buyer has taken the time to inspect your property. Wouldn't he be willing to take just a little more time to look at your colorslides? Have you pictures of the property showing it when all the flowers are in bloom? Or possibly you have slides of last summer's garden; or a favorite shot showing your place after a snowfall.

If spending $1,000 or more in fixing up and painting up results in your getting a buyer at your price instead of a "no sale," or a buyer at a reduced price, you have made a wise investment.

In addition, although fix-up costs aren't tax-deductible, they may be deducted from the amount you realize from the sale of your property in arriving at the adjusted sale price for determining your taxable gain on the sale of the property. (See pages 157–158 for fix-up costs.)

For example, if you sold the house for $60,000 but invested $2,400 in fixing it up for the sale, your adjusted sale price will be $57,600 ($60,000 less the $2,400 fix-up costs). Then if you buy another house for $55,000, your taxable gain is based on $2,600 (the difference between the adjusted sale price of $57,600 and the cost of your new house at $55,000).

However, if you have no fix-up costs, still selling the old house for $60,000 and buying the second for $55,000, your taxable gain is based on the difference of $5,000. Before fix-up costs are allowed as a deduction against your gain, you must have records and receipts to prove that the work was done no earlier than ninety days before the sale and that the work was paid for not later than thirty days after the property was sold.

More important than the few dollars you may save is being able to sell the property at your price. Fix it up, clean it up, and show it to greatest advantage. And do show your property as a home and not merely as a structure.

Your prospective buyer will be visualizing your house as a future home for his family. Will it be a comfortable place to live in? Have a cheerful log burning in the fireplace if it's a gray day. You don't need to fake anything, just have it cozy. It was Edgar Guest who said, "It takes a heap o' livin' in a house t' make it home."

Show a home.

CONSIDERATIONS WHICH CAN RESULT IN EXTRA PROFITS WHEN SELLING REAL ESTATE

On pages 21–22 we discussed the advantages of a property owner's getting an appraisal before trying to put a fair market value selling price on his property. We warned about the tendency of a property owner to add a sentimental value to the true value of land and buildings, resulting in an inflated selling price and in the property's not being sold.

However, it is possible for a seller to be too realistic—or should we say depreciatory—when he puts a value on his real estate. For example, a person wants to sell his house and three acres of land. He has found another four acres on which he would like to build a new house. These four acres are being offered for $3,000 an acre.

To him both pieces of land are of equal value so he offers his three acres for sale at $3,000 an acre. But are the two pieces of land identical? They have different aspects, are on different sites. Possibly one piece of land will someday be an ideal spot for a shopping center, whereas the other piece of land might be better for a colony of retirement homes.

Land cannot be created by man. This is the age of filled lots, of forming land from swamps, of diverting waterways to make land on which houses can be built, and of moving soil from high spots to lower spots. This is not creating land, this is merely moving land. Basically, we can say that there is only so much land in this world for the ever increasing number of people who want that land.

The one who will ultimately enjoy the use of a piece of land is the man who is willing and able to pay the price necessary to buy it. The price he pays for the land is determined by the urgency of his desire to be the owner of that unique piece of land—not duplicated anywhere else in the world—and not by what price he would have to pay for a similar, but not identical, piece of land.

Let's imagine that the land you wish to sell includes a knoll which terminates in a steep cliff. It looks as though a huge apple is sitting up there with one half of it sliced off, resulting in an almost vertical bluff.

In your opinion, anybody wanting to build a house and live up there would have to be crazy. The soil is too shallow for growing shade trees. All it will ever be is just a bare knoll. It is cold and windy up there most of the year. The rest of the year it is too hot for comfort. It would be very costly to build and maintain a road of access.

But, is there another knoll identical to it anywhere else in the world? How many people can own and live on such a knoll? The number of such locations is not changing. The number of people looking for unique pieces of land on which they can build their houses is rapidly increasing. Property considered worthless by you may be considered invaluable by someone else.

Aren't city lots and properties close to shopping centers and schools usually worth more than comparable properties farther away from them? Why? Because the number of sites close to these centers is limited.

Don't corner lots usually cost more than lots crowded into the center of the block? Why? The number of corner lots is limited. Remember that there is only this one lot that you have for sale. Nobody else can offer a prospective buyer exactly what you have to offer him.

Extra profits often aren't realized because a property owner puts too much emphasis on the value of the buildings, which can be duplicated, and not enough emphasis on the land itself, which has certain features and a locale which cannot be duplicated.

Did you ever consider that your property could be sold for some purpose other than the use you have made of it? Possibly you wish to sell because your house is too large for your family. Could you realize more from the sale if you offered it on the basis that it could be converted into a duplex, a nursing home, or an office building? Notice how many offices and even retail sales outlets are in buildings which were once private houses.

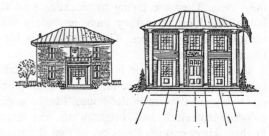

Possibly the location and land you have to sell would be an attractive package to a person interested in starting a business—a grocery, a filling station, or a drive-in restaurant. Many places of business are now on properties which at one time were home sites.

Advertising your property for sale, perhaps on the basis of the opportunities it presents because of the land and location, might produce a buyer willing to pay more than the buyer who was looking solely for a residence. You can interest prospective buyers with different buying motives by altering the presentation of your property in the ad:

FOR SALE: 12-room modern house close to schools and new shopping center.

(or)

FOR SALE: 12-room house close to shopping center and schools—could be converted into a duplex, office building, or retail store.

(or)

FOR SALE: 1½ acres of land on heavily traveled thoroughfare—ideal location for any retail business.

Your twelve-room house can be duplicated. A prospective buyer will not be willing to pay more for the house to be used as a residence than it would cost him to duplicate it in another comparable area. In the first ad, you appeal only to buyers who are looking for a house.

In the second ad you appeal to prospective buyers looking for business opportunities. But again, it is doubtful if anyone will be willing to pay more for the property than he would have to pay for a similar twelve-room house in a comparable location.

Your one and a half acres of land in that particular location *cannot* be duplicated. In the third ad, you appeal to a prospective buyer who possibly has no interest in the property as a house, but who has an interest in the opportunities which exist because of the location of your land. Only you can offer him this land, this opportunity.

Farms need not necessarily be sold as farms:

FOR SALE: 250-acre dairy farm with 40-cow-stanchion barn, two silos, five-year-old modern house.

(or)

FOR SALE: recreational property, 250 acres, 60 acres wooded, running stream, beautifully rolling land, ideal for development into a recreational area.

In the first ad you appeal only to buyers looking for farms. The buyer will not pay more for the property than he would have to pay for another farm which offers him comparable buildings, land, and location.

In the second ad, you make a unique offer. How many properties offer sixty acres of wooded land, a running stream, and beautifully rolling land? You offer the farm as an opportunity to someone interested in developing the land into a recreational area.

Your broker, knowing what you have to sell, will advise you as to what the possibilities are of selling your property for a use other than the one you have made of the property. If you decide that all you have to sell is a conglomeration of buildings, materials, and the land on which these materials are located, should you hope to sell for more than the cost of similar properties in the same area?

Possibly you live in a quiet community of seven thousand people where properties similar to yours are selling for $40,000. However, properties similar to yours—and you know that there are very few—are selling for $60,000 in Chicago. There is no way of moving your $40,000—land and dwellings—to Chicago in an effort to sell it for $60,000.

A prospective buyer from Chicago, possibly retired and wishing to escape to a small community, might be interested in buying your property. He expects to pay less than the $60,000 he would have to pay for a similar property in Chicago, but does he expect to be able to buy such a property for as little as $40,000? He might jump at the chance and consider it a bargain if he is able to buy your property for only $45,000.

Possibly you have a farm you want to sell. The price for farms in the area is established at between $1,500 and $2,500 an acre depending upon the kind of land, the number of acres, and the condition of the buildings.

In another area, similar farms are selling for $4,000 an acre because of rapid urbanization. The fact that farms are being subdivided to provide building sites results in fewer and fewer farms for sale as such.

Shouldn't buyers looking for farms be glad to offer you $2,500 to $3,000 an acre for your farm knowing that they will have to pay $4,000 an acre for similar farms in a different area? Why not offer your farm for sale in an area where farm prices are soaring?

Another example of how the availability of land plays a role in determining land prices is shown in the cost of recreational land.

Most people would love to own a second place where they could build a cabin or house, on part of an acre, and to which they could escape on weekends and during vacations.

Usually those people who are seeking a site for a second house prefer that the property be wooded and close to water. (Possibly such property would not be worth more than $1,000 an acre, offered as property to be used for agricultural purposes.) But what is an acre of this land worth to a person who wants to build on it his long-dreamed-of weekend or vacation cottage?

What would an acre of wooded land, with its own brook, cost in the vicinity of Chicago? There is none available, so no price can be put on it. But if a person is willing to pay $7,000 or more for a lot in Chicago on which to build a house, shouldn't the same person be willing to pay more than $1,000 for an acre of wooded land with a stream running past it?

Are you sure that your property can't be sold for much more if it is offered on a market where similar properties are less available and much higher-priced? Are you sure prospective buyers in a different locality wouldn't be willing to pay more for your property than you can possibly get by offering it for sale on a local market?

For what prices are city lots in your area selling—$1,000, $6,000, $12,000, or more? What sizes are the lots? If the lots are selling for $3,000 and they are of such a size that five of them—with allowances for streets, alleys, and utilities—make up an acre, the land is selling for $15,000 an acre ($3,000 a lot, five lots in each acre).

Since the original patent (grant of that acre by the U. S. Government to its first private owner) that acre has probably been used at one time for agricultural purposes—to raise crops or for livestock grazing—and probably has sold for less than $100.

As houses began to appear in the area, the land became worth more and more until today, according to our example, it is selling—after being subdivided—for $15,000 an acre. It seems logical that you can earn a handsome profit if you own land that cost you only $1,000 or even $3,000 an acre and you are able to sell that land for $15,000 an acre after having it subdivided.

Many owners of small tracts of land have interpreted the words "subdivision" and "lots for sale" to mean sudden riches. These words can mean disappointment and heartache to the landowner. Whether or not you can realize a profit by having your land subdivided and selling lots depends upon:

1. Whether you originally bought the land at a low enough price, and

2. If your cost of having the land surveyed, subdivided, and platted, plus the cost of having roads put in and utilities brought to the area, isn't more than the difference between the price you paid for the land and your selling price, and

3. If there is enough demand for the lots in your neighborhood so that you are able to sell them at a profit.

If you are seriously pondering the possibility of quick riches by having your property subdivided and selling it in lots, first check with the register of deeds in the county where your property is located. Learn the location of other subdivisions in the area. Have the owners been successful in selling lots? At what prices were they able to sell their lots? How attractive to a prospective buyer will your lots be as compared to other lots still available in the community?

Don't be surprised when you learn from the register of deeds that the vacant piece of land just outside of town which you always thought would be an ideal location for a subdivision had been subdivided several years ago. The owner spent a lot of money advertising the lots for sale but none sold.

Your real estate broker is an excellent source of advice as to the possibility of selling lots. He knows what the demand is for lots in your community and for what prices lots are selling. Also, he can refer you to a surveyor—familiar with the subdivision requirements for your area—who can give you an estimate of what the cost will be to have your land subdivided.

Remember, if you have land subdivided and then are unable to sell the lots, you lose. For example, you originally bought the land for $2,000 an acre. You had it subdivided, planning to sell five lots from each for $3,000, thus selling the land for $15,000 an acre. Subdividing plus putting in utilities and roads cost $3,000 an acre, raising your total investment in the project to $5,000 an acre.

If you are unable to sell lots in your subdivision, will a prospective buyer be willing to pay a premium for your land because it has been subdivided? Probably not. The fact that you were unable to sell your lots may even cause a pro-

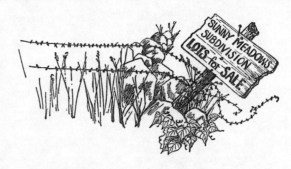

spective buyer to put a value on your property lower than your original cost of $2,000 an acre.

Possibly the buyer was interested in buying your property, thinking that someday he would have it subdivided and sell lots. You have already proven to him by not being able to sell the lots that this opportunity doesn't exist. Under these conditions it is doubtful that a prospective buyer will gamble on the possibility of being able, in the near future, to sell the lots.

Before deciding to have your land subdivided, ask a surveyor what your costs will be. Check with a real estate broker as to the demand for lots and as to what you can expect to receive for the lots. Subdividing land and selling lots is not a task for the amateur; check with the professionals.

TRADING PROPERTIES

Trading properties—rather than selling one property and then buying another property—can sometimes be very rewarding. Properties are usually traded on the basis of what value the parties to the trade put on their respective properties instead of on the basis of equal fair market values.

For example, possibly you consider your property worth only $55,000 but have offered to sell it for $60,000. You wish to sell in order to buy another party's property in a different school district.

It seems to you that his property is ideal for you and that your property is of the type and in the location he wants.

You trade properties with him!

You are satisfied. You were able to trade your property, which you considered to be worth about $55,000, for a property offered for sale at $62,000.

The other party to the trade is also satisfied. He didn't really consider his property worth $62,000 but was hopeful of selling it for that because he thought that the special type of property he wanted to buy would cost at least that much.

Even though each property was traded for a value greater than would have been considered its fair market value, each party to the transaction is satisfied. Each thought he received more in exchange for his property than he could have if he had sold it outright and then bought the particular kind of property he wanted.

Before offering your property for sale, ask yourself these questions:

Can I sell my property for a higher price if I offer to sell it for a use other than the use I have made of it?

Can I sell my property for a higher price if I offer it for sale on a market where similar properties are less available and priced higher?

Can I sell my land for a higher price if I have it subdivided and then sell lots?

Can I make a better deal by trading properties?

PART II

Be a Wise Buyer

Chapter Four

BEFORE YOU BUY, EXPLORE ALL THE ANGLES

TO RENT A HOUSE OR TO BUY ONE

There is no one answer to the age-old question of whether to rent a house or to buy one. As the social and economic circumstances affecting each family differ, so do the reasons that determine their decisions.

You might suppose that a book dealing with the buying and selling of real estate would naturally recommend buying instead of renting.

Not so. Under some circumstances, there are disadvantages in owning a house. Families seek property ownership when their personal incomes are greater than needed for day-to-day living, when they are making more money, perhaps, than in previous years, and when the economy is following an inflationary trend. The price of houses, under these conditions, is usually higher than during a recession.

But families who buy houses during inflationary periods may find themselves, for personal reasons, having to sell these houses in a declining economy. The result is disappointment and some financial loss, since real estate values inevitably decline during recessions.

The key to any profitable transaction is to buy low and sell high. If you have bought high and been forced to sell low, you have paid too high a price for ownership.

When you rent, on the other hand, you are not tied to the property; you can probably move easily enough, depending upon the terms of your lease. This is important when your employment requires that you move frequently or when promotions are contingent upon moving.

How many people do you know who have refused promotions or better jobs because to accept would involve selling their houses and moving? Owning property can be more costly than renting when frequent buying and selling are involved.

For example, even though your property appreciated and you are able to sell it for more than you paid for it, you may end up with less than your original investment because of the costs involved in selling your property—broker's commission, title search and insurance, and lawyer's fees. (Refer to pages 3–7 for cost of selling.)

In some cases a young husband and wife are wise first to establish their insurance program, delaying the purchase of a house until their family size and needs are established. Life insurance premiums are based on the age of the insured when he takes out the policy. The cost of home ownership is dependent upon the fluctuations of the economy. Through delaying the purchase of their first house, a young couple can sometimes avoid the cost of buying and selling houses as the size and needs of their growing family change.

Some people rebel against routine maintenance chores. Either they are not adept at them or they simply hate to be bothered with them. Also, maintenance chores which a person may once have enjoyed doing can become burdensome with advancing age. The person who looks upon maintenance as a burden will possibly be happier as a renter. Don't, however, think that renting automatically releases you from these chores. Often because a landlord is slow to make repairs or because he simply ignores his tenant's pleas to have repairs made, a tenant can wind up with the same maintenance chores he would have had if he had owned the place.

The upkeep required in owning a house will usually take more of your time than the upkeep required of you as a renter. Possibly as a renter you have plenty of time for your golf game. Surely as a proprietor you will have less time. Are you willing to dedicate the necessary hours out of your schedule to the maintenance of your house?

The costs of maintaining your own house remain the same regardless of your income or of fluctuations in the economy. Your house is not going to wait until your salary goes up before it needs a new roof. The hot water heater will need to be replaced someday regardless of your employment or income status.

The cost of maintaining a house can be a burden when a person's income has declined because of bad luck, changes in the economy, or retirements being too large, he can find himself in the budget can become a big obstacle when the budget is reduced.

A couple who, after studying their income and income potential, decide that they can afford to rent a $40,000 house will probably buy a $50,000 house. People tend to buy more costly houses than they would rent, primarily because they feel that they will be willing to put more of their income into a house they own rather than into use of a property through a lease.

Buying implies forced savings, payments toward the house, but when the buyer is too optimistic about his income, resulting in his payments' being too large, he can find himself in the position of being house poor. After making payments on the house the family has too little left over for other investments or for enjoying the life they were able to enjoy as renters.

Regardless of the economics involved, there are many qualitative benefits to be realized from ownership. Some people get a lot of satisfaction out of owning a house—from the right to do with the property as they wish, from being free from the authority of a landlord.

Some enjoy remodeling, fixing up, and even making additions to the house. They take a lot of pride in their work and feel great satisfaction in knowing that it is theirs.

For this person, owning the house fulfills his basic need to express himself. He projects this through the improvements he makes on the property. For example, building a fence around the property to contain the children would be his way of expressing his desire to protect his family.

Some people are wise to buy a house because it forces them into a savings program. Each payment they make toward the purchase price of the property represents just that much more equity acquired in the property. Each payment is like putting so many dollars into a savings account.

Ownership can provide the family with an estate, provided an amount of insurance is carried which is at all times equal to the unpaid balance owed on the property. The owner who is properly insured need not be concerned about how his rent will be paid next month if he is not around, or is unable to pay it. Owning the house, the knowledge that shelter has been provided for his family, brings with it inestimable peace of mind.

The owner can confidently buy furnishings, rugs, appliances, and furniture to suit the house. The renter must temper his selections knowing that any furnishings he buys may possibly have to be fitted into several other very different interiors. Thus when the owner buys furnishings, he buys particular articles for particular parts of his house and considers that these are to be permanent. As compared to the renter, the owner is able to buy furnishings better adapted to the house.

Further, when you own your house, there is no landlord to put restrictions on the size of your family. You are the king of your castle and if you wish to bring up a family of twelve in a three-bedroom house, that is your privilege.

Also, as the owner, you are allowed, within reason, to enjoy such pets as you please. If you want to have dogs or cats, or a pony for the children, this too is your privilege.

Moreover, ownership gives you complete control of your children's home environment. If you want to remodel a room specifically for their pleasure, do so. In our house, we installed the knobs on certain doors at lower than standard levels just to make it easier for the children to open and close the doors. Surely we wouldn't have been allowed to do this as renters.

As the owner, if you wish to install facilities for your children's outside recreational uses, do so. Perhaps you would enjoy building a playhouse for them next summer, with their help, of course.

Many creditors and employers look upon property ownership as a sign of financial stability. It demonstrates a person's sincerity in trying to provide for his family. It shows a man's willingness to accept responsibility. Most application for employment forms ask whether you own your house or rent it.

Owning property is a step toward financial independence. It is a financial move which entails your being involved, being forced into a savings program represented by the payments you make toward ownership of the house. Buying a house is establishing a financial goal, the ownership of your house, and your acceptance of a program to achieve this goal.

Tax benefits are available to the property owner. He may deduct interest which he pays on money he borrows. He is allowed a deduction for the real estate taxes he pays. Property ownership is one of the safest investments there is since you are always guaranteed a dividend on your investment. Your guaranteed dividend is the use of the property.

In addition to this guaranteed dividend, you have complete control of your investment. After you have paid for your house, you are the only stockholder and you may do whatever you wish with your investment.

When showing the cost of renting as compared to the cost of buying a house, it is easy to sway the example in favor of property ownership simply by ignoring the buyer's potential loss of income due to his forfeiting a choice as to what use he may make of the dollars represented by his down payment and annual payments thereafter.

It is possible that, with your investment experience you can invest these dollars and earn 10%; or, possibly because of your lack of investment knowledge, you can earn only 6% with these dollars. The cost of ownership will be greater for the person who can earn 10% on his investment dollars than it will be for the person who can earn only 6% on his investment dollars.

Looking at an example in which we consider only a down payment of $10,000 made the first year, the amount of forfeited income is:

To a person who can earn 10% on his investment dollars ($10\% \times \$10,000$ used as a down payment) . . . $1,000 investment income forfeited the first year.

To a person who can earn only 6% on his investment dollars ($6\% \times \$10,000$ used as a down payment) . . . $600 investment income forfeited the first year.

When honestly figuring the cost of property ownership, the formula should include an allowance for the income you lose through forfeiting the use of the money used as a down payment, plus an allowance for income lost through forfeiting the use of money which will be directed toward payments on the property in future years.

THE COST OF OWNERSHIP VERSUS RENTAL

Statistics are available to show the cost of renting compared to the cost of home ownership in different areas:

ANNUAL COSTS OF A MODERATE URBAN LIVING STANDARD FOR A 4-PERSON FAMILY: 1976

Source: Dept. of Labor, Bureau of Labor Statistics

Area	Rental Cost	Home Ownership Cost
New York, N.Y. Northeastern N.J.	$1,732	$2,466
Boston, Mass.	$2,030	$4,266
Philadelphia, Pa. New Jersey	$1,513	$2,672
Chicago, Ill. Northwestern Ind.	$1,949	$3,050
San Francisco Oakland, Calif.	$2,446	$2,964
Washington, D.C. Maryland-Virginia	$1,893	$2,818
Minneapolis St. Paul, Minn.	$1,689	$2,598

(On today's market these costs are higher, but the differences still exist depending upon what items are included in the comparisons.)

Items included in the above "cost" figures:

Rental Cost	= cost of rent		
Home Ownership Cost	= cost of house repair, maintenance, taxes, interest and principal payments	(PLUS)	cost of gas, heating fuel, electricity, water, and insurance on household contents

It appears that everything has been included in the "costs" and that in these areas it costs more to own than to rent.

But no allowance is made in the Home Ownership Cost figures for an adjustment on your taxable income for real estate taxes, interest on your mortgage, and for equity gained (increased ownership) through your payments on the mortgage principal.

Our worksheet following this chapter forces you to make an allowance for the tax advantages of home ownership plus your increased equity through your payments on the mortgage principal.

After making these allowances you will see that it would possibly cost you less to own in the Boston, Massachusetts, area than to rent. Complete the worksheet before deciding whether you should buy or rent.

The following example shows how the factors of income loss, tax benefits, and equity gained can be worked into a worksheet to determine if home ownership is a wise financial investment.

	Cost of home ownership (per month)	Dollar benefits through home ownership (per month)
Real estate taxes	$100	
Deduction on taxable income for the payment of real estate taxes. (30% tax bracket)		$30
Home maintenance	$50	
Mortgage		
Monthly payment of principal and interest	$155.06	
Equity gained based on average part of the mortgage payment that monthly goes toward payment of principal		$83.34
Deduction on taxable income for the average part of the mortgage payment that monthly goes toward interest. (30%×$71.72)		$21.52
Interest you could earn monthly with your money if you hadn't used it for a down payment. $30,000 down payment×7% interest÷12 months	$175	
	$480.06	$134.86
Total cost of home ownership	$480.06	
Less dollar benefits received	$134.86	
Net cost per month of home ownership	$345.20	

Cost of house	$50,000
Down payment	$30,000
Mortgage	$20,000
Mortgage interest	7% per annum
Mortgage term	20 years
Income tax bracket	30% combined state and federal

(Over the twenty-year life of the mortgage the monthly payments will average $83.34 toward principal and $71.72 toward interest.)

Assuming it cost you $345.22 a month to own this property, wouldn't it cost someone else the same amount per month to own the property and rent it to you?

This is not always true, since a landlord is allowed deductions other than those allowed a property owner who uses the property as his residence. Referring back to our example, in addition to the deductions you are allowed as a residence owner, a landlord is allowed the following:

A deduction for maintenance and repair costs. In our example this cost is $50 monthly. Putting the landlord in the 30% combined tax bracket, this deduction becomes $50 a month ×30% tax bracket	$15.00
A deduction for depreciation. Using the straight-line depreciation (no salvage value) on a $50,000 property over 30 years, we arrive at $1,666 depreciation a year or $138 a month× 30% combined tax bracket	$41.40
Monthly value to the landlord of these additional deductions	$56.40

Although your cost of owning the property is $345.22 a month, a landlord's cost to own the same property is only $288.82 (your cost of $345.22 less $56.40, the value of the additional deductions allowed a landlord).

If the landlord rents this property to you for what it costs you to buy it, $345.22 a month, his net return for renting you his $50,000 property is only $676.80 a year.

Rent he receives monthly	$345.22
(less) landlord's monthly cost of ownership	$288.82
	$ 56.40 net return per month, or $676.80 return per year

If the landlord rents to you for $345.22 a month and only realizes $676.80 annually on his $50,000 investment, he receives only 1.3% net return on his investment. The landlord will certainly want and expect to receive a greater net return than 1.3%. What percentage he wants will vary with individuals, but for our example, let's assume that he will be satisfied with a 7% net return on his investment.

The landlord's monthly cost of ownership	$288.82
The net return the landlord wants on his investment per month is 7%× $50,000 investment÷12 months	$292.00
Monthly rent when the landlord wants only a 7% net return on his investment	$580.82

Regardless of what figures are used, a landlord will want a profit from the rental of his property. Part of your rental payments will be his profit. Through your rental payments you buy the property for your landlord. As to whether you should buy or rent, which do you prefer?

| Rent receipts (or) | A savings represented by the profit which the landlord would ordinarily make from your rental payments. |

Ninety-nine out of every hundred real estate investors are gambling with confidence that the selling price of single-family houses will go up faster than these houses will depreciate.

There is a sound basis for this premise:

PER CAPITA INCOME

(*Source:* Dept. of Commerce, office of Business Economics)

	1970	1973	1974	1975	1976
U.S.	$3,966	$5,049	$5,486	$5,902	$6,441

(These figures represent the total U.S. personal income divided by the total U.S. population.)

Conclusion: Personal and family incomes are rising. Our population consistently has more money to spend per year.

COST OF BUILDING MATERIALS AND LABOR

(*Source:* Dept. of Labor, Bureau of Labor Statistics)
Index base: 1947–49

	1973	1974	1975	1976
All construction materials	138.5	160.9	174.0	187.7
Union hourly wage scale in the building trades	160.8	173.4	188.8	200.5

Conclusion: The cost of building materials and labor is rapidly rising. It costs more to build a house today than it did in previous years, and there is every indication that it will cost even more in the future.

PRICES OF BUILDING LOTS

(*Source:* Dept. of Housing and Urban Development)

1965	$3,400
1970	$5,000
1974	$5,500
1975	$6,400
1976	$7,000

Conclusion: Each year building lots cost more, and again there is every indication that costs will continue to rise in the future.

COST OF HOUSING

(*Source:* Bureau of Labor Statistics)
Index base: 1967—100

1972	129.2
1973	135.0
1974	150.6
1975	166.8
1976	173.2
1977	187.6

Conclusion: The cost of property ownership is rapidly rising because families have more money to spend and the cost of building materials, labor, and building lots has increased.

Based on these trends, the cost of building in 1990 a house that could have been built for $45,000 in 1976 is $65,000.

Cost

1976	$45,000
1980	$50,850
1985	$57,500
1990	$65,000

These trends will continue.

There will be more and more people to occupy the land available and the population will have more money to spend toward buying their own houses. The cost of property ownership will increase along with the increases in the cost of construction materials, labor, and building lots. The value of most existing houses will increase along with the increases in the costs necessary to replace them.

ARE YOU SURE THAT OWNING REAL ESTATE ISN'T ONE OF THE BEST BUFFERS AVAILABLE TODAY AGAINST INFLATION?

The choices are yours. Which do you want?

Rent receipts (*or*) A savings represented by the profit which a landlord ordinarily makes off your rental payments.

Buy your house now, at today's prices (*or*) Wait and sometime in the future for your house pay a higher price

WORKSHEET FOR DETERMINING MONTHLY COST OF OWNERSHIP

Cost of house $_____

Down payment $_____

Mortgage $_____

Mortgage interest $_____

Mortgage term $_____

Your income tax bracket   _____% (combined state and federal)

	Cost of home ownership (per month)	*Dollar benefits through home ownership (per month)*
Real Estate Taxes Yearly taxes $_____ ÷ 12	$_____	
Deduction on taxable income for the payment of real estate taxes. Monthly taxes $_____ × _____% tax bracket		$_____
Home Maintenance Estimate at 1½% annually for new houses and 2% annually for old houses	$_____	
Financing Monthly payment of principal and interest	$_____	
Equity gained based on average part of the mortgage payment that monthly goes toward payment of principal. Take amount from an amortization table		$_____
Deduction on taxable income for the average part of the mortgage payment that monthly goes toward interest. Average interest $_____ × _____% tax bracket		$_____

	Cost of home ownership (per month)	Dollar benefits through home ownership (per month)

Interest you could earn monthly with your money if you hadn't used it for a down payment. Down payment $_____ × _____% return ÷ 12 months $_____

$_____ $_____

Total cost of home ownership $_____
Less dollar benefits received $_____
Net cost per month of home ownership $_____

Chapter Five

YOU DECIDE TO BUY

WHICH TO BUY—AN OLD HOUSE OR A NEW ONE?

Whether you should buy an old house or a new house depends upon what is available, what the several costs are, and how you evaluate what each has to offer. There are definite advantages and disadvantages with both. These should be explored by anyone confronted with the decision, to buy an old house or a new one.

Old Houses

Carpeting and draperies are usually already installed and included in the purchase price at a reasonable figure. Built-ins such as cabinets and appliances are usually also included in the price at very reasonable cost.

The landscaping is already done, the property has matured. If you've had the chore of establishing a new lawn, you know that it can take years. Note how many new houses on new lots have no trees, or very few, and those that have been planted are small.

Usually the stores and services in the neighborhood are well established, as well as shopping centers and churches. You will not be gambling on what will move into the neighborhood as it matures. In an already established area, you know what the zoning laws permit.

When you build a new house in an area that is not yet established, you often are taking a chance on what future use will be made of adjoining areas. Also, with an older house, the price and value of the property have been established, since the property has possibly been bought and sold several times. You don't pay a premium simply for newness, as you do with a new car.

Taxes, too, have been established on an older house. Check with the city clerk to learn what the taxes have been during the previous years. What has been the pattern? Have they remained about the same or have they been increasing? In most cases with an older house you can anticipate fewer special assessments for such things as the installation and maintenance of streets, alleys, water mains, and sewage systems.

In an established neighborhood you can decide before you buy whether you are acquiring the sort of neighbors you like. Often with a new house, in a new neighborhood, you are gambling on your future neighbors. Will they be the kind of people you will enjoy having as friends?

With an older house, the cost of insuring the property is established. Also, the seller should be able to show what his costs have been for heating, electricity, water, and sewage.

Most old houses offer opportunities for the home craftsman to improve the property by fixing up and painting up. A few hundred dollars spent on remodeling will usually add twice that amount to the value of the property.

With older houses, you are usually buying more

total space for your money. You can buy more square footage of floor space and more cubic footage of space with your property-buying dollars.

New Houses

When you buy a new house, on the other hand, you are less likely to be buying somebody else's problems. The wise seller of an older house is an expert at covering faults with a little paint and plaster. To the dismay of the new owner, these blemishes too often recur. And buying a new house allows you to choose a design you like. You can select your own floor plan and style.

If you're the home craftsman type, you can buy a mere shell of a house and finish it with your own labor. This can considerably reduce the cost of buying the house. And when you buy a new house you should have no problem with the building's conforming to current building codes.

With personal income going up, young folk are looking toward starting out their married lives in new houses. There is usually a greater demand for new houses and they are easier to resell.

Usually you can finance a larger percentage of the total purchase price of a new house; usually less down payment is required when you buy a new one. With improved skills and materials, a new house should be better constructed than an older one.

There is always the price of owning something new. An often-used selling point when older houses are offered for sale is that the reduction in price is greater than the depreciation; the buyer will be getting more for his money when he buys an older house. Actually this is often true and on this basis older houses can be "good buys."

But depreciation is not dependent solely upon the physical condition of the buildings. An older house, which often is in poorer condition when it is sold than it was when it was new, instead of having depreciated in value may have appreciated. It may be worth more now than when it was originally built. And a new house may be worth less when it is offered for a sale than the cost of the labor and materials that went into its construction.

Every person who is contemplating the purchase of a house should temper his final decision with the thought that someday he may want to resell that house. Whether he started with a new house or a used one, what will that property be worth when he wants to resell it?

To what extent will the property depreciate? How much less will the property be worth five to ten years from now?

The depreciation which the house owner should expect will come from three sources:

1. Economic depreciation;
2. Functional depreciation;
3. Physical depreciation.

Economic Depreciation

Economic depreciation results from social and economic changes which occur quite aside from any physical changes in the real estate.

For example, when a new neighborhood was started, most of the houses built were in the $35,-000 price range. Recently, houses in the $20,000 price range have been cropping up in the same neighborhood. Obviously the lower-priced houses in the neighborhood will tend to drag down the resale value of the higher-priced houses. The existence of the higher-priced houses will tend to raise the value of the lower-priced houses.

A house in one neighborhood may actually increase in value because of the increased desirability of the neighborhood, while the same house in another neighborhood could rapidly depreciate in value because of the social or economic deterioration of the neighborhood. Or, a new house in a deteriorating neighborhood may rapidly depreciate in value while an older house in an adjoining neighborhood, which is becoming a more and more desirable place to live in, may increase in value.

Although the buildings are depreciating, the value of the land or lot can be appreciating fast enough to offset the depreciation, resulting in a steady increase in the aggregate value of the total property.

Functional Depreciation

Functional depreciation results from the design or construction of the building's not being acceptable to the market on which the property is offered for sale.

The house with large rooms, high ceilings, even with bay window and cupolas, was once very much in demand. It would be difficult to sell such a house today even for construction costs. It is simply not the type of house today's buyer wants.

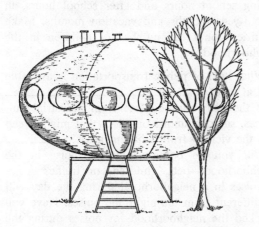

A new house which is "different," which is not in conformity with the ideas of today's buyer, may be obsolete the day it is completed. Even though it is situated in a desirable neighborhood in which older houses are appreciating, the offbeat house may rapidly depreciate because its basic design and construction are not of a kind sought after by the average modern buyer.

Most older houses, regardless of the soundness of their construction and the standard at which they have been maintained, suffer from functional depreciation. For today's market they lack enough bathrooms and they have outdated plumbing and heating systems. They are just not what is wanted today.

The value of houses—old and new—and their rate of functional depreciation are constantly changing as the desires of buyers change. It is difficult to forecast what the property buyer ten years from now will want, but it is usually wise not to invest in a house that is eccentric in style.

Physical Depreciation

Physical depreciation is the result of a property's becoming less valuable and less desirable because of the deterioration of the materials used in its construction. This is the easiest type of depreciation to detect and to evaluate. Unfortunately, it is often the only kind of depreciation the buyer really studies before buying a house.

Evidences of physical deterioration are: dry rot in wood-frame buildings, termite damage, cracking of concrete work, corrosion of plumbing

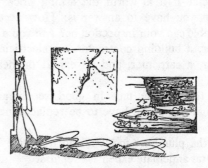

and heating systems, and over-all obsolescence due to age and lack of upkeep. (Refer to pages 52–58 for what to look for when buying a house.)

To some degree the owner has control over the rate at which his property suffers physical depreciation. Does he do a conscientious job of maintaining his house? Is he continually fixing up and painting up?

Although he can judge physical deterioration, the owner of the house will not realize how much economic and functional depreciation the house has suffered until he offers his property for sale. Only then can he accurately gauge how desirable the property is to a prospective buyer, including the neighborhood and the architecture and construction of the building.

Whether he is looking at an old house or a new house, a prospective buyer should study what effects economic and functional depreciation of the property would have on its resale value.

Is the property located in a neighborhood in which other properties are appreciating due to the neighborhood's becoming more desirable? Will this trend continue?

Are the buildings of a design and construction that appeal to today's buyers? Will it be a desirable type of house for buyers five to ten years from now?

There can be no one answer as to which to buy—an old house or a new one. Either one can be a very profitable or a very unrewarding experience, depending upon how well the property satisfies the needs of the family, how wisely the property was originally purchased, and what the market will be for that particular property when it is eventually resold.

WHAT TO LOOK FOR WHEN BUYING A HOUSE

The best we can do is to supply you a check list of the things you should inspect and the inquiries you should make about a house before you decide if it is worth the asking price. The question you have to answer is: How accurate or valuable can your inspection be? Are you a civil engineer, a building contractor, an electrician, a plumber, a carpenter, and an expert on heating units?

Is the heating unit in good repair and adequate or will it have to be replaced next year?

Is the plumbing modern and adequate or can you anticipate expensive repairs?

Does the wiring conform to the building code or can you look forward to having it replaced?

These questions should definitely be answered before the decision is made to buy a house, and in most cases it is wise to go to the small expense of having an expert answer these questions for you.

If you have progressed to the point where you definitely like the neighborhood, you have made a general inspection of the property and your family likes it, and you still think the asking price is what the house is worth, have a civil engineer, a contractor, or someone whose business is building or home repairs give you an opinion as to the value of the house. The few dollars this will cost is cheap compared to the risk of not learning about needed repairs until after you own the property.

The first step is to learn if you are really interested in the property. This starts with an inspection of the neighborhood.

Things to Check in the Neighborhood

Make these checks both by day and by night.

Are the adjoining property owners the sort of people you would like to have as friends? _____

Will you be comfortable living in a neighborhood with the present number of children about the neighborhood? _____

Is the neighborhood predominantly made up of older people or of young couples just starting their families? _____

Entire neighborhoods can change in the periods during school hours and after school hours, in school-year months and vacation months. Make inquiries about the number of children in the neighborhood.

What type of public transportation is available and at what cost? _____

Is the neighborhood free from industrial nuisances, such as smoke or odors that might creep into the vicinity from adjacent areas? _____

Will you be bothered by the noise in the neighborhood—pets, children, or traffic? _____

Noises in a neighborhood during the day will be different from the nighttime noises. Have you checked the neighborhood for noises during the day and at night? _____

How close are the churches, schools, and shopping centers you prefer? _____

Can your children reach school and recreation grounds without crossing heavily traveled streets or intersections? _____

Take a walk. Look around. Ask questions.

How close are you to community recreational centers and to facilities for adult recreation? ___

Do the property owners in the neighborhood show a pride in ownership? _____

Are their lots neat and their houses painted? Is there evidence that they make a conscientious effort to maintain their houses? _____

What medical facilities, services and personnel will be available to you? _____

Where are the hospitals and what kind of ambulance service will be available? _____

What are the police and fire protection available to you? _____

These matters could make a difference in the cost of your property insurance. Are the streets in the neighborhood regularly patrolled by the police? Where is the closest fire hydrant? _____

Will qualified house repair and other services be available to you in the area? _____

If your washing machine breaks, will you be able to have it quickly repaired or will you have to wait your turn for a serviceman from the other end of town? _____

Are the trees, shrubs, flowers, and lawn permanent? _____

Were they planted only last year, or six months

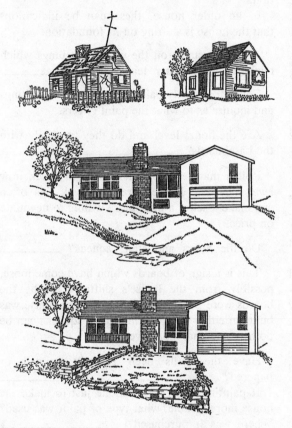

ago, or even more recently just to make the property more salable? Are they well established and free from disease? _____

Is municipal garbage collection offered free in the area, and if not, what is the cost and what type of service can you expect? _____

How hard is the water in the area and what type of water softener will be necessary?_____

After you get inside the house you may find that a water softener has already been installed and is practically new. Is it adequate for the hardness of the water? Is there a guarantee on it? Where was it originally bought? _____

What type of snow removal service will there be? _____

Are the streets in this neighborhood the last ones cleaned? Could this result in your having to miss work, or be late for work, following heavy snowfalls? _____

How does the house you are buying compare with the other houses in the neighborhood? _____
_____

If the other houses in the neighborhood seem to be worth a little more than the one you are considering, that may help to pull up your property value.

If the other houses appear to be worth less, they will tend to pull down the value of the house you are considering.

What is the value of the houses in the adjoining neighborhood? _____

Usually a moderately priced house will appreciate in value if it adjoins an area of higher-priced houses.

Is the neighborhood in the older end of town where houses have been depreciating and will continue to do so?_____

Things to Check Outside of the House

Is the slope to the lot sufficient for adequate drainage? _____

With most soil types, 1″ to every 10′ is considered adequate.

Is the foundation of the house sound and in good repair? _____

The foundation should extend at least 6″ above the ground level and the house should sit squarely upon its foundation.

Is the lot large enough for your children to play outside and not be in the street? _____

Is the entrance to the house well sheltered and well lighted? _____

Is the main entrance door wide enough? How about the back door and possibly the entrance to the cellar? _____

It could be frustrating to have to buy new furniture because you are unable to get your old furniture through the doorways and into the house.

Are the garage doors wide enough so that you can easily get your car in and out of the garage? How easily do the garage doors open and shut?

_____

Is the lot well lighted at night? Where is the street light? _____

What is the condition of the surfacing material used on the exterior of the house? When will it need repainting? Was it recently repainted with a cheap paint just to make the house more attractive? _____

Is the flow of traffic past the lot at a reasonable speed? Are there adequate stop lights, stop signs, and traffic control? _____

This definitely should be checked both during the day and at night. Sometimes a street that is quiet and peaceful during the day is like a freeway during other hours.

Are the windows and door openings located so as to give you the winter sun and to shade the interior of the house in summer? _____

Is the chimney in good repair? What is the condition of the flashings over the doors, windows, and covering joints on the roof? _____

Is the roof in good repair? When was the last new roof installed? Who did the work? What weight of material was used? _____

Look for the number of repaired or replaced shingles. Note the number of curled-up and fried-out shingles; when will a new roof be needed?

_____

Are there enough outside water taps?_____

Is the soil of a type and at a depth adequate for you to maintain a lawn, grow shrubs and trees, and plant a garden? _____

Borrow a spade and check the soil.

Are the outside buildings suitable for storage? What are the uses you could make of these buildings? _____

Can you expect problems in maintaining a lawn or garden because of neighborhood pets—dogs and cats? _____

Are there any burned spots on the lawn or any evidence of digging? _____

Are there enough storm doors, windows, and screens? Where are they stored when not in use?

_____

Look for their tunnels around the foundation of the house. Check again for termite damage when you are inside the house. Is there any evidence of termites? _____

Things to Check Inside the House

FLOORS AND WALLS

Are there opened trim joints, buckled wallboard, or cracks in the plaster? _____

In a relatively new house, these can be indications that green lumber was used in its construction.

In an older house, these can be indications that the house is shifting on its foundation.

Are there stains on the walls or ceilings which might indicate water leaks? _____

Check for freshly painted-over areas on ceilings and inquire as to what the paint covers.

Are the floors level and do they fit snugly with the baseboards? _____

Roll a marble across the floors to check how level they are. If they are not level, this often can make a seller a little more willing to negotiate on price.

Do the floors and stairs squeak? _____

This is a sign of boards which have come loose, possibly from the house's shifting. Maybe the boards were poorly installed when the house was built. In either case, getting rid of squeaks can be bothersome and expensive.

Have the walls been recently painted or papered? _____

If painting was recently done just to make the house more salable, what type of paint was used? Where was it purchased? _____

What is under the wallpaper? Before putting it on, did they remove the old wallpaper or did they put the new wallpaper over the old? Are there any extra rolls of the wallpaper? Where was it bought? _____

Have the floor coverings been recently installed? _____

If there is carpeting and if it is to be included in the price, what is its value? Was it recently installed to make the house more impressive? Where was it purchased? _____

What is under the recently installed linoleum or tile? Did they bother to remove the old tile or linoleum before installing the new? This will make a difference as to the problem you may expect in making the floor covering adhere to the floor. _____

If tile was used, is there any extra tile of the same pattern? Where was the tile bought? _____

Do all windows and doors open and shut freely?
_____

Often it is interesting to check upstairs windows and windows in rooms which are seldom used.

Shake the windows. Do they fit snugly? _____

What is the condition of the glass in the windows and doors? _____

Raise some window shades and open some draperies. You might be interested in what you find. Does the glass fit snugly into the frames? Is the glass old and discolored? _____

Is there damage around the windows caused by weather leaks? _____

Are the windows weather-stripped? Is there evidence of damage around the windows due to accumulated moisture? _____

ATTICS AND BASEMENTS

To what degree have the joists and beams rotted and what caused the rot? _____

Using a knife, a nail, or an ice pick, when you see a rotted spot, dig into it. To what extent have the structural members rotted? _____

If the rot was caused by excessive moisture due to poor ventilation, what will it cost to ventilate the basement or attic properly? _____

What will it cost to supplement rotted joists or beams with additional ones or to replace them with new ones? _____

This is a good time to check for signs of leaks in the roof. Look for watermarks on the floor of the attic. Using a flashlight, check for holes in the roof. Is there any evidence of leaks? _____

If there is evidence of structural damage due to termites, what will it cost to correct it? _____

Is there any evidence that the house has a wet basement? _____

Are there watermarks on the basement walls indicating that at some time water has stood in the basement? _____

If there is a sump pump in the basement, it is a good sign that the basement leaks. Why else would the pump be there?

Is the basement structurally sound? _____

If jack posts are used in the basement to support the floors in areas where heavy appliances or furniture is kept, it is a good sign that the floors are not structurally sound.

If there are large cracks in the foundation, it is wise to have a specialist check the basement. Don't gamble on the basic soundness of the house.

INSULATION

Is the house properly and adequately insulated?
_____

As a minimum there should be two inches of insulation on the floors and walls and between three inches and six inches of insulation over the ceilings.

Check in the basement and attics for insulation.

By removing electrical outlet plates or switch plates you can sometimes determine if the walls are insulated and what type of insulation was used.

Things to Note About the Floor Plan of the House

Are the traffic patterns adapted to your family?
_____

Is the house broken up into living, sleeping, and working zones? _____

The housewife will be making the trip from the kitchen to the front door many times daily. How far is it? _____

Into what zones does the entrance from the basement or garage enter? _____

Is access to the bathroom facilities easy without passing through the living zone? _____

Can you move directly from the kitchen to the sleeping zone without passing through the living zone? _____

You should not have to pass through the center of any one room when moving from one zone to another.

For example, you should be able to pass from the living zone to the sleeping zone to the working zone without having to pass through the center of any one room.

Is the kitchen roomy and so situated that it receives a maximum of natural lighting? _____

Small kitchens with little exposure to outside lighting—resulting in the housewife's working most of the time by artificial light—make for grumpy wives.

Windows should be so situated that they are easy to keep clean. Is there a window over the sink? Turn on the faucet. Does the water splash on or close to the window? Will keeping this window clean be a problem? _____

Is the kitchen small enough and organized well enough so that the housewife need not pay the high price of extra steps just for roominess? _____

Large kitchens are usually appealing, but unless they are properly organized, they may mean many extra steps for the housewife.

Where are the cabinets or storage units? Are they adequate? Are they handy to the working areas? _____

Are the zones so situated that there is a minimum of noise from one zone to another? _____

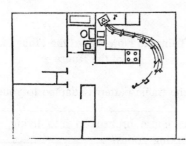

Take along a portable radio. Turn it on in the kitchen and then walk through the house.

Move the radio into the living room. Again walk throughout the house. Are the sleeping zones quiet? _____

If you plan to have a playroom or hobby center in the basement, move the radio into the basement and then again walk through the house.

Are the sleeping areas adequate for the family you plan on? _____

Will there be enough bedrooms for your family next year? How about five or ten years from now? Are the rooms large enough for dressers and desks? Does each room have adequate closet space? Are the closets well lighted? _____

What other areas in the house could be converted into bedrooms? Could additional bedrooms be easily added and would they tie in with the present sleeping zone? _____

What rooms do you have to pass through to get from the sleeping zone to the bathrooms? _____

Is the family room in the best location for your family? _____

Most people with young children prefer that the family room be close to the kitchen.

When the family does a lot of entertaining, it is sometimes best that the family room adjoin the living room so that both may be used as one room for big parties.

In some cases it is desirable that the family room be completely separated from the living room and kitchen. This creates two separate living zones—the family room and the living room.

Things That Should Be Checked by a Professional

PLUMBING

Is the water pressure adequate for the facilities in the house at present and for any additional bathrooms you will install? _____

Open the drains and turn on all the faucets in the house. Flush the toilet. Is there an even flow of water from the faucets? Is there a steady flow of water from the upstairs faucets? _____

If a faucet spits and sputters when you open it, it usually is an indication that there is inadequate water pressure in that line.

Is the drainage system adequate for the facilities at present in the house and for any additional facilities you may install? _____

Open all drains, turn on all faucets, and then flush the toilet. Does the toilet empty properly? ___

Is the plumbing modern, in good repair, and does it conform to the building code? _____

Does each faucet have its own turnoff? Or does the entire plumbing system have to be shut off and drained to repair a dripping faucet? _____

How easily can the plumbing traps be removed for cleaning? Are they so old and have they been disconnected for cleaning so infrequently that they have cemented themselves into place?

Check the manufacturer's name on the toilet bowl, the bathtub, and the plumbing fixtures.

Are they of quality materials or the cheapest that could be bought? _____

If the property has a septic tank, when was it installed? What is its capacity and when was it last cleaned? _____

Will the hot water heater be adequate for your family needs? _____

Where was it purchased and who installed it? The firm can tell you if it will be adequate for the needs of your family. _____

Is there a guarantee on the hot water heater? Can the guarantee be transferred to you? What is the name and address of the person who has serviced the unit? _____

Will the water softener be adequate for the needs of your family? _____

Where was it bought and who installed it? ___

_____

Is there a guarantee on the unit? Can the guarantee be transferred to you? What is the name and address of the person who services the unit and what is the monthly cost of having the unit serviced? _____

HEATING

Is the heating system adequate for the house?

_____

Turn up the thermostat. Learn how long it takes to raise the temperature throughout the house. Check in an upstairs room. Does the house heat evenly? _____

Is the heating system designed so that you can easily connect it to extra rooms added to the house? _____

If the heating unit requires air filters, how are they replaced? _____

Is the heating unit equipped with a humidifier and can an air conditioning unit be adapted to it? _____

Is the humidifier or air conditioner adequate for the house? Who is available to service them? How often do they require cleaning and how are they cleaned? _____

What has been the cost of heating the house?

_____

Are there any existing guarantees on the heating unit? What repairs or conversions have been made on the unit and who made them? Where was the unit purchased? Where has fuel been purchased? _____

Will the noise made by the heating unit bother your family? _____

Each unit is individual and has its own particular noises.

Turn on the heating unit and walk throughout the house. Check for noises in the bedrooms.

ELECTRICITY

Is the electrical system throughout the house modern and does it conform to the building code?

_____

Any contractor or electrician should be able after a brief inspection to advise you on this subject.

Is the electrical system adequate for the use you plan to make of the house? _____

Where are the switches? Are there enough outlets and are they located where you will need them for the use of your appliances? _____

Imagine that you are preparing an elaborate meal. Are there enough outlets conveniently located for you to enjoy using your appliances? What would it cost to install additional outlets?

_____

Imagine you are vacuum-cleaning the entire house. Where are the outlets? _____

Check as to What Uses You Will Be Allowed to Make of the Property

What restrictions do the local zoning ordinances put on the uses you may make of the property?

_____

Check with the city clerk. Is the area zoned as a residential one? If so, is it restricted to single or multifamily units? Is it zoned for commercial or for manufacturing purposes? _____

This will make a difference as to what use you may make of the property and also as to what you may expect to have as current or future neighbors.

How are the areas adjoining this property zoned? Will you be enclosed by manufacturing or commercially zoned areas? _____

Does the property conform to local building restrictions? _____

Check with the city clerk and building inspector.

Restrictions might include minimum lot size for the size of buildings on it, or setback requirements dictating that buildings be a certain number of feet or inches from the front line of the lot.

Is the building in conformity with safety codes?
_____

Check with the local building inspector.

The purpose of these codes is fire prevention and sanitation. They usually cover such things as plumbing, ventilation, and electrical wiring.

Will the property be affected by future changes in the layout of the community? _____

Some communities have "official maps" which show where the beds of future streets will lie. These maps also show the widening lines along existing streets. Possibly someday a street will pass through what is now the back yard of the property.

Are there any planned changes that might affect the property you are considering buying? Check with the city clerk. _____

Are there any restrictive covenants that might limit the uses you may make of the buildings or property? _____

Such a covenant would be written into the deed by which the seller received ownership of the property. It is possible that such a covenant could put restrictions on what uses you, as the new owner, could make of the property.

If there are any restrictive covenants on the property, it is wise to have your attorney clarify just how they will affect uses you may make property? _____

When inspecting a house, try to determine if it is the type of *home* your family will enjoy.

Sit in the living room, then take a trip to the bathroom. Imagine you are sitting in the living room watching TV. Will you hear noises from the kitchen? _____

How convenient is the kitchen refrigerator for a late-evening snack? _____

When you want to go to bed early, will you be bothered by noises from the kitchen or by the children watching TV in the family room? _____

Imagine that the house is your own home.

SHOULD YOU PAY THE SELLER'S PRICE OR DICKER?

If you have decided that you definitely want to buy the property and your only problem is that you haven't decided what price you are going to have to offer in order to buy it, answer these questions:

Is the seller's listed price the very lowest price he will accept? If the seller will accept a lower price, what is the rock-bottom price he will accept?

Recall that one of a broker's duties to a buyer is to reveal to him the lowest price the seller will accept for the property. For example, the seller lists the property at $60,000 but tells the broker that he will accept an offer for $55,000. The broker is duty-bound to reveal to the buyer that the seller will accept $55,000 for the property.

If the broker has told you the lowest price

the seller will accept and you still consider the price too high, is there any sense in making a lower offer? Definitely, yes! The broker has been completely honest with you but the seller may change his mind and accept your lower offer.

How long has the property been listed for sale? Possibly the seller is disgusted because the property hasn't been sold and will consider an offer at a lower price but hasn't yet mentioned this to the broker. Make your offer.

Recall that no matter how much your offer differs from the price the seller is asking for the property, the broker's duty is to submit your offer to the seller.

When you make your offer to purchase, you introduce yourself through the broker to the seller. You show the seller that you are interested in buying his property. You are telling the seller at what price and on what terms you are interested in buying his property.

You have started to NEGOTIATE. Until you submit your offer this is not possible. Many sales are never made because a buyer considers it useless to make an offer at his price. Price is usually the one big factor in determining whether a seller accepts an offer. However, the "conditions" under which you are offering to buy the property can very well influence the price the seller will accept.

For example, you offer a price of $5,000 less than the seller's asking price and in addition you ask that the seller personally carry a mortgage for a portion of the selling price.

The seller is agreeable to knocking the $5,000 off his original asking price but is unwilling to do any of the financing personally. Simply by arranging your financing elsewhere, you could become the new owner of the property at the price you wanted to pay.

Just as some people respond to money, some to praise, and some to titles, sellers of real estate take widely differing attitudes on what is of real importance to them. For example, although he doesn't say so in his listing, a seller may be unwilling to make any concessions on his selling price but may be willing to help a buyer with financing.

Another seller may not be willing to help out with financing but may be willing to lower his selling price in exchange for an all-cash transaction. Still another seller, although he has not said so in his listing, may be attracted by a trade-in deal.

Until you make an offer to purchase you have no way of knowing what concessions the seller will make. You do not know what he included in the listing because he considered it the right thing to do, as compared with what he will actually accept for the property.

When the seller fails to accept your offer, you should find out what it was that he didn't like about your offer. You can always submit another offer if the seller refuses to accept your first offer. Just because a girl refuses to accept your proposal of marriage the first time you proffer it doesn't mean that you can't propose again.

The broker is of necessity a student of people. He understands the seller's psychology, exactly what he is aiming for. The broker will help in every way possible to bring about a meeting of minds between you and the seller. This is the only way he can earn his commission.

Make your offer. If it isn't accepted, find out why it wasn't, select alternatives, discuss possible solutions with the broker, and make another offer. Remember, though, that dickering for a lower price can result in your losing the property even though you would have been willing to pay the seller's price; you were dickering just in the hopes of saving money.

Remember that a seller of real estate is not bound to sell to you on the terms of your offer until such time as he has accepted your offer and the acceptance has been personally delivered or mailed to you. For example, you submit an offer to the seller to purchase his property at a price of $5,000 less than his listed price. Before the seller has made a decision as to whether he should accept your offer, a third party offers to buy the property at the seller's asking price. Naturally the seller accepts this offer.

You earn yourself a bundle of disappointment through your efforts to save $5,000. You were willing to pay the asking price but were just trying to save $5,000 by dickering.

Possibly you considered the property worth even more than the price the seller was asking. You considered it a good deal at that price but you were trying to save money by submitting an offer at a lower price. Again, a third party offered to buy the property at the seller's asking price. Because you considered the property underpriced, you might be willing to make another offer for an amount in excess of the original listed price. You could end up paying more for a property than you would have if you had been willing to pay the original asking price and then pushed for a quick acceptance of your offer by the seller.

Many times at personal property auctions I have seen people quit bidding on an object only to buy the same object later, at a higher price, from the person who originally bought it.

The person who failed to buy the object by submitting the highest bid was uncertain as to how badly he wanted it. He needed time to think about it and didn't like the idea of being rushed into making a decision. After having time to think about it, such a person often is willing to pay a higher price for the same object than he would have had to pay if he had been willing in the first place to make the highest bid for it. He just needed time to think about it.

In the typical real estate transaction this situation need not exist. A buyer may reserve the exclusive right to buy a property on his terms and still be allowed time to reconsider his offer and possibly later withdraw his offer. When a seller accepts the buyer's offer to purchase and that acceptance has been delivered to the buyer, the buyer has the exclusive right to buy that property on the terms outlined in his offer.

If at this stage the buyer changes his mind—decides that he doesn't want to go ahead with the purchase of the property—he may back out of the deal.

However, when a buyer defaults or fails to go ahead with an offer that has been accepted by the seller, the seller may:

1. Demand that the buyer's earnest money be forfeited to him as liquidated damages, or
2. Sue the buyer for specific performance of the contract in an effort to force the buyer to go ahead with the terms of the contract, or
3. Sue the buyer for damages resulting to the seller because the buyer failed to go ahead with the terms of the contract.

When the buyer's sole objective is to preserve the exclusive right to buy a property and not to establish a basis for negotiation, he should use an option instead of an "offer to purchase."

OPTION
Seller gives the buyer an opportunity to buy his property on the seller's terms.

Buyer accepts the seller's offer.

Usually very little negotiation takes place. The seller has set his price and terms and the buyer either accepts them or pays a penalty.

Earnest money payment is required for a valid option.

OFFER TO PURCHASE
Buyer offers to purchase the seller's property on the buyer's terms.

Seller accepts the buyer's offer.

An excellent starting point for . means through which buyer and seller can each learn what the other wants, then make compromises to result eventually in a meeting of minds and a sale.

Earnest money is recommended but not always required.

OPTION
Buyer must exercise his right to buy the seller's property by the date set in the option or else the buyer forfeits his earnest money to the seller as liquidated damages.

If the buyer doesn't go ahead with the purchase, he loses his earnest money.

OFFER TO PURCHASE
After the offer has been accepted, the closing may take place at any reasonable time after the agreed-upon date and the buyer will not be asked to forfeit his earnest money. However, when time of closing has been made an essential part of the contract, if the buyer cannot close the deal by the date agreed upon, he may lose his earnest money.

If the buyer backs out of the deal after the seller has accepted his offer, the seller may (1) keep the buyer's earnest money as liquidated damages, or (2) sue the buyer for specific performance, or (3) sue the buyer for damages.

It certainly appears that the logical way to preserve the exclusive right to buy a property while given time to decide if you really want it, or will be able to buy it, is through the use of an option. The most you can lose if you decide not to buy the property is your earnest money.

However, when a seller lists a property for sale, his objective usually is to expose what he has for sale to as many prospective buyers as possible, in hopes of receiving from one of them an offer to buy that conforms with the terms of his listing.

Why should a seller give a buyer an option—the exclusive right to buy his property—at any price or on any terms other than those on which he wants to sell the property?

Doing so denies him the right to sell to another buyer who might be willing to purchase the property at the seller's price and on the seller's terms. On this basis, when they have had their properties listed, many sellers are reluctant to give options unless the option is to buy the property at the price and on the terms outlined in the seller's listing.

One way of using a purchase offer so as to reserve the exclusive right to buy a property is to write into the offer the provision that you are willing to go ahead with the terms outlined in your offer but only subject to the approval of your offer by a third party. (Refer to pages 58–59, 67 for special conditions in the offer to purchase.) Even though the seller accepts your offer and the acceptance is delivered to you, you have the right to withdraw from the contract if the third party does not approve of your offer. You reserve the exclusive right to purchase the property but allow yourself time to reconsider your offer and possibly withdraw from the contract.

Do not expect to be allowed much time to reconsider your offer, and possibly withdraw it, on the basis that you aren't bound to it until the seller accepts it and the acceptance is delivered to you. When you give your offer to the broker, he is going to present it to the seller as quickly as possible.

As already noted, the biggest single factor as to whether a seller will accept an offer usually is the offered price. On this basis, sellers will often give a little to get a little. For example, the seller lists the property for $60,000 but tells the broker that he will accept as little as $55,000. Although he doesn't tell his broker, the seller will actually consider an offer of $52,000.

On the basis that the broker tells you that the lowest price the seller will accept is $55,000, you make an offer in which you are willing to pay $55,000 but only if the seller will (1) finance part of the purchase price, (2) provide you with a survey of the property, and (3) supply you an owner's policy of title insurance.

The seller does not intend to do any of these things. They each represent an expense to him and will reduce the final number of dollars he will receive from the sale of the property, but you are offering him the price he wants—$55,000— so he is willing to bend a little by going ahead with your requests.

Should a buyer submit an offer asking a seller to accept a price lower than the listing price and in the same offer ask the seller to make additional concessions?

It is necessary first to understand the seller. He may have little interest in your offer because he thinks that you are asking him to concede too much. Usually, though, he will be willing to negotiate, to express what he definitely will not go along with and on what points he possibly will make concessions.

Sometimes after the buyer has made a few concessions to the seller, the seller will accept the offer thinking that he has made a good deal. He compares the offer he finally accepts to the offer that was originally submitted but not to what he originally wanted for the property.

Most people have been involved in making a purchase in which they offered a price much lower than was asked, only to end up paying a price somewhat between the original asking price and their original offering price. Both parties to the transaction are probably content in that each received concessions from the other.

After the offer to purchase is submitted to the seller and the seller says he will accept it, but only subject to certain changes, two points have to be clarified:

What the seller actually wants as compared to what he will accept, and

What the buyer will actually give as compared to how he would like to buy the property.

Confusion at this stage as to what each party actually wants often results in the failure to consummate a deal that otherwise could have been rewarding to both parties.

The real reason why one or the other party to a transaction is unwilling to go ahead with the deal is often hidden in the terms, the conditions, and the provisions of the offer and the listing.

The reason or reasons why a seller will not accept an offer must be explored and clearly understood so that they can be discussed, possibly modified or eliminated, resulting in a contract acceptable to both buyer and seller.

The biggest problem is often in simply isolating and defining the real problem. We are hopeful that the following worksheet will be helpful in isolating the problem or problems to be solved in your real estate transaction.

WORKSHEET FOR ISOLATING PROBLEMS

Lowest price seller will accept $_____

    Seller will accept the lower price of $_____

    but only if _____

Highest price buyer will pay $_____

    Buyer will pay the higher price of $_____

    but only if _____

Conditions the buyer has listed in his offer that are not acceptable to the seller:

_____

_____

_____

Proposed alternatives by the buyer to conditions in his offer that are not acceptable to the seller:

_____

_____

_____

Conditions the seller has in his listing that are not acceptable to the buyer:

_____

_____

_____

Proposed alternatives by the seller to conditions in his listing that are not acceptable to the buyer:

_____

_____

_____

Chapter Six

EVALUATING THE PROPERTY

WHAT IS THE PROPERTY REALLY WORTH?

Do you want to be convinced that the property you would like to own is really worth the price the seller is asking for it?

Ask the seller's neighbors and, provided they like him, they will agree that the property is worth as much or even more than he is asking for it. They will want him to make a "good deal."

Or, if you really want to sell yourself on it, compute the total cubic footage of the buildings and multiply that figure by what it will cost to reproduce it on today's market. Add to that figure an inflated value on the land. You can make the seller's price look favorable or unreasonable depending upon what adjustment you make on the final figure for the depreciation of the property.

Or simply ask the seller why he wants to sell the property. He must have a reason for selling it at so low a price. Why is he making this sacrifice? Possibly he has to move because of the climate, because of his employment, or because his family has grown too large for the house.

Unfortunately many buyers use this kind of information as a basis for determining whether a property is really worth the asking price. The result may well be that they learn, when they try to resell the property, that they actually paid too much for it.

In the typical real estate transaction the price the seller is asking is the price he thinks he can get and that price doesn't necessarily have any relationship to the actual value of the property. Usually the seller will have his price "puffed up," leaving him room to negotiate with the buyer.

The seller's asking price is sometimes inflated by memories and emotional values he attaches to the property. This often occurs when a family has been reared in the house.

The lowest price the seller will accept often

changes during the duration of the listing. The broker is required to reveal to the buyer the lowest price the seller will take for the property, but the seller may change his mind. As a prospective buyer, you may make an offer to buy the property at any price you wish.

The broker is required to submit your offer to the seller no matter how much it is below the seller's asking price. Only by accepting or refusing your offer to purchase the property does the seller reveal the lowest price at which he will sell. The selling price should be comparable with the prices on similar properties in similar neighborhoods or with the prices on similar properties in the same neighborhood.

Buying your house may be the biggest financial transaction of your life. Certainly it will be one of the most important in that it involves providing shelter and security for your family. With that thought in mind, let's agree that you are not going to base your offering price on such slim evidence of value as the opinion of a neighbor, the opinion of the seller, or on a figure arrived at through mathematical gymnastics.

Don't gamble on receiving your dollar's worth when you make an offer to purchase a property. In every community there are groups of people well qualified to advise you as to the fair market value of any property you may be considering. Lending agencies, because they are involved in lending money to borrowers for buying houses, usually have people on their staffs who are well qualified to give property appraisals.

If you approach them on the possibility of procuring a loan to be used toward the purchase of a particular property, they will give you their opinion as to the value of that property. If they are doing or have done business with the seller, they probably will be reluctant to say that he is asking too much for the property. However, if in reply to your request for a loan the lending agency asks for a larger than normal down payment it ought to be a good indication that they think the property is overpriced.

Insurance companies also often have experienced people on their staffs who are well qualified to give opinions as to the value of real estate. A request for an opinion as to what it will cost to insure a property will get you an opinion on the value of the property. An insurance company will be reluctant to insure a property for more than its true market value.

When requesting the opinion of a lending agency or an insurance company, consult one which is familiar with costs and values in the area where the property is located. The cost of labor and materials varies greatly in different parts of the country and even in different communities. The opinion as to the value of a piece of property is valid only when it is based on values and costs for the area where the property is located.

If you required an operation on your knee, would you go to the butcher, the baker, the candlestick maker, or would you go to a surgeon? Naturally you would go to the person whose profession is solving your particular problem, the surgeon.

Certainly when you are contemplating an offer to buy property, you have a problem. You do not want to offer more for the property than it is worth. You want to preserve your family's dollars and you want a dollar's worth of value for every dollar you spend. Your problem is to know the true value of the property so that you can make a reasonable offer for it and not end up hating a house after you learn that you paid too much for it and are now stuck with it.

Appraisers

Fortunately there are experts—real estate appraisers—whose profession is determining the value of real estate. Their fees are based on an approved schedule which in turn is based on how much of their time will be required in making the appraisal. In some cases their fee may be as low as $25, which is surely a small price to pay for the reassurance that you aren't offering more for a property than it is actually worth.

Appraisers can be located by looking in the Yellow Pages under "Appraisers" or by asking at any bank or lending agency. Or you may telephone the county courthouse and ask for the probate secretary to the county judge. This person has the list of people appointed as appraisers for the county plus their fee schedule.

The appraiser does not simply drive past the property and arrive at a value. He uses any one of or a combination of all of the different approaches to appraising real estate.

THE SALES APPROACH

When using this approach the appraiser studies what similar properties have sold for and then makes an adjustment in his final appraisal for any changes in the economy that have taken place since those properties were sold.

THE COST APPROACH

When using this approach the appraiser adds the value of the land to the cost of reproducing the buildings. From this total he deducts an amount for depreciation.

In determining the cost of reproducing the buildings, the appraiser learns what the cost was per cubic foot to construct similar buildings and then multiplies that figure by the total number of cubic feet in the building he is appraising. He then adjusts that figure for depreciation.

He learns the value of the land by studying the prices being paid for similar pieces of land.

THE INCOME APPROACH

This method is rarely used in appraising residential properties, as it involves arriving at a value on the property on the basis of the income that can be derived from the ownership of the property.

The appraiser may use any one of these approaches or his final appraisal may be a composite of all of these approaches, but in every case his final figure will be based on the approach that will result in the most reliable figures for you.

Possibly you are 90% sold on a property's being a "good buy" and are afraid that if you don't get your offer made the owner may sell the property to another buyer. But you still would like to have an appraisal made before you fully commit yourself to buying the property. Is this possible?

Certainly! Write into your offer to purchase that your going ahead with the provisions in your offer is dependent upon an appraisal.

"The buyer's going ahead with the provisions in this offer is dependent upon the results of an appraisal to be completed by _____."

Provided the seller accepts your offer, this type of contingency reserves for you the right to buy the property and at the same time makes it possible for you to withdraw your offer without penalties if the value put on the property by the appraiser is enough lower than the listing price to make the property unattractive to you. (Refer to pages 58–59, 67 for using special contingencies in the offer to purchase.)

Possibly you are sold on the value of an appraisal but aren't comfortable with accepting an opinion as to value from a stranger—the appraiser. You are more comfortable with the opinion of a friend and neighbor who has bought and sold several houses.

Remember that real estate values vary greatly in different communities. The appraiser is trained in determining the true fair market value of properties based on their value in relationship to their location.

The appraiser, a stranger to your desires and whims, places a value on the property according to his experience and training, and his final opinion is devoid of any (exaggerated) value you or a friend might put on the pretty flower bed or well-kept lawn.

The appraiser has nothing to gain through making the appraisal, other than his fee. He sees the property as being worth so many dollars regardless of who is selling and who is buying. The fact that the seller has to move because of his employment, or that the buyer's wife desperately wants the house, does not enter into the value put on the property by the appraiser.

Possibly you are afraid of putting too much weight on an appraisal because you are from a neighboring community and you aren't sure the appraiser isn't working with the seller's broker.

It is unethical for an appraiser to make an appraisal when his employment or fee is dependent upon the outcome of that appraisal when he has any interests in the property unless his interests are fully explained in the appraisal certificate.

Your appraiser's sole objective is to give you as honest and accurate an opinion as possible as to the fair market value of the property. His reputation depends upon this.

If you should go to a surgeon—instead of to a butcher, baker, or candlestick maker—for a knee operation, you certainly should go to an appraiser for an opinion as to the value of a property before you make an offer to spend your family's money to purchase that property.

A BROKER'S DUTIES TO THE BUYER

Even though in most real estate transactions the broker receives his commission from the seller, the broker has certain duties and obligations to prospective buyers.

The warning, *caveat emptor*—let the buyer beware—does not apply to a real estate transaction. If this had an application here, it would be the buyer's duty to determine if all the facts presented to him about the property were true.

The doctrine of "elementary fair conduct" applies to real estate transactions. By this tradition a buyer is entitled to fair and honest representation of the facts by the seller and the broker. It is not the buyer's duty to ascertain that these

representations are true. It is the duty of the seller and the broker to present all facts to the buyer as honestly and fairly as possible.

Some of the broker's duties and obligations to you as the buyer are:

Returning Your Earnest Money

The broker will return your earnest money payment to you if you wish to withdraw your offer to purchase at any time before the seller accepts your offer and the acceptance has been personally delivered to you or mailed to you. (Refer to pages 83–86 for earnest money.)

Actions of the Real Estate Salesman

The broker is responsible to you for the actions of his salesmen.

If a real estate salesman misrepresents facts to you about a property and you are damaged because of this misrepresentation, the real estate broker-employer is liable for the misrepresentation.

For example, a real estate salesman told you that a property was suitable for a two-family dwelling. On that basis, you purchased the property only to suffer damages later on because the property was actually only suitable for use as a one-family dwelling.

The broker-employer is liable for this misrepresentation by his salesman and any effort to collect damages should be made directly against the broker-employer.

Commitments by the Broker to the Buyer

Even though the broker is the employee-agent of the seller, he is duty-bound to fulfill any commitments he makes to you as the buyer.

For example, a broker told you that he would have a lien on a property removed before title to the property was transferred to you. If he failed to have the lien removed as promised, he violated his duty to you. In this example, you possibly could collect directly from the broker for any damages you suffered because of the broker's failure to have the lien removed as promised.

Revealing Lowest Price to the Buyer

The broker's duty is to get the best possible deal for his principal (the seller), but he is also duty-bound to reveal to a prospective buyer the lowest possible price the seller will accept for the property. For example, although a seller listed the property with the broker for sale at $50,000, the seller mentioned to the broker that he would accept as little as $45,000.

You, as buyer, asked the broker what the lowest price the seller would accept was, and the broker, referring to the listing, quoted you $50,000 even though he knew that the seller would accept $45,000. In so doing the broker violated his duty to be truthful and fair with you

at all times. He violated his duty to reveal to you the lowest possible price the seller would accept.

You possibly could sue the broker for the difference between the price you paid ($50,000) and the lowest price the seller would have accepted ($45,000).

Intentional Misrepresentation

The broker's duty is not to distort or misrepresent to you any material fact about the property. Remember that the doctrine of elementary fair conduct applies to real estate transactions and that by this doctrine you are entitled to fair and honest representation by the seller and broker at all times.

When a broker distorts or misrepresents material facts to a buyer it is a breach of faith and the broker can be held liable for any damages a buyer suffers as a result of the broker's failure to deal honestly and fairly with him.

Misrepresentation by Silence

The broker's duty is to present honestly to you all the facts about a property whether or not your knowing the facts will reduce the possibility of your buying the property.

The broker should not remain silent about facts known to him, even though informing you of the facts may reduce his chances of earning a commission. For example, one thing that appeals to you about a property is that there is a school within two blocks. The broker knows that the school is going to be closed and replaced by a new school in a different neighborhood.

The broker remains silent, not telling you that the school will be closed, and lets you buy the property. The broker can be held liable for any damages you suffer as a result of this misrepresentation by silence.

Accuracy of Information

A broker's duty is to exercise reasonable care in determining that all of the information given to him about a property is factual. For example, the seller told the broker that the area was zoned as residential but actually the zoning had been changed and now the area is zoned as commercial.

The broker failed to check the zoning ordinances and passed on to the buyer what the seller had told him—that the area was zoned as residential. If you purchased the property relying on the statement that the area was residential and you suffered damages because the area in fact was zoned as commercial, the broker could possibly be held liable for damages.

The broker was careless when he failed to check the zoning ordinances and passed on information without first checking the accuracy of that information.

Duties of Broker to Buyer Under an Oral Contract

Even though your agreement with the seller to buy the property is oral, and oral contracts for the sale of real estate cannot be enforced in most states, the doctrine of elementary fair conduct still applies. You are still entitled to fair and honest representation by the broker.

Even though your contract to purchase the property is oral, a broker has the same duties and obligations to you as are imposed upon him when the contract is written.

Submitting Your Offer to Purchase

A broker's duty is to submit to the seller all offers to purchase the property. In some cases this may be considered a waste of the broker's time, but nevertheless it remains his duty to submit all offers.

For example, the property is listed for $50,000 and you submit an offer to the listing broker for only $30,000. The broker is required to accept your offer and to submit it to the seller. On the day the broker presents your offer to the seller, the seller may be in such a mood that he will accept your $30,000 offer.

Copies of Forms

After you sign the offer to purchase, the broker will give you a copy of that form.

After the seller accepts your offer to purchase, a contract for the sale of the property has been created. The broker will give you a copy of this contract.

In addition to the duties and obligations a real estate broker has to a buyer, there are limitations and restrictions upon the functions a real estate broker may perform for a buyer.

Return of the Buyer's Earnest Money Payment

If you wish to withdraw your offer to purchase after the seller has accepted it, and the acceptance has been either personally delivered to you or mailed to you, the broker may return this earnest money to you only when he has the written consent of the seller.

If the seller refuses to give the broker his written consent to returning the earnest money to you, the broker should retain the money in his real estate trust account until both parties agree in writing to the disposition of the money or until a court makes a decision and issues an order as to the disposition of the earnest money.

Representing Both Buyer and Seller

The broker may not act as an agent for you as the buyer while at the same time acting as an agent for the seller without the knowledge and consent of both buyer and seller.

For example, you agree to pay the broker $2,000 if he can talk the seller into accepting $40,000 for a property the seller has listed to sell for $50,000.

If the broker agrees to accept your $2,000 while at the same time accepting a commission from the seller, he violates his fiduciary duty to his principal (the seller) in that he is not acting in good faith and with complete loyalty to his principal.

A broker may not act for the two parties to a real estate transaction and collect commission from both parties without the knowledge and consent of both parties.

Giving Legal Advice to the Buyer

The real estate broker, provided he is not an attorney, may not give you an opinion as to:

1. Your legal rights in a transaction.
2. The legality of any instrument or form used in a real estate transaction.
3. The validity of a real estate title.

The real estate broker may do no more than fill out the approved forms involved in a real estate transaction and he may do this only when he is the participating broker in the transaction.

Taking a Lien on the Property for Commission

The real estate broker may not put a lien on the real estate because he is not able to collect his commission from the sale of the property.

For example, you purchase a property for $50,000 and the title to the property has been transferred to you. The seller has not paid the broker his commission on the sale of the property. The broker may not put a lien on your real estate in an effort to collect his commission from the seller.

Discrimination

It is unlawful for a real estate broker or salesman to refuse to negotiate with, or to refuse to sell, rent, or lease to any person because of his race, color, creed, or national origin.

Chapter Seven

FINANCING THE DEAL

THE COST OF BORROWING MONEY

Buying real estate usually involves borrowing money.

The price of your real estate will vary depending upon the manner and the terms by which you finance the purchase.

Loans are classified on the basis of how they are to be repaid. The three main groupings are unamortized loans, fully amortized loans, and partially amortized loans. Amortization is the method by which a future obligation is diminished by periodical payments.

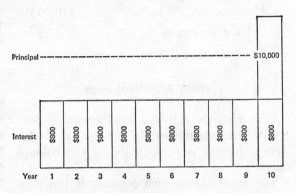

Unamortized Loan

With an unamortized loan, the entire amount borrowed is repaid in one payment at a specified date, usually at the end of the period for which the money is borrowed. The interest is paid at stated interest-paying intervals.

Because the amount of the principal due on the loan does not change during the term of the loan, the amount of the interest payments does not change. For example, with a $10,000 loan at 8% interest per annum to be repaid in ten years, the payments are:

Fixed interest payment. . .$800 year per year Principal to be repaid at the end of the loan period (10 years) $10,000

The total interest is $800 per year×10 years or $8,000.

This is a lot of interest to pay on a $10,000 loan, but the borrower has the use of the $10,000 for the entire ten years. Money earned through the use of the $10,000 can offset the $8,000 of

the total interest. In other types of loans the borrower doesn't have the use of the entire amount borrowed for the entire term of the loan.

Fully Amortized Loan

With this common type of loan, the borrower pays a fixed amount at set intervals. The payments remain the same throughout the loan period and each payment represents a payment on both the principal and the interest.

As the unpaid balance on the loan decreases— as more and more payments are made—the amount of the payments that goes toward reduction of the principal increases and the amount of the payment that goes toward the payment of interest decreases.

For example, on a $10,000 loan at 8% interest per annum to be repaid in 10 years, the payments are:

Yearly payments of $1,455 (rounded off) except for payment in final year when interest payment has to be adjusted because it was rounded off in the other years.

Interest	$775	$718	$657	$591	$519	$442	$357	$266	$168	$57
Principal	$680	$737	$798	$864	$936	$1,013	$1,098	$1,189	$1,287	$1,394
Year	1	2	3	4	5	6	7	8	9	10

Total interest for the 10 years is $4,550

Total paid in 10 yearly payments
at $1,455 each $14,550
less amount originally
borrowed $10,000
Total interest is . . . . $ 4,550

Partially Amortized Loan

With this type of loan, a fixed amount is paid toward the reduction of the principal at set intervals. Interest is paid on the unpaid balance only.

The result is that each payment is less than the preceding payment. The amount paid toward principal on each payment remains the same but the amount of interest on each payment steadily declines as the unpaid balance is reduced.

For example, on a $10,000 loan at 8% interest per annum to be repaid in ten years, the payments are:

Fixed payments on
principal . . . . $1,000 each year.
Payments on the interest are calculated on the unpaid balance and decline each year.

Interest	$800	$720	$640	$560	$480	$400	$320	$240	$160	$80
Principal	$1,000	$1,000	$1,000	$1,000	$1,000	$1,000	$1,000	$1,000	$1,000	$1,000
Year	1	2	3	4	5	6	7	8	9	10

Total interest for the ten-year period is $4,400.

Each example involves a loan of $10,000 with interest at 8% per annum with the loan to be repaid in ten years.

But, depending upon the repayment method selected, there are differences in the total yearly payments and total interest on the loans.

Type of loan	Yearly payment	Total interest
Unamortized Loan	$ 800*	$8,000
Fully amortized loan	$1,455	$4,554
Partially amortized loan	$1,080 to $1,800†	$4,400

A mere reference to the amount of the payments is not a valid method of evaluating a loan. By referring solely to the amount of the payments, the completely unamortized loan with a yearly payment of only $800 is the most attractive. But the completely unamortized loan also requires the most total interest. Of the three loans compared, it is the most expensive.

When comparing offers from prospective lenders, to determine the amount of interest the use of the money will cost, total the amount of the payments and then subtract from that total the amount you originally borrowed. The answer is the amount of interest it costs to borrow the money.

The formula is:

Total of payments for principal
and interest. . . . . $———
(less) original amount borrowed . . $———
Amount of interest. . . . . $———

Let's see how we can use this formula to determine the total interest on the three loans we used as examples. In each case, the amount borrowed is $10,000 at 8% interest per annum, which is to be repaid in ten years.

UNAMORTIZED LOAN

10 interest payments of $800 each	$8,000
(plus) lump sum principal payment	$10,000
Total of payments for principal and interest	$18,000
(less) original amount borrowed	$10,000
Amount of interest	$8,000

* With the unamortized loan the yearly payment represents interest on the entire amount borrowed and, because the principal of the loan isn't reduced, the amount of interest due on each payment remains unchanged. The final payment is for the interest plus the amount of the original loan.

† With the partially amortized loan, the amount of the scheduled payments varies. Each payment is for a set amount of the principal but the interest included is based on the unpaid balance, which is less with each payment.

FULLY AMORTIZED LOAN

10 payments of principal and interest with each payment being $1,455

Total of payments for principal and interest	$14,550
(less) original amount borrowed	$10,000
Amount of interest	$4,550

PARTIALLY AMORTIZED LOAN

10 payments but each one is different, so total all 10 payments

Total of payments for principal and interest	$14,400
(less) original amount borrowed	$10,000
Amount of interest	$4,400

Using this formula requires that you know the total amount you have to pay toward principal and interest. Arriving at this figure is simple with an unamortized or a fully amortized loan, as they have unchanging payments. Multiply the number of payments by the amount of each payment to arrive at a total.

With the partially amortized loan, each payment is different, so it is necessary to total all of the payments for principal and interest.

Note that we are not comparing the loans on the basis of the stated interest or the amount of each payment. We compare the loans on the basis of the cost of borrowing the money.

This prevents you from being trapped by what sounds like a low interest rate but which actually requires you to pay more interest than you would pay at a higher interest rate. The difference is the method by which the money is to be repaid.

Which loan sounds more attractive to you?

Loan A

An unamortized loan of $10,000 at 7% interest per annum for ten years with each payment to be only $1,000 and the principal to be repaid in a lump sum with the final payment.

—or—

Loan B

A fully amortized loan of $10,000 at 9% interest per annum for ten years with each payment to be $1,520 (rounded out).

Loan A offers a 7% interest rate as compared to the 9% interest rate for loan B. Loan A also requires payments of only $1,000 whereas loan B requires payments of $1,520. Both loans require the same number of payments. Loan A requires, however, that the total amount borrowed be repaid in a lump sum at the end of the loan.

Based on the interest rate and the amount of each payment, it appears that loan A is the better one for you with its lower interest rate and smaller annual payments.

When we apply our formula based on the total amount that has to be repaid, the picture changes:

Loan A

10 interest payments of $700 each	$7,000
(plus) lump sum principal payment	$10,000
Total of payments for principal and interest	$17,000
(less) original amount borrowed	$10,000
Amount of interest	$7,000

Loan B

(10 payments of principal and interest with each payment being $1,520)

Total of payments for principal and interest	$15,200
(less) original amount borrowed	$10,000
Amount of interest	$5,200

If your main concern is paying the least amount of interest, loan B with the higher interest rate and higher payments is the better loan for you.

You arrive at the true picture only when you total the amount which has to be repaid and then subtract the original amount borrowed from this total to arrive at the total interest.

Interest usually is and should be quoted on a per annum (annual) basis.

Although quoted on a per annum basis, interest may be calculated on different time intervals, which makes a difference in the total amount of interest you will pay on a loan. Interest usually is calculated, and payments made, on a monthly basis, a quarterly basis, a semi-annual basis, or on an annual basis.

How it is calculated makes a difference in how much interest you will ultimately be required to pay.

METHODS OF CALCULATING INTEREST ON THE LOAN

Let's look at examples of how much interest you will have to pay depending upon whether you make payments monthly, quarterly, semi-annually, or annually.

In each example you borrow $1,200 for one year at 9% interest. The only difference is the intervals at which you repay the loan.

Interest Calculated Monthly

With this method you pay back monthly a part of the principal plus making a payment that represents interest on the unpaid balance.

Nine per cent interest per annum if calculated monthly (monthly payments of principal plus interest) is equal to ¾ of 1% or .75 interest per month (9% ÷ 12 months is .75 interest per month).

Month	Monthly payment on principal	Unpaid balance on the loan	Monthly interest on unpaid balance
1	$100	$1,200	$ 9.00
2	"	$1,100	$ 8.25
3	"	$900	$ 7.50
4	"	$1,000	$ 6.75
5	"	$800	$ 6.00
6	"	$700	$ 5.25
7	"	$600	$ 4.50
8	"	$500	$ 3.75
9	"	$400	$ 3.00
10	"	$300	$ 2.25
11	"	$200	$ 1.50
12	"	$100	$ .75
		Total interest	$58.50

Interest Calculated Quarterly

When payments are made quarterly (every three months), each quarter the amount of the unpaid balance on the loan declines so that the amount of the interest due each quarter on the unpaid balance also declines.

Nine per cent interest per annum, when calculated quarterly, is equal to ¾ of 1% per month×3 months or 2¼% of the unpaid balance each quarter.

Quarter	Quarterly payment on principal	Unpaid balance on the loan	Quarterly interest on unpaid balance
1st 3 months	$300	$1,200	$27.00
2nd 3 months	$300	$900	$20.25
3rd 3 months	$300	$600	$13.50
last 3 months	$300	$300	$ 6.75
		Total interest	$67.50

Interest Calculated Semiannually

When payments are made semiannually, each six months, the amount of the unpaid balance is reduced so that the amount of interest due on the unpaid balance declines with each payment period.

Nine per cent interest per annum when calculated semiannually is equal to ¾ of 1% per month×6 months or 4½% of the unpaid balance every six months.

Payment period	Semi-annual payment on principal	Unpaid balance on the loan	Semi-annual interest on unpaid balance
1st 6 months	$600	$1,200	$54.00
2nd 6 months	$600	$600	$27.00
		Total interest	$81.00

Interest Paid Annually

When the interest is paid annually and the loan is for one year, there is no reduction in the amount of the principal during the term of the loan and interest is paid on the total amount of the loan.

	Annual interest on the loan
Amount of the loan	$1,200
9% interest on the loan	×.09
Total interest	$108

In each case $1,200 is borrowed for one year at 9% interest. The interest on the loan varies according to the interval on which the loan is repaid.

Method by which the loan is repaid	Total interest on the $1,200 loan at 9% for 1 year
Interest calculated monthly	$58.50
Interest calculated quarterly	$67.50
Interest calculated semiannually	$81.00
Interest paid yearly	$108.00

Again, if your objective is to pay a minimum of interest, it is necessary to apply the formula:

Total of payments for principal and interest	$————
(less) original amount borrowed	$————
Amount of interest	$————

Which loan sounds more attractive to you?

Loan A
$1,200 loan at 9% per annum with the interest calculated quarterly, or

Loan B
$1,200 loan at 7% interest per annum with the interest calculated annually.

Without referring to the formula to determine the total interest the loan of $1,200 costs, you might conclude that the loan at 7% costs less. But applying the formula, you learn that the loan at 9% costs less in interest charges than does the loan at 7%.

Loan A
(Interest payments on $1,200 loan when the interest is calculated quarterly at 9%: $27—$20.25—$13.50—$6.75—plus repayment of the $1,200 principal.)

Total of payments for principal and interest	$1,267.50
(less) original amount borrowed	$1,200.00
Amount of interest	$67.50

Loan B
(Interest payments on $1,200 loan when the interest is paid annually: $1,200 at 7% is $84 interest—plus repayment of the $1,200 principal.)

Total of payments for principal and interest	$1,284.00
(less) original amount borrowed	$1,200.00
Amount of interest	$84.00

Again, if your concern is in paying a minimum of interest, loan A at the higher interest rate is the better loan for you.

From this analysis, it is clear that when evaluating loan possibilities from different lenders, it is necessary to go one step further than simply weighing the loans on the basis of the interest rates charged. The length of the loan, the manner in which it is to be repaid, and the repayment schedule all play a role in determining what your total interest will be.

Sometimes a borrower is given the choice of repaying a loan over various lengths of time—possibly a choice of repaying a loan over a fifteen-year period as compared with repaying the loan over a ten-year period. What are the relative advantages and disadvantages?

When the payments are spread over more years, if the interest remains the same, the borrower has smaller annual payments but pays more total interest.

For example, compare a self-liquidating loan on $10,000 at 8% interest per annum spread over fifteen years as compared to ten years:

Number of years to repay the loan	Yearly payment	Total interest
15 years	$1,146.00	$7,194.00
10 years	$1,455.00	$4,554.00
Differences	$ 309.00	$2,640.00

By spreading the loan over fifteen years instead of over ten years, the borrower reduces the amount of his annual payments by $309 and increases the total amount of interest he pays by $2,640.

Whether this is favorable depends upon the needs of the borrower. Perhaps he needs the smaller, constant payment schedule and is willing to pay the extra interest for it.

In some cases a would-be borrower may be given this choice: $10,000 at 9% interest to be repaid in ten years, or $10,000 at 8% interest to be repaid in fifteen years.

If the borrower's concern is paying a minimum of interest, possibly he will be attracted by the loan at 8% interest instead of the loan at 9% interest for a shorter period.

Is he really saving interest money by accepting the longer-term loan at the lower interest rate—$10,000 at 8% for fifteen years instead of $10,000 at 9% for ten years?

Number of years to repay the loan	Per cent interest	Total interest
10 years	9%	$5,196.00
15 years	8%	$7,194.00

In this example his total charge for interest is greater if he accepts the loan at the lower interest rate.

However, when he is offered a loan of $10,000 at 6% for fifteen years instead of $10,000 at 9% for ten years, the pictures changes:

Number of years to repay the loan	Per cent interest	Total interest
10 years	9%	$5,196.00
15 years	6%	$5,182.00

In our example the total interest charge is greater at the lower interest rate when the loan is made for fifteen years at 8% instead of for ten years at 9% interest.

However, when the interest rate is low enough —in our example, at 6%—a borrower actually saves on total interest by selecting the longer repayment schedule.

To compare the cost for different loans you must know what payments you have to make to repay the loans. The total should include all principal and interest payments.

Then apply the formula:

Total of payments for principal and interest	$_____
(less) original amount borrowed	$_____
Amount of interest	$_____

Unlike prices on many other products, the cost of, or the value of, money cannot be raised to absorb part of the financing costs or interest.

An automobile dealer who ordinarily sells a particular car for $3,000 and finances the sale at 10% can sell the same car for $3,150 and finance the sale at 5%. There are some who will be attracted by the lower interest-paying rate. They don't realize that somehow, somewhere the dealer has to make up the income he is losing by offering to finance at 5% instead of at 10%.

Of course, the dealer does this simply by charging $3,150 for the car instead of $3,000. The buyer doesn't know that he is buying a product worth only $3,000 and is paying $3,150 for it.

The situation changes when you borrow money. You know the value of the product you are buying—money. One thousand dollars from one lender has no more purchasing power than has $1,000 borrowed from a different lender. Where to borrow money becomes a matter of who will sell money to you at the lowest price.

Unfortunately it is not always this simple. True, the lender is not able to say that his money is worth more than an equal amount of money you may be able to borrow from another lender, but by charging for "extras" a lender may sell you his money for a seemingly lower price than a competitor. These extras are given many names —debt service, origination fees, and loan installation fees—but in every case they add to the cost of borrowing money. When comparing the cost of borrowing money from various sources, include the cost of these extras as a part of the total cost.

For example, one lender is willing to lend you $10,000 at 9% for ten years. You figure that the total interest you are required to pay on this loan will be $5,196.

Another lender is willing to lend you $10,000 at only 8% for ten years. You have figured that the total interest you are required to pay is only $4,554.

$10,000 for 10 years at 9%	$5,196 total interest
$10,000 for 10 years at 8%	$4,554 total interest
Difference	$642

It appears that you can save $642 over the ten years by borrowing at the 8% interest rate as compared to borrowing at the 9% interest rate.

But the lender who is so willing to lend you the $10,000 at the 8% interest rate also charges an "origination fee" of 7% of the amount of the original loan. So refigure the deal.

Total cost when the only charge is the 9% interest rate $5,196	
Total cost when charges are 8% interest plus a 7% origination fee:	
Interest at 8%	$4,554
7% origination fee	$700
Total cost	$5,254

In this example it costs more to borrow the money at the lower interest rate due to the 7% origination fee than it costs to borrow the same amount of money at the higher interest rate.

$10,000 for 10 years at 8% interest plus a 7% origination fee	$5,254
$10,000 for 10 years at 9% interest	$5,196
Difference	$58

Again it is clear that when comparing costs of borrowing money, first learn the total amount that has to be repaid—principal and interest. From that subtract the original amount borrowed. Add to your answer the cost of extras and you have the total cost of borrowing the money.

Total of payments for principal and interest	$———
(less) original amount borrowed	$———
Amount of interest	$———
(plus) cost of any extras	$———
Total cost of borrowing $——— is	$———

This is the age of credit buying and there are those who will take advantage of the uninformed borrower by making it easy for him to borrow at seemingly very low interest rates. We have all seen money advertised:

"Borrow up to $500 for 3 months—only 3% interest."

"Buy on credit and save—only 1½% interest per month—no carrying charges."

Knowing that local sources of money are charging less interest, these mail order offers of quick money at low interest rates seem attractive. But are all of the interest rates quoted on the same basis—on a per annum basis? Three per cent interest for three months is the same as 1% for 1 month, which is the same as 12% for a year.

One and one half per cent for one month—no carrying charges—is the same as 18% for a year. (1½% per month×12 months=18% per year.)

What the interest charge is depends upon how the interest is quoted:

How quoted	Total interest for 3 months	3-month interest on a $1,000 loan
3% for 3 months	4½%	$30
1½% per month	3%	$45
6% per annum	1½%	$15

The very attractive 3% for three months and only 1½% per month become rather tarnished when compared to interest quoted and charged on the more reasonable per annum basis.

When interest is quoted on other than a per annum basis, use the following formula to learn what the actual charge is for interest on a per annum basis:

$$\frac{(\quad)\times(\quad\%)}{12 \text{ months in a year}}=\text{interest per year}$$

Time period for which interest is quoted

For example, when interest is offered for only 3% interest for three months, it actually costs 12% a year.

$$\frac{(4)\times(3\%)}{12 \text{ months in a year}}=12\% \text{ per year}$$

Time period for which interest is quoted 3 months

Surely a prospective borrower should quickly desert this source of money for money from more legitimate sources at more reasonable rates.

Every effort to borrow money should originate with your local banker. Even though you are not able to come to terms with him, he can supply you with the guidance necessary for you to obtain the best possible loan for your needs.

Chapter Eight

JOINT TENANCY—IS IT FOR YOU?

Only you can decide if you should take title to a property in the name of the husband only, in joint tenancy, in tenancy in common, or in tenancy by the entireties.

But authorities agree that your decision should be made only after you discuss with your attorney (1) the different types of assets you own, (2) in whose name or names these assets are held, (3) the dollar value of your assets, (4) your income and investment plans, and (5) your personal desires.

What is candy for one couple may be poison for another couple. For example, in some cases co-ownership of property in joint tenancy will result in tax savings. In other cases you can end up paying an inheritance tax on property you thought you already owned.

The cost of having an attorney to review your estate and make recommendations as to the form in which you should take title to additions to your estate is small compared to the cost of making a wrong decision.

If you as a couple wish to own property together, you should consider taking title either as tenants in common, as joint tenants, or as tenants by the entireties. In some states, if you do not specify otherwise in the conveyance by which you take title to your property, it is presumed that you want to own the property jointly.

Usually, in community property states, when the conveyance by which a couple takes title to a property lists them as husband and wife and does not specifically declare in what form they are taking title, it is presumed that they intend the property to be community property. (See pages 154–155 for community property.)

In other states, for example, in Florida, Massachusetts, Maryland, and New York, unless the conveyance says otherwise, when the title passes to husband and wife it is presumed to be in tenancy by the entireties.

In most states, when title passes to two persons not listed as husband and wife, and the conveyance doesn't specify otherwise, it is presumed that they are accepting title as tenants in common.

States differ in what form they presume the title to be held when property passes to two or more persons and the conveyance doesn't specifically state in what form they are accepting title. Be sure to understand the consequences of the different forms of ownership; have your title made out so that your interests will pass on to whomever you wish—your heirs or your spouse.

Tenancy in common is ownership of real estate or personal property by two or more persons, each having an undivided equal or unequal interest in the property. Upon the death of one of the owners, his share goes to his heirs.

Joint tenancy is the ownership of real estate or personal property by two or more persons, each having an undivided equal interest in the property. Upon the death of one of the owners, his share goes to the other owner or owners.

Tenancy by the entireties is similar to joint tenancy in that upon the death of one of the owners, his share goes to the other owner. Where tenancy by the entireties is recognized, the husband and wife are treated as one person. This makes a difference when the title is made out to a husband, his wife, and a third person. For example, when the title is made out to John Doe and Mary Doe, husband and wife, and Jim Smith, a single man:

With joint tenancy each party receives an undivided equal interest in the property; each party would receive title to an undivided ⅓ of the property.

With tenancy by the entireties John Doe and

Mary Doe, because they are treated as one, would receive an undivided ½ interest and Jim Smith would receive an undivided ½ interest in the property.

Except for this difference, tenancy by the entireties and joint tenancy are very similar, so we shall restrict our discussion to joint tenancy and tenancy in common.

DIFFERENCES BETWEEN JOINT TENANCY AND TENANCY IN COMMON

	Joint tenancy	Tenancy in common
The share each owner has	Undivided equal share	Undivided equal interest or possibly an unequal interest
Upon the death of one of the owners, who gets his share?	The other owner or owners	The heirs of the deceased owner, but only subject to possible widow or widower's dower or homestead rights
Right of a person to direct in his will who is to receive his share	Right doesn't exist in joint tenancy	The right exists but the transfer may be subject to the widow or widower's dower or homestead rights
Right of one owner to sell his share	*Homestead property* One owner may not sell without consent of the co-owner *Non-homestead property** Selling will sever the joint tenancy and create a tenancy in common.	A co-owner may sell subject to possible dower or homestead rights

* With tenancy by the entireties a co-owner may not transfer his interest in the property without the consent of the other owner or owners.

The distinguishing difference between joint tenancy and tenancy in common is the right of survivorship, which accompanies ownership in joint tenancy. The right of survivorship provides that when you own property in joint tenancy with another his share, upon his death, belongs to you regardless of any provisions he may have made to the contrary in his will.

Usually a co-tenant may convey his interest in property owned in joint tenancy without the co-owner's consent, providing it is not homestead property. This destroys the joint tenancy and the owners then have title as tenants in common.

The result of destroying the joint tenancy and creating a tenancy in common is that no longer will a co-owner's share, upon his death, pass to the surviving co-owner. Instead, upon his death, a co-owner's share will go to his heirs or as directed in his will, subject to dower and homestead rights.

A co-tenant gains very little when he sells his interest in property held in joint tenancy. He receives the revenue from the sale of his interest in the property but he loses an equal amount by forfeiting his right of survivorship to the remaining part of the property.

Usually the conveyance through which you receive your interest in a property makes it clear, by the way in which the names are listed, as to whether a couple holds title as joint tenants or as tenants in common.

Joint tenants	*Tenants in common*
". . . as joint tenants" (or) ". . . as joint tenants and to the survivor of either" (or) ". . . as joint tenants and not as tenants in common and to the survivor of either"	". . . as tenants in common"

Sometimes it will not be so clearly spelled out. In such cases, the laws of your state will dictate in what form you receive title. Note that in all cases where the property is given in unequal shares it is presumed to be as tenants in common.

Even though the original conveyance gave you title to the property as joint tenants, it is possible for you to have voluntarily or involuntarily changed the form in which you now hold title.

SEVERING JOINT TENANCY

Joint tenancy is usually terminated when one co-owner transfers his interest to a third person. The co-owners then hold title as tenants in common. When a co-owner transfers his interest to the other co-owner the joint tenancy is severed. Providing there were only two co-owners, the owner to whom the interest was transferred now has fee simple title to the entire property.

Provided there are only two co-owners, upon the death of one co-owner the survivor has fee simple title to the entire property.

A joint tenancy is severed when a money judgment is entered against one of the co-owners and the writ of execution has been issued by the court.

Co-owners may break a joint tenancy arrangement through a severance action, which results in each one's owning in fee simple a half interest in the property.

DISADVANTAGES OF JOINT TENANCY

Irrevocable Gift

You deny yourself the right to control, through your will, who is to receive upon your death the property you own in joint tenancy with another.

Prior to your death, by putting the property in joint tenancy, you gave a half interest in it to the co-owner and you agreed that the co-owner was to receive your half interest in the property upon your death.

Gift Taxes

You may possibly subject yourself and your estate to a gift tax.

When you put the property in joint tenancy, you made a gift of one half the value of the property to the co-owner. Unless the co-owner can prove that he contributed toward the purchase price of the property, you possibly will have to pay a gift tax on the value of the property you originally transferred to the co-owner when you put the property in joint tenancy.

Possibly the value of the half interest you transferred to the co-owner is small enough so that it will be exempt from tax through your state's gift tax exemption laws. Check this with your attor-

ney. He can tell you after studying your estate if you will be liable for a gift tax if you put your property in joint tenancy.

Inheritance Taxes

You may have to pay an inheritance tax on property you thought you already owned.

State inheritance tax laws differ, but usually when the property is owned in joint tenancy, upon the death of one of the owners, the survivor can be taxed on the value of the half interest in the property he inherited from the deceased.

Regardless of whose name the real estate is held in, it is possible that there will be no inheritance tax due because of the state's inheritance tax exemptions. Again it is wise to get your attorney's opinion as to the form in which you should take title in order to keep these possible taxes at a minimum.

Property Management

When you put the title to property in joint tenancy, besides transferring an undivided equal interest in the property, you relinquish the ex-

	Real estate title in husband's name only	Real estate title held in joint tenancy
If husband dies first, for inheritance tax purposes usually the property is valued at	full value	One half total value of the property
If wife dies first, for inheritance tax purposes usually the property is valued at	No tax as the husband owns fee simple title to the property and inherits nothing.	One half total value of the real estate

clusive right you would have had as an owner in fee simple to make all decisions as to the use and management of the property.

With the property in joint tenancy, disagreement between the co-owners as to the use and management of the property can cause friction and quarrels.

These could have been prevented had the title been in one person's name only and such person had the exclusive right and duty to make all decisions pertaining to the management of the property.

ADVANTAGES OF JOINT TENANCY

Probate Costs

By holding title to property in joint tenancy, you usually reduce the cost of settling your estate upon your death.

However, even though you owned all your assets in joint tenancy with your spouse, court proceedings will be necessary to establish inheritance taxes and to perfect the title to the property.

Property held in joint tenancy escapes executor or administrator fees but not attorney fees.

Happier Wives

It is probable that by putting the title to your house in joint tenancy, you will have a more appreciative wife than if you hold title in your name alone. Wives often mistakenly think that joint tenancy is the one way they can protect themselves against being left with nothing from your estate in return for a lifetime of maintaining a home for you and rearing your children.

In most states this definitely is not true. State laws of descent usually provide a widow with certain rights in real estate owned in fee simple by her husband no matter what provisions he has made in his will. Refer to pages 153–156 for who will inherit your property.

Without exception, the decision as to the form with which you should take title to your property should be answered only by you and your attorney, after he has thoroughly reviewed your assets and desires.

Chapter Nine

THE DEED TO THE PROPERTY

QUIT CLAIM DEEDS

Send me a self-addressed envelope and ten cents and I'll send you a deed to our nation's White House.

Really, don't bother. You would be wasting your time, postage, and dime, because all I'd send you is a quit claim deed, which wouldn't transfer to you any ownership in the White House other than that you already have as a taxpayer.

Your deed is proof that you own the property. In your offer to purchase, specify what type of deed you want the seller to give you.

With a quit claim deed the grantor transfers to the grantee his interest in the property without guarantees. A person does not have to be an owner in fee simple to give you a quit claim deed to a property. The grantor simply transfers to you whatever interest he may have in the property. He does not guarantee you that he has an interest in the property.

If I gave you a quit claim deed to the White House, I should be transferring my interest in it to you. I have no interest in it to transfer and hence should be giving you nothing; however, in the quit claim deed I guaranteed you nothing.

If you ever bought the Brooklyn Bridge and were given a deed to it, it probably was a quit claim deed. Buyers will rarely accept quit claim deeds as evidence of ownership, since they guarantee nothing. However, quit claim deeds sometimes are used in real estate transactions to clear a title.

For example, upon examination of the abstract to the property (history of the owners of the property) it is found that a Mary Smith at one time had been willed a $\frac{1}{10}$ interest in the property.

Because it cannot be found where or when Mary Smith ever relinquished or transferred her interest in the property, the buyer refuses to go ahead with his offer to purchase the property on the basis that he considers Mary Smith's interest a cloud on the title.

Mary Smith is sought and found. It seems that many years ago she sold her interest to the present owner but the deed had never been recorded. By giving a quit claim deed of her interest to the seller, she now relinquishes any claims she might have against the title to the property. She guarantees the transfer of any interest she had in the property. She does not guarantee what her interests were. She no longer has any claims against the title to the property.

SPECIAL WARRANTY DEED (or) GRANT, BARGAIN AND SALE DEED WITH COVENANT AGAINST GRANTOR'S ACTS

With this type of deed the grantor transfers legal title and legal possession of the property to the grantee and in addition the grantor guarantees his acts only.

For example, if the grantor put a mortgage on the property and then in the deed guaranteed the grantee that he was transferring the property to him free and clear of all liens and encumbrances, it would be the grantor's duty to remove the mortgage before giving title to the grantee. The grantor put the lien (mortgage) on the property. It existed only because of his act.

With this type of deed the grantor is not liable for any defects in the title caused by a previous owner.

GENERAL WARRANTY DEED (or) DEED WITH
FULL COVENANTS

With this type of deed, the grantor transfers legal title and legal possession of the property to the grantee and makes the following guarantees:

That he is the lawful owner of the property.

That he has the lawful right to convey or sell the property.

That there are no liens or other encumbrances against the property except for those mentioned as exceptions in the deed.

That there are no lawful claims against the property.

That the grantee will have peaceful possession of the property.

That no person shall make demands upon the grantee in an effort to force him to vacate the property.

If you prefer a general warranty deed—a deed with full covenants—over a quit claim deed or special warranty deed, specify in your offer to purchase that the seller convey the property to you with a general warranty deed (a deed with full covenants).

Usually statutes require that for a deed to be valid it must be signed, sealed, and delivered.

Signed

The deed should be signed by the grantor and his name should appear on the deed in the same form as it appears on the instrument by which he originally acquired his interest in the property.

For example, if my name appears as Jens E. Nielsen, Jr., on the deed by which I acquired my house, my name should also appear as Jens E. Nielsen, Jr., on the instrument by which I transfer to another my interest in my house.

Having my name appear as Jens Nielsen on one instrument and as Jens E. Nielsen, Jr., on a subsequent instrument could raise doubts. However, just because there is a difference in the way a name appears does not void a deed. If it can be proved that the different signatures refer to the same person the deed will be valid.

If a husband holds title to property in his name only and wishes to sell that property, his wife should sign the deed to release her dower rights in the property. (Refer to pages 155–156.)

If the seller's wife refuses to sign the deed, a buyer at the discretion of the court may refuse to accept the deed and sue the seller for damages. Damages result because the buyer thought he had bought the property and that he was going to receive a fee simple title to it.

Or, when the seller's wife refuses to sign, the buyer may accept the deed signed by the husband only and ask the court to deduct from the buying price an amount equal to the value of the seller's wife's community property rights or dower rights in the property.

In some states when the property is in the wife's name only, she can transfer her entire interest in the property through a deed without her husband's having also to sign the deed.

Sealed (not required in all states)

This simply involves having the word "seal" appear after the signatures of the grantor or the grantor and his wife.

Delivered

What constitutes delivery of a deed varies from state to state.

Remember that unlike a will, a deed cannot be changed. If you deed your property to another, when the deed is delivered you have made an irrevocable transfer of your interests in the property.

A will takes effect upon your death. A valid deed becomes effective when it satisfies the legal requirements for delivery. After a deed has been delivered, it is too late to change your mind. Generally, it is considered that the deed has been delivered if any one of the following events has occurred:

>The grantor gives the deed to the grantee or to a person acting as an agent for the grantee.
>
>The grantor gives the deed to the grantee but the deed is subject to the occurrence of a certain event.
>
>The grantor gives the deed to a third person to hold until certain events occur and only after these events have occurred is the third person to deliver the deed to the grantee.

Witnessed (not required in all states)

This is simply verification by others that it is your signature that appears on the instrument.

Acknowledged (not required in all states)

This is verification by a notary public that you voluntarily and under no duress signed the instrument.

RECORDING YOUR DEED

In some states it is possible that, unless you record your deed, you may lose the legal title and legal possession of your property. For example:

>August 1—the grantor delivered your warranty deed to you
>
>September 1—the grantor delivered another warranty deed to the same property to another person, a purchaser in good faith
>
>October 1—the second purchaser of the property recorded his warranty deed
>
>November 1—you recorded your warranty deed

Even though you were given your warranty deed to the property first, the second purchaser of the property could possibly be declared the owner of the property because he recorded his deed prior to the time you recorded yours.

In order for this situation to be resolved in his favor, the second purchaser of the property—the second one to receive a deed to the property but the first to record his deed—will have to prove that he acted in good faith. He will have to prove that he had no knowledge or notice that another had a prior right or claim to the property.

For example, if you were living on the property, even though you failed to record your deed, the second purchaser could not be declared a purchaser in good faith if he failed to inquire of you as to any claims you had on the property.

DESCRIPTION OF PROPERTY IN THE DEED DIFFERENT FROM DESCRIPTION IN THE SALES CONTRACT

Remember that when a seller accepts an offer to purchase, a contract for the sale of the property is created. This contract describes the property you want to buy and outlines the conditions under which you agree to buy the property. When the seller signs the contract, he agrees to sell you the described property on the terms outlined in your offer.

What if the description of the property in the deed differs from the description in the sales contract? For example, what if in the sales con-tract the lot is described as being 120' by 200' but the deed describes the lot as being 100' by 200'?

Usually the buyer has several alternatives when the description in the deed differs from the description in the sales contract:

>The buyer may refuse to accept the deed, or
>
>The buyer may accept the deed but, if he does, he may not at a later date sue the seller

to have the deed changed. The acceptance is usually considered a waiver on the buyer's behalf to the variances between the deed and the sales contract.

When both buyer and seller agree that it is a mutual mistake, they can usually have the deed changed.

Possibly you have saved for years to accumulate enough money to buy your first house. The cost of having your attorney check your deed is small compared to the value of a good and sufficient deed.

In most cases the deed will be drafted by the seller's attorney, but only you, following the advice of your attorney, can answer such questions as:

Should you have the seller's interest in the property transferred to you as joint tenants or as tenants in common?

Is the seller's interest in the property really being transferred to you free and clear of all liens and encumbrances? Or, possibly, should you be satisfied with accepting the property subject to certain liens or encumbrances as outlined in the deed?

Usually before a deed may be recorded it has to be witnessed, acknowledged, the names of the grantors typed or printed under their signatures. And the deed should identify the person who drafted it.

Sounds complicated? It is. Have your attorney check the deed to make sure it complies with the statutes of your state.

EARNEST MONEY OR BINDER

When you sign an offer to purchase, the real estate broker will ask you for earnest money. Earnest money is money paid by the buyer to either the broker or the seller when he signs the offer to purchase, which money is a guarantee that the buyer will perform as outlined in his offer to purchase and which is to be applied toward the purchase price of the property.

When you sign an offer to purchase, you in effect say to the seller that you are willing to purchase the property he listed for sale but only on the terms you outlined in your offer to purchase. Your earnest money represents your guarantee that you will go ahead with the offer if he accepts it.

The seller can accept your offer and you can have a firm contract even though you make no earnest money payment. Earnest money is not essential to a valid contract for the sale of real estate. However, it can act as a sales tool for a buyer to use in persuading a seller to accept his offer. For example, the seller lists his property for sale at $60,000. You definitely want to buy the property but consider it worth only $55,000, so you make an offer to buy the property for $55,000. The seller does not have to accept your offer.

Wouldn't the seller be more inclined to accept your offer if the broker can show him a check for $20,000 earnest money when he presents your offer to him? The earnest money payment will show your sincerity.

If I wished to sell you on the idea of buying a steak, wouldn't I stand a better chance if I could show you the steak instead of just telling you about it?

What happens to your money when you use a substantial earnest money payment as a sales tool to persuade the seller to accept your offer?

In the listing contract the broker signed with the seller, the broker agreed to hold any money given him by a prospective buyer in his authorized real estate trust account. Also in the offer to purchase signed by you at the time you made the offer, you specified that the broker is to retain all money paid by you on the contract in his real estate trust account. It should also be spelled out in what bank the broker maintains his real estate trust account.

It is your money until the seller accepts the offer or the money is returned to you because the seller doesn't accept your offer or, possibly, the money is distributed as liquidated damages.

If you are dissatisfied with the bank in which the broker maintains his real estate trust account, you have the right to insist that the broker keep your money in an authorized real estate trust account in the bank of your choice. This is seldom considered necessary, as real estate brokers' trust accounts are under the rigid control of the Real Estate Commission and the same controls are exercised no matter what bank handles the account.

In addition to specifying in your offer to purchase where your earnest money is to be held, you should be given a receipt signed by the broker for your earnest money. This signed receipt should specify where the money is to be held and should include the name of the bank in which the broker maintains his authorized real estate trust account.

You sign an offer to purchase and your earnest money payment is resting securely in the broker's real estate trust account. If you change your mind, decide you do not want to purchase the property, what happens to your earnest money payment?

Return of Earnest Money Before the Offer Is Accepted

Usually you are allowed to withdraw your offer to purchase at any time prior to its acceptance by the seller. When you withdraw your offer, you are entitled to a full refund of your earnest money.

Return of Earnest Money After the Offer Is Accepted

What happens to your earnest money if you decide to withdraw your offer after the seller has accepted it?

Ordinarily the offer to purchase stipulates that even though the seller has accepted the offer, the buyer is not bound to it until the accepted offer is mailed or personally delivered to the buyer. Check any offer you make to purchase a property to learn if the offer contains this type of provision. The freedom to withdraw your offer without forfeiting your earnest money is valuable to you.

For example, you make an offer to purchase a property which is *almost* what you want. Later, but before the seller accepts your offer and the acceptance is mailed or delivered to you, you find a property for sale which is exactly what you want. Have you the right to withdraw your offer, and if so, are you entitled to a full refund of your earnest money?

Return of Earnest Money with Oral Contracts

You enter into an oral contract to purchase another's property, make an earnest money payment, and then decide you do not want to go ahead with the transaction even though the seller accepted your offer and you received his acceptance. What happens to your earnest money?

In most states oral contracts for the sale of real estate are unenforceable. If the parties to the contract wish to go ahead under an oral contract, the transfer of the property will be valid. But neither party under an oral contract can sue the other for specific performance of the provisions in the oral contract, as he could do with a written contract.

When you back out of an oral contract after the seller has accepted it, the seller will probably be entitled to an amount of your earnest money represented by any damages he suffered by entering into the oral contract with you, and you will be awarded the remaining balance of the earnest money.

Return of Earnest Money When Buyer Defaults on Written Contract

What happens to your earnest money payment if after the seller accepts your offer and you receive his acceptance, you decide you do not want to go ahead with the written sales contract?

Usually there is a provision in the offer to purchase that dictates that if the buyer fails to carry out the terms of the contract, all the money he has paid on the contract, at the option of the seller, will be forfeited as liquidated damages.

This forfeited money will be retained by the seller subject to the broker's commission, if any, and subject to reimbursement to the broker for any disbursements he made on the seller's behalf. For example, the broker may have paid an attorney on the seller's behalf for having title to the property perfected. The broker is entitled to reimbursement for this expense.

In the absence of a "forfeiture of earnest money" provision in the offer to purchase, what happens to your earnest money if you decide you do not want to go ahead with the purchase after the seller accepts your offer and you receive his acceptance?

The seller may simply return to you all or part of your earnest money. This is unlikely, however, as usually a seller will have suffered damages in that he lost the opportunity of negotiating with other buyers during the period he thought he had sold the property to you.

In some cases when the earnest money payment is large in comparison to the total purchase price—for example, $20,000 earnest money payment on a $60,000 property—a buyer could have part of his earnest money returned to him because the total earnest money payment was in excess of the damages suffered by the seller.

The seller may return the earnest money to you and attempt to sue you for specific performance of the contract. He could attempt through a court action to force you to act as agreed upon in the offer to purchase contract. The seller would be most likely to attempt this if your earnest money payment were small and he thought your offer to purchase was reasonable.

Return of Earnest Money When Seller Defaults on Written Contract

What happens to your earnest money payment if, after the seller accepts your offer to purchase, he decides not to go ahead with the provisions of the contract?

Possibly the seller is unable to deliver to you the type of title you requested in your offer to purchase as one of the provisions of your offer. One of three things could occur:

1. You may be satisfied if the seller simply returns all your earnest money to you, or
2. You may sue the seller for damages. You could have suffered a loss inasmuch as you ceased looking at other properties when the seller accepted your offer. You possibly missed an opportunity to buy another property which would have been just as satisfactory to you.
3. You may sue for specific performance.

You may attempt to get a court action to force the seller to go ahead with the provisions of the contract.

When you make an earnest money payment, the money will usually be held in trust in the broker's real estate trust account until one of the following occurs:

1. The seller accepts your offer and your earnest money is applied toward the purchase price of the property.
2. The earnest money is returned to you because the seller is unable or unwilling to go ahead with the provisions of the sales contract.
3. You forfeit the earnest money to the seller because you are unable or unwilling to go ahead with the provisions of the sales contract.
4. The earnest money is returned to you because the seller does not accept your offer.

Time Given Seller to Accept the Offer

When making an offer to purchase accompanied by an earnest money payment, how much time should you allow the seller to consider your offer before he either accepts it or refuses it and returns your earnest money to you?

Should you give him six months or six days or less to consider your offer and to make a decision?

A reasonable amount of time is considered the time necessary for the broker to consult with the seller and explain your offer to him, plus any time a seller may need to consult other parties.

How long this will take depends upon how accessible to the seller are the broker and other people he might want to consult as to your offer.

For example, if all parties involved live in the same community, it is reasonable to expect the broker to be able to be in touch with the seller and for the seller to reach the other parties and to make a decision within two weeks.

If the seller refuses your offer, when do you want your earnest money returned to you? This usually is by not later than the day after the seller refuses the offer.

Be reasonable and allow the seller ample time to consider your offer. If you are sincere about wanting to buy the property, show the seller proof of your sincerity by making a sizable earnest money payment.

Before making an offer to purchase a property, answer the following questions and make your decisions a part of your offer:

In what bank is the broker to hold my earnest money payment?

_____

By what date is the seller to accept my offer or else return my earnest money to me?

_____

If the seller does not accept my offer, by what date is my earnest money to be returned to me?

_____

By what date and under what conditions may I withdraw my offer and still be entitled to a full refund of my earnest money?

_____

Does the offer to purchase contain the provision that I shall forfeit all of my earnest money if I back out of the contract after it has been accepted by the seller and the acceptance has been mailed or delivered to me?

_____

DEMAND A SURVEY

Your friend and neighbor is selling his house. His buyer has demanded a survey of the property before he will proceed with the deal, so your neighbor has had his property surveyed. A survey is a diagram of a property showing all encroachments. An encroachment is anything that extends over another's lot line.

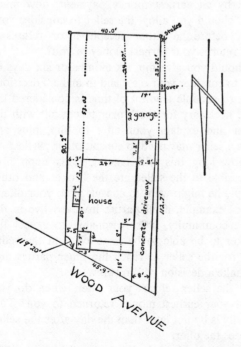

PLAT OF SURVEY

Your neighbor telephones, asking to meet with you and your wife to discuss an important problem. That evening he tells you that according to the survey he had made of his property, you built your picket fence on his property and now you have to remove it. Or possibly your new garage extends onto his lot, or part of your flower garden is on his property.

This wouldn't have happened if you had insisted that the seller supply you with a survey of your property before you bought it. The survey would have shown you the exact location of your lot lines.

When you buy a property, the sales contract and title transfer papers should contain a complete and accurate description of the property. Unless a survey is made, the description will probably be the same as the one used in the instrument by which the seller received his title to the property.

What guarantee do you have that the seller really owns the property you propose to buy? You have only the seller's guarantee that he is transferring the property as described in the title transfer papers to you, free and clear of all liens and encumbrances.

If the seller is deceased or can't be reached, what good is this guarantee when you learn that the description of the property is wrong and you built your fence on your neighbor's property?

Only with a survey are you guaranteed that you will receive the exact property the seller guarantees you through the title transfer papers.

The cost of a survey is determined by how long it takes the surveyor to complete it. This varies with locations, the size of the property, how much information is available to the surveyor, and what information you want included in the survey.

Usually a survey of a residential property includes only a diagram of the lot showing the location of the buildings that occupy the lot, and will cost from $50 to $100.

As a part of your offer to purchase the property, you may possibly want to include the provision that the seller is to provide you with a survey of the property at his cost. If you do this, list whatever information you want included in the survey.

For example:

"The seller is to supply me with a survey made by a licensed surveyor of the property showing lot lines and buildings."

If you aren't acquainted with a competent surveyor, ask your banker or real estate broker to refer you to one.

Know what you are buying! Have a survey made of the property!

Chapter Ten

TITLE TO THE PROPERTY

ABSTRACT OF TITLE OR OWNER'S POLICY OF TITLE INSURANCE?

With a deed the seller transfers his interest in the property to you in exchange for the purchase of the property.

What is the seller's interest in the property? What can he give you as a guarantee that he actually owns and has the right to transfer this interest to you?

In the deed the seller declares that he is transferring legal title and legal possession of the property to you, but what happens if the seller misrepresents his ownership? Your deed is only good to the extent that the seller can be held financially liable to you for the damages you suffer from any misrepresentation.

The typical real estate transaction involves two instruments to guarantee that you will actually receive what you are buying:

1. A deed by which the seller conveys his interest in the property to you, and

2. An abstract of title which is evidence that the seller actually owns the property, or an owner's policy of title insurance by which the seller guarantees you through an insurance policy that your title will be protected against any claims to it.

Exceptions are that in some areas only a certificate of title is used. Rather than draw up a formal abstract or title policy, the attorney examines the recorded instruments pertaining to the property and issues a certificate declaring that he examined the records and stating what liens and encumbrances are held against the title, or else declaring the title free and clear of all liens and encumbrances.

In other areas a Torrens certificate is used.

All who could possibly have any claims against the property are publicly invited to declare their claims and sue to have them satisfied. After the suits are dismissed or settled, the court orders a title recorded in the new owner's name and issues the new owner a Torrens certificate.

Under this system, if there are attacks against the title after the certificate is issued, usually the register of title who originally issued the certificate is not held liable.

Because of the widespread use of abstracts and owner's policies of title insurance, our discussion is restricted to them.

Abstract of Title

An abstract of title is a history of the recorded documents pertaining to a piece of real estate.

"Recorded documents" refers to documents available to the public through the office of the county recorder in the county where the property is located and such other records as may be available through other public offices.

Some of the recorded documents that may appear in an abstract of title are deeds, recorded leases, liens, foreclosure actions, special assessments, and judgments.

The abstract company is liable for any mistakes in the abstract only to that person—usually the seller—who contracted with them for the abstract.

After examining the abstract, your attorney will give you his written opinion stating that:

1. The title to the property is merchantable, or

2. The title to the property is not merchantable, and a list of what has to be done to make the title merchantable.

If in your attorney's opinion the title is merchantable, purchase the property and accept the abstract.

If in your attorney's opinion the title is not merchantable, you have three choices:

1. Buy the property and accept the abstract even though you will not be receiving a merchantable title, or

2. Demand that the seller at his expense have the necessary changes made in the title so that he will be able to deliver to you a merchantable title, or

3. If you and the seller agree, accept an owner's policy of title insurance in lieu of an abstract of title.

Most states where the abstract of title is used specify in their approved sales contract forms what periods will be covered by the abstract and by what dates the abstract is to be processed.

The abstract is to show a history of the recorded documents pertaining to the property from the time the patent was issued to within *twenty* days of the closing date.

By not later than *fifteen* days prior to the date set for closing the seller is to deliver a complete abstract of title to the buyer for examination by the buyer's attorney.

The buyer is to be allowed *ten* days to have his attorney examine the abstract and in writing notify the seller of any objections to the title.

The seller is to have not more than *sixty* days to have the title rectified and to furnish the buyer a marketable title. (The dates and time periods entered are those usually used in Wisconsin.)

Even though you specify in your sales contract a date by which you want the transaction closed and request that the seller is to deliver to you an abstract at least fifteen days prior to that date, a late delivery of the abstract to you by the seller will not necessarily void the contract.

Late Delivery of the Abstract to the Buyer

When you wish to be allowed to withdraw from a contract for the sale of property if the seller is unable to perform in the manner required by the contract and by the dates outlined in the contract, you should specify in the contract that "time is of the essence of the contract."

In addition you should outline the consequences if either buyer or seller fails to perform as required in the contract by the dates as outlined in the contract.

Usually if the seller fails to perform as stated in the sales contract:

1. The buyer's earnest money is returned to him, and

2. The buyer is possibly awarded liquidated damages, and

3. The contract is canceled.

If the buyer fails to perform as stated in the sales contract, usually:

1. The buyer's earnest money is forfeited to the seller, and

2. The seller possibly is awarded liquidated damages, and

3. The contract is canceled.

How important to you are the dates you have specified in your offer to purchase? For example, how important to you is the date by which the seller is to deliver a marketable title?

If these dates are so important to you that you might wish to withdraw from the contract if the seller is unable to perform as required by these dates, specify in your offer to purchase that "time is of the essence of the contract" and outline the consequences in the event either buyer or seller is unable to perform as required by these dates.

Seller Unable to Deliver a Merchantable Title

What if at the date set for the closing, in your attorney's opinion, the title delivered to you by the seller is still not a merchantable title?

Ordinarily the sales contract will contain a provision that allows the seller a set number of days to have the title rectified or to furnish the buyer with an owner's policy of title insurance.

In some states the seller is usually allowed a maximum of sixty days, from the date he receives the written objection to the title, to have the title perfected. The original date for the closing of the transaction is delayed to allow the seller this time.

What happens if at the end of the time allowed the seller, he is still unable, in your attorney's opinion, to deliver a merchantable title to you?

The contract is void. The law does not require you as the buyer to accept anything other than a merchantable title. All money you paid on the sales contract will be returned to you.

In review of abstracts, if the seller elects to furnish you an abstract of title, you will receive:

1. The abstract of title, which is a history of the recorded documents that pertain to the property. The abstract company is liable for any mistakes in the abstract only to the person who contracted with them for the preparation of the abstract.

2. A letter from your attorney stating that the title to the real estate is either merchantable or not merchantable. The attorney is liable for his opinion only to the person who retained him to examine the title to the property.

As only a history of the recorded documents pertaining to the title to the property, neither your abstract nor your attorney's written opinion that you have a marketable title protects you against hidden defects in your title such as forged or illegal deeds, undiscovered heirs, frauds, and impersonation by the owners, nor do they protect you against the interests of unknown persons.

For the added protection against these possible defects, in lieu of an abstract of title, you may wish to specify in your offer to purchase that the seller furnish you an owner's policy of title insurance.

Owner's Policy of Title Insurance

This is an agreement between a title insurance company and usually a property owner in which the title insurance company agrees to protect or defend the title to the property against claims not excluded in the policy.

Just as an accident insurance policy gives you only the coverage outlined in the policy, an owner's policy of title insurance protects you only to the extent outlined in the policy. However, usually the following guarantees and exclusions are made a part of the policy:

Does guarantee you a marketable title. (In some cases the title insurance company may only agree to defend you against any loss resulting from defects in your title.)

Does guarantee the person named in the policy—usually the buyer—that they will defend him in any court action brought against him as pertains to the title to the property described in the policy.

Does guarantee that they will defend the title only as it existed on a certain date. Usually this is the date when the title to the property is conveyed to the buyer.

Does guarantee that they will defend the title only up to the dollar amount specified in the policy. Usually this amount is the price the buyer paid the seller for the property.

Does guarantee the insured against any loss or damages from liens and encumbrances on the property at the time the policy was issued and which aren't listed in the policy as exclusions.

Does guarantee the insured against any defects in any mortgages or trust deeds put on the property by the insured at the time or prior to the time the policy was issued.

Does not insure against taxes or assessments that act as liens on the property but which aren't listed on the public records.

Does not insure against those things that are listed as being exclusions in the policy.

Does not insure against claims that can be determined by an inspection and survey of the property.

For example, by visiting the property, you can learn who is at present in possession and what their rights are to the possession of the property. By having a survey made of the property, you can learn where the lot lines are and if there are any encroachments— structures extending over the lot lines.

As you should with all insurance policies, read carefully your owner's policy of title insurance.

To demonstrate how an owner's policy of title

insurance protects you, let's imagine that the seller and you agree that you are to receive an owner's policy of title insurance in lieu of an abstract of title. You pay $50,000 for the property and agree that the policy is to be written for $50,000. Also you agree that the policy is to protect your title as it exists up to the time the seller conveys title to the property to you.

If after the policy is issued to you, a court action is brought against you pertaining to a defect in the title, which defect existed on or prior to the time the seller conveyed the title to you, the insurance company will defend you in court at no cost to you, provided the defense does not cost more than $50,000.

Ordinarily you will not be given an owner's policy of title insurance prior to date set for the closing of the transaction. Instead you will receive a "commitment" by a title insurance company.

The commitment or "preliminary report" is a report issued by a title insurance company in which the company states that it will issue an owner's policy of title insurance to the person to be named in the policy. With a commitment or preliminary report you may proceed as though you had actually been issued the owner's policy of title insurance. You are assured that you will receive the policy.

Let's compare the value to you of an abstract of title and an owner's policy of title insurance:

Even though the offer to purchase form may give the seller the right to choose between an owner's policy of title insurance and an abstract of title, you may specify in your offer which one you want.

For example, in your offer to purchase specify that the seller is to furnish you, at his expense, with an owner's policy of title insurance and that his furnishing this be an essential part of the contract.

Check with your attorney as to which you should request or even demand as a part of your offer—an owner's policy of title insurance or an abstract of title.

Abstract of Title and Owner's Policy of Title Insurance (Compared)

	Owner's policy of title insurance	Abstract of title
Guarantees you merchantable title	Sometimes	No
Guarantees you against any loss as a result of any claims against your title	Yes, but with exceptions and only up to the amount stated in the policy—usually the purchase price.	No, but in some cases the attorney who examined the abstract can be held financially liable for his written opinion of the abstract.

ZONING—HOW IT AFFECTS YOUR TITLE

No matter what type of title you receive to the property, there will be restrictions and limitations on what uses you can make of the property. Easements for public utilities give servicemen the right to enter upon your property to service such items as electrical, telephone, and water and sewage facilities.

Local building restrictions limit the type and size of the structures you may have on your property. These restrictions frequently dictate, for example, how many feet your residence must be from the edge of your lot line.

Zoning is the division of a governmental unit—city, town, or county—into districts, assigning prohibited and permitted uses to the real estate in such districts. The most common categories are residential, commercial, manufacturing, and agricultural.

Recall that one of the broker's duties to you is to exercise reasonable care in determining that all the information given to you by him and by the seller is factual. This releases you from the chore of searching public records for information as to easements against the property, local building restrictions, and zoning ordinances.

Simply ask the broker.

If you are going to invest your savings in a house, shouldn't you know if there is the possibility of a laundry's being started across the street from your house? Or are you buying a house that will appreciate because of big handsome houses cropping up on adjoining lots?

Before making an offer to purchase a particular property, have answers to these questions:

What effect will the present zoning ordinances have on what use I may make of the property? _____

_____

What changes are planned in the present zoning ordinances? _____

_____

Even though an area is zoned for one particular use, properties that do not conform to the zoning ordinances may exist in that area and may be bought and sold.

For example, while the area was zoned as commercial, you owned and operated a very successful coin laundry. The zoning was changed to residential only. Does this mean that you have been put out of business because of the change in the zoning?

This wouldn't be fair to you, since when you started the laundry, the use you were making of the property was in conformity with the zoning ordinances.

Non-conforming Use

Usually when a property does not conform to the zoning ordinances because of a change in the zoning ordinances, the property is declared a non-conforming use property and the owner is allowed to continue making the original use of the property provided:

1. He does not expand on the non-conforming use he was originally making of the property. He probably will not be allowed to make any additions to the laundry.

2. He does not try to re-establish the business or use after abandoning it—usually for twelve months. If he closes his laundry for thirteen months, he probably will not be allowed to reopen it.

3. He will not be allowed to re-establish the use when the property has been damaged and the cost to restore it to its original use is more than one half of the assessed value of the property. If a fire partially destroys his laundry and the loss is more than half of the value of the property, he probably will not be allowed to re-establish the business.

Buying a non-conforming use property is like buying an egg only to learn that it has no yolk. When you look at the egg, it looks complete. It is only when you try to use it that you learn of the limited uses you can make of it. When you buy a non-conforming use property, you are held to the same restrictions as was the original owner on what uses you may make of the property.

Ask the broker if the property conforms to the zoning ordinances. If you are willing to buy a non-conforming property, be sure you thoroughly understand what restrictions exist as to what uses you may make of the property.

Illegal Use

When a property is used contrary to the zoning ordinances and the contrary use is not the result of a change in zoning ordinances, it is called "illegal use."

For example, even though the area is zoned as residential and disallows any commerce, you start a laundry. You start the laundry after the area has been zoned as residential.

You or any buyer of the property can be forced, at any time, to discontinue using the property as a laundry. When you started the laundry, you should have known that the use you were making of the property was an illegal use, contrary to the zoning ordinances.

You, as well as any buyer of your laundry, will not be protected, since you voluntarily put yourself in this position. It was not the result of any change in the zoning ordinances over which you had no control, as is the case with non-conforming use of properties.

Even though you know that the use made of a property is an illegal use you may wish to buy the property and continue making such use of it.

Special Use Permit

You may be able to sell the zoning authorities on issuing you a "special use" permit, which will allow you to make this use of the property contrary to existing zoning ordinances.

Do not buy the property intending later to ask about a special use permit. Zoning ordinances are passed to establish definite uses for properties and most zoning authorities are very reluctant to make any exceptions, to issue any special use permits.

Official Maps

One year after you buy a property, the city street commissioner tells you that they are going to put in a new street that will pass within ten feet of your back porch. Can the city do this?

Most communities have "official maps," which show the beds of future streets and planned widening lines along existing streets.

It is the duty of the builder or buyer of real estate to determine how these additional streets and changes in existing streets will affect his property. If you build a new house in the bed of a planned street, the community is not liable for your loss when you have to remove the house to make way for the street. The official map was available. It is not the city's fault that you failed to make inquiries.

Perhaps you want to get away from the congestion and confusion of city living. You want to buy a lot in the country and build a new house on it. You notice that a few desirable new houses have been built recently in a scenic area just outside of town only fifteen minutes' drive from where you work. You make an offer to buy a lot in that area.

Is the lot a part of an approved subdivision?

Subdivisions

Laws differ from state to state, but usually once a subdivision has been established and the plat showing the division of the land into lots and blocks has been approved and recorded, the platting code will dictate such things as:

1. Lot size allowed in the subdivision.
2. What the street layout is to be.
3. What access is going to be available to the main highways
4 In what manner the streets are to be surfaced and maintained.
5. Uses which may be made of the properties in the subdivision.

Discuss the platting code with the broker. Learn what uses you will be allowed to make of the property. Learn when and in what manner streets, water and sewage, and utilities are going to be available and how they are going to be maintained.

If you buy a piece of land that is not a part of an approved subdivision, you lose the benefits that would otherwise come to you through the platting code.

For example, a farmer sells you an acre of land with the assurance that someday he is going to have the land platted. Six months pass and much to your disappointment nothing has been done about putting in the streets. You are not protected by the platting code, as the seller has not yet had the area platted. Are you stuck?

To protect the buyer who thinks the piece of

land he bought is someday to be a part of an approved subdivision, state statutes usually provide that, if over a certain number of parcels of land of a certain size are sold within a limited time, the land must be surveyed and the plat approved and recorded.

For example, if an owner of real estate sells five or more parcels of land of 1½ acres or less each within a five-year period, the land must be platted and the plat approved and recorded.

Usually if the seller fails to satisfy the requirements established by his state, a buyer can back out of the deal, but only provided he acts within a limited time from the date of the contract.

This type of statute prevents the chaos that would result if clusters of houses cropped up without benefit of platting codes or zoning ordinances. The broker is familiar with local building restrictions, easements, platting codes, and zoning ordinances. Ask him how these affect the uses you wish to make of the property you want to buy.

INFORMATION TO HAVE AND DECISIONS TO MAKE
BEFORE MAKING AN OFFER TO PURCHASE A PROPERTY

Remember that when you make an offer to purchase a property, the broker is going to submit that offer to the seller. If the seller accepts that offer you are bound to the terms of that contract. Always assume that the seller will accept your offer. Be sure that you will be content to go ahead with the terms in that offer.

Always have the questions on the worksheet that follows this chapter answered before making your offer. Do not delay completing this worksheet until after you have made your offer. Each unanswered question is a potential irritant and pitfall in your sales contract.

How Much Are You Willing to Pay
for the Property?

Should you offer to pay the listed price or should you submit an offer at a considerably lower price? What is the property really worth to you? (Refer to pages 63–65 for what a property is really worth.)

Remember, though, that the broker is going to submit your offer to the seller and if the seller accepts it, you are bound to the contract. Don't make a low offer on a property you really don't want just because you think that if you can buy it at that low price, it is a good deal.

Remember also, when determining the number of dollars you want to spend, that in addition to the purchase price, you will have expenses for (1) recording of documents, (2) attorney fees, and (3) an expense in taking over the seller's property insurance or in acquiring new insurance.

The price I am willing to pay for the property is $_____

Under What Terms Are You Willing
to Pay for the Property?

You may offer to buy the property on any terms suitable to you; you are not committed to the way in which the seller has said he wants to be paid for the property.

For example, the seller says in his listing that he wants the total selling price of $55,000 in cash. You offer the seller $10,000 and ask that he finance the other $45,000 on a land contract or a purchase money mortgage. (Refer to pages 142–148 for land contracts and to pages 128–139 for mortgages.)

You make this proposal by stating in your offer to purchase that you are willing to go ahead with the other provisions in your offer only if the seller will accept the $10,000 cash and finance the balance of $45,000 with your choice of either a land contract or a purchase money mortgage. The seller might accept this, possibly because of a change in his own finances, or because it is the most attractive offer he has received.

Possibly the seller has a mortgage on the property that he is willing to allow you to assume and agree to pay as part of the purchase price. For example, the seller wants $50,000 for the property and is willing to sell on the following terms: The buyer is to pay $10,000 cash and is to assume and agree to pay a mortgage for $40,000 that the seller owes to a third party.

Often because of rising interest rates, it will

cost a buyer less to assume and to pay an existing mortgage than it will cost him to take out a new mortgage. In every case, explore thoroughly what your financing costs will be. (Refer to pages 69–75 for the cost of money.)

The terms under which I am agreeable to paying for this property are ————————
————————————————————————————

Conditions Under Which You Are Willing to Go Ahead with the Provisions in Your Offer to Purchase

When making the offer to purchase, specify in the offer the conditions under which you are willing to go ahead with the provisions in your offer. When the seller accepts the offer, thereby creating a contract to sell you the property, he agrees to sell you the property subject to the conditions you outlined in your offer.

Let's look at some of the ways in which you can exercise your right to specify in your offer the conditions under which you are willing to go ahead with the deal.

SURVEYS

If you want the seller to supply you with a survey of the property at his expense, state this in your offer:

"Seller to supply the buyer a survey of the property at the seller's expense."

When the seller accepts the offer, he agrees to supply this survey at his expense. You will not be required to go ahead with the other provisions of the purchase contract unless the seller supplies you with the survey at his expense. (Refer to pages 86–87 for surveys.)

SALE OF OTHER PROPERTY

Possibly you want to go ahead with your offer but only provided you are able to sell another property for a certain amount by a certain date.

In your offer state:

"This offer is subject to the buyer's being able to sell (complete description of the property) for (dollar amount) by (date by which you want to have the property sold)."

After the seller accepts your offer, you still are not bound to the contract if you are not able to sell your property for the amount and by the time you stated in your offer.

SUBJECT TO SECURING NECESSARY FINANCING

You want to buy the property but you haven't enough cash; somehow, somewhere, therefore, you have to arrange financing. For example, you consider $60,000 a very reasonable price to pay for the property, but you have only $15,000.

You figure that with your income you can handle a $45,000 mortgage for a term of fifteen years and at not more than 9% interest.

State in your offer:

"This offer is subject to the buyer's being able to procure by (date) a mortgage for $45,000 for a term of not less than 15 years and at not more than 9% interest."

After the seller accepts your offer, if you are not able to procure the mortgage as described in the offer by the date given in the offer, you are not bound to the contract.

WAIVER OF CONTRACTORS' LIENS

Remember that a person who supplies labor, services, and/or materials for the improvement of real estate may file a lien against the real estate for the collection of any amounts due him. (Refer to pages 125–127 for liens.)

The lien when properly filed becomes a lien against the real estate regardless of who owns the real estate. Surely you are entitled to every assurance that no liens have been overlooked. One way to handle this is to include in the offer to purchase the following type of provision:

"This offer is subject to the seller's furnishing the buyer with an affidavit listing all contractors and/or subcontractors who have supplied materials, labor, and/or services for the improvement of the real estate within the last _____ months."

Fill in the period of time your state grants to a contractor or subcontractor to file a lien after completing any work or furnishing any materials for the improvement of real estate.

"Also this offer is subject to the seller's furnishing the buyer with a full waiver of lien from each of the contractors or subcontractors on the list."

This type of provision will not put too great a burden on the seller if he is sincere about wanting to accept your offer. It will be comforting to you to have the assurance that you will be receiving the property clear of any contractors' or subcontractors' liens.

TIME IS OF THE ESSENCE OF THE CONTRACT

In your offer to purchase, state by what date you want the transaction closed, the title transferred to you, and the purchase price paid to the seller.

If you wish to be allowed to withdraw from the contract in the event the seller is unable to perform in the manner and by the dates outlined in your contract, specify in your offer that:

"Time is of the essence of the contract."

Also outline what penalties you want imposed on the seller if he cannot perform by the dates outlined in the contract. Possibly you will want to specify that you be allowed to withdraw from the contract if the seller is unable to close the transaction by a given date.

Remember, though, that if you make "time is of the essence" a part of the contract, it can also impose penalties on you if you are unable to perform in the manner and by the dates outlined in the contract.

SUBJECT TO APPROVAL BY ANOTHER

Perhaps there is some uncertainty in your mind as to whether the property is really suited to the use you plan to make of it. You have a friend whose advice you would like to have, but he is out of town for two weeks. Simply put into your offer:

"This offer is subject to approval by (name and address of the person) by not later than (date)."

Such a provision will make your being bound to the contract subject to your friend's approval of the offer.

This certainly is not a complete list of all the possible special conditions you might wish to include in your offer to purchase. These examples are offered simply to demonstrate the flexibility of the special provisions you may put into your offer.

If you are faced with a special circumstance that is going to determine whether you will be able to buy a property, go ahead and make the offer. Include the special circumstance as a condition that must be met or an event that must occur before you will be required to fulfill the other provisions in your offer:

The conditions under which I am agreeable to going ahead with the provisions in this offer are _____
_____

How Much Earnest Money Do You Plan to Put on Deposit with the Broker When You Make Your Offer to Purchase?

When you make an offer to purchase a property you will be asked to make an earnest money payment. This payment represents your guarantee that you will go ahead with the provisions in your offer if the seller accepts your offer. (Refer to pages 83–86 for earnest money.)

Normally you will be asked for an earnest money payment equal to 10% of the purchase price of the property. A more substantial earnest money payment is usually helpful in encouraging the seller to accept an offering price that is lower than his listed price.

Often in addition to earnest money, you will be asked to make an additional payment toward the purchase price of the property when the seller accepts your offer. If you wish to use "offering an additional payment when the seller accepts the offer" as a sales tool to encourage the seller to accept your offer, state the amount of this additional payment in your offer.

The amount of earnest money payment I am willing to make is $_____
I am agreeable to making an additional payment when the seller accepts the offer of $_____

Where Will Your Earnest Money Payment Be Held?

Ordinarily a buyer's earnest money payment is held in the participating broker's authorized real estate trust account, which is under the control of the Real Estate Commission. (Refer to pages 83–86 for earnest money.)

You will receive a receipt for your earnest money payment and the receipt should specify the name and address of the bank in which the broker has his real estate trust account.

If you prefer that your earnest money payment be retained in a real estate trust account in a bank other than the one in which the broker has his, you may make this request in your offer to purchase.

My earnest money payment is to be retained in the _____

By What Date Is the Seller to Accept Your Offer or Else Return Your Earnest Money Payment to You?

Recall that your earnest money payment is your guarantee that you will go ahead with the provisions made in your offer if the seller accepts your offer to purchase the property.

The time a buyer should allow a seller for making a decision will vary with every offer. The broker needs time to present the offer to the seller. Possibly the seller needs time to consult others. When the buyer, the broker, and the seller live in the same community, two weeks is usually ample time to allow the broker to reach the seller and for the seller to make a decision.

If the seller does not accept your offer by the date specified in the offer, you are entitled to the return of your earnest money payment. You should specify in your offer by what date you want this payment returned to you.

Often a buyer specifies that if the seller does not accept the offer by the date specified in the offer, the buyer's earnest money payment is to be either personally delivered to him or mailed to him the following day:

I wish for my earnest money payment to be applied toward the purchase price only if the seller accepts the offer on or before
_____
If the seller does not accept this offer by the above date, I wish my earnest money payment to be returned to me by _____
_____

When May You Withdraw This Offer and Still Be Entitled to a Full Refund of Your Earnest Money Payment?

After making your offer will you be allowed to change your mind without losing your earnest money payment?

Offer to purchase forms usually provide that the buyer may withdraw his offer without penalty at any time prior to the time the seller accepts it and that acceptance is mailed or personally delivered to the buyer.

This provision reserves for you the right to change your mind provided you do so before the seller accepts your offer and his acceptance has been mailed or personally delivered to you. Have clearly written into your offer to purchase the conditions under which you may withdraw your offer without losing your earnest money payment:

I may withdraw this offer and get a full refund of my earnest money payment if I do so by _____

What Will Happen to Your Earnest Money If You Withdraw Your Offer After the Seller Has Accepted It and the Acceptance Has Been Delivered to You?

After the accepted offer has been mailed or delivered to you, you have entered into a contract to buy the property. Your earnest money payment was your guarantee that you would go ahead with the provisions of your offer if the seller accepted your offer.

If, after the seller accepts your offer, you wish to withdraw, you are breaking your contract.

On this basis, most offer to purchase forms have written into them the provision that when the buyer wants to back out of the sales contract, the seller at his option may keep the buyer's earnest money payment.

Other alternatives available to the seller are to sue the buyer for specific performance or to sue for damages. (Refer to pages 84–85 for earnest money-buyer defaults.)

Before signing an offer, discuss this matter with the broker. Have an understanding of what it can cost you and what actions the seller can take against you if you change your mind about your offer after the seller has accepted it and the acceptance has been delivered to you.

If I wish to withdraw my offer after the seller has accepted it and the acceptance has been delivered to me, my earnest money payment shall be _____ _____

What Is to Be Included in the Purchase Price?

The seller includes in his listing contract an accounting of what is to be included in the selling price, but the listing is only the employment contract between the seller and the broker. It is no guarantee that you will receive the items he included in his listing contract.

Your offer to purchase after it has been accepted by the seller and the acceptance has been delivered to you is the actual sales contract. When the offer is accepted by the seller, the seller is agreeing to sell you the property described in the offer on the terms you outlined in the offer.

To avoid confusion and possibly friction, your offer should clearly and completely describe just what you expect to receive in exchange for paying the purchase price. The offer should contain a complete and accurate description of the real estate you are offering to buy. For example, a complete description could be:

"The property located at 1125 John Street in the City of Milwaukee, County of Milwaukee, known as Lot numbered Four (4) in Block numbered Five (5) in the XX Subdivision with such lot having a frontage of _____ feet with a depth of _____ feet."

Such a description would leave little doubt as to what real estate you are offering to buy.

Usually when problems arise as to what is to be included in the purchase price, they result from a failure to have an understanding as to whether certain items are fixtures (considered a part of the real estate) or whether such items are personal property and as such are not to be included in the purchase price. (Refer to pages 121–123 for fixtures.)

To prevent any misunderstandings, list in your offer to purchase the items you expect to receive in exchange for paying the purchase price.

The following items are to be included in the purchase price:

(circle either "yes" or "no")

Attached antennas	yes	no
Water conditioner	yes	no
Draperies	yes	no
Curtains and rods	yes	no
Venetian blinds	yes	no
Window shades	yes	no
Awnings	yes	no
Carpeting	yes	no
Hot water heater	yes	no
Heating unit	yes	no
Linoleum	yes	no
Lighting fixtures	yes	no
Bathroom accessories	yes	no
Screen doors and windows	yes	no
Storm doors and windows	yes	no
Others _____	yes	no
_____	yes	no
_____	yes	no

The real estate I am offering to buy is (complete detailed description of the real estate) _____ _____ _____

What Method Do You Want Used to Prorate Taxes, Rents, Utility Bills, and Prepaid Insurance Premiums?

If title to the property changes hands on July 1, who owes the property taxes for that year?

The new owner will receive the tax bill for the entire year although he owned the property only for the last six months of the year.

Through the process of prorating, the seller will pay the new owner an amount equal to the taxes for six months and then, when the taxes for that year are due, the new owner will pay the entire amount.

Too often this process and the provisions for it aren't discussed before the buyer makes his offer. He learns about it only after it has actually happened at the closing, and too frequently he is disappointed because he thinks that somehow he has been cheated.

Before signing your offer, discuss with the broker and include in your offer to purchase what method of prorating you want used. (Refer to pages 117–121 for prorating.)

The prorating method I want used is_____
_____

Who Will Pay Future or Existing Special Assessments?

Special assessments are charges levied against a property by a city or village for improvements made for the benefit of that property.

Examples are special assessments for street improvements, gutter and sidewalk improvement, and the installation of water and sewage systems.

Special assessments usually are made payable over several years so that at any one time there may be payments remaining due on an assessment for work started or already completed plus future payments for work planned but not yet started.

Any planned public improvements that could result in special assessments against the property should be noted in the offer. For example, possibly the seller has received notice that the sidewalk is to be repaired next year at a cost of $500 to the owner of the property. As the new owner you probably will be expected to pay that $500.

You are entitled to know about any planned public improvements that will affect the property. Ask the broker or seller about them.

Normally special assessments for work started prior to the date of the offer are paid by the seller.

Special assessments for work that is to be started after the date of the offer are paid by the buyer.

For example, if there is a special assessment of $300 payable at $100 a year for three years against the property for street improvement and the work had started prior to the date of the buyer's offer, the seller is responsible for paying the entire $300.

Discuss special assessments with the broker, make your decision, and specify in your offer to purchase just how you want the payment of special assessments handled.

Planned public improvements that will result in special assessments against the property are _____
_____

Special assessments for work started prior to the date of this offer to be paid by _____
_____

Special assessments for work that is to be started after the date of this offer are to be paid by _____

By What Date Do You Want Physical Occupancy of the Property?

Generally it is specified in the offer that you will be given "legal possession" of the property on the date of closing. Legal possession is your right to the property but only subject to the rights of tenants or others legally in occupancy.

For example, you could have title to a property (legal possession) but not be able to occupy the property (physical occupancy) because of some tenant arrangement.

When will you want physical occupancy of the property—the actual use of the property— the right to move into and occupy the property?

Some people never accomplish anything as scheduled. Imagine that you had all your belongings packed and on the moving van, ready to move into your new house. But the seller just hasn't got around to moving his things out yet. Disappointment and hard feelings! Specify in your offer by what date you want to be allowed to move into and occupy the property.

What if the seller is not able to move out by the date of closing when legal possession of the property is transferred to you? He will still be living there and using your property. Shouldn't you be entitled to some compensation? Specify in your offer what you expect the seller to pay daily, as a use and occupancy charge, if he plans to live there after the closing date. Also specify how many days you are willing to allow him the use of the property.

For example, for $10 a day you might allow the seller the use of the property for ten days after the date of closing. If after ten days the seller is still not able to deliver physical occupancy of the property to you, you are entitled to damages. You were ready to move in and the seller had agreed in the sales contract to give you physical occupancy of the property by that date.

Normally a provision is made in the offer whereby a part of the purchase price is held by a third party to guarantee that the seller vacates as agreed. If the seller does vacate as agreed, this money is then given to him. However, if the seller fails to vacate as agreed, this money is awarded to the buyer as liquidated damages.

For example, you asked that $500 from your purchase price be held in escrow (safekeeping) by the broker. If the seller does not deliver physical occupancy of the property to you by the agreed-upon date, the $500 will go to you as liquidated damages. If the seller does deliver physical occupancy of the property to you by the agreed-upon date, the $500 is returned to him.

Don't be the victim of owning a property and not being able to use it. Have the following decisions made before you make your offer to purchase:

The date by which I want physical occupancy of the property is _____
I will allow the seller use of the property for _____ days after the day of closing in exchange for a use and occupancy charge of $_____ a day.
$_____ is to be withheld from the purchase price to be held in escrow by _____
_____
If physical occupancy of the property is not delivered to me by _____, this money is to be awarded to me as liquidated damages. If physical occupancy of the property is delivered to me by the above date, the money is to be returned to the seller.

When and Where Do You Want the Closing to Take Place?

In your offer to purchase you agreed to buy the property. Naturally you are anxious to close the deal and become the new owner. The work has just started. Before the deal can be closed the seller has to arrange to furnish either an acceptable abstract of title or an owner's policy of title insurance. You will probably have to arrange financing and make arrangements to take over the seller's property insurance or to make arrangements for a different policy.

Don't be so anxious to close the deal that you pick a closing date that is impossible for both you and the seller.

If in your offer you made "time of the essence as to the date of closing" and the seller is not able to close on the agreed-upon date, you may back out of the deal and have your earnest money returned to you or you may sue the seller for damages.

But if "time is of the essence as to the date of closing" and you are not able to close the deal on the agreed-upon date, the seller may also back out of the deal or sue you for damages. Both parties have agreed to the contract. Do not cause friction by hastening the closing date.

The place of closing is selected after considering the location of all the people involved in the transaction. Ordinarily closings take place at the office of either the buyer's or seller's attorney or mortgagee.

The closing is to take place on or before ___
The closing is to take place at _____

What If the Property Is Damaged After the Offer Has Been Accepted by the Seller and Delivered to the Buyer but Before Legal Possesion of the Property Is Transferred to the Buyer?

Most states have laws to handle this situation, so check with the broker before making any decisions. Normally if damage to the property resulting from fire or the elements is not more than 10% of the selling price, the seller pays to have the property restored. This may not be used as an excuse for the buyer to back out of the deal.

If the damage is more than 10% of the selling

price, the buyer may withdraw from the contract and have his earnest money returned to him, or he may go ahead with the contract and be entitled to the insurance proceeds not in excess of the purchase price.

If the damage occurs after the buyer has been given legal possession as the new owner, he is liable.

If the property is damaged prior to the time of closing, it will be handled in the following manner: _____ _____

Do You Want the Seller to Furnish You an Abstract of Title or Owner's Policy of Title Insurance?

You should specify in your offer to purchase which you want. When the seller accepts your offer he will be required to supply the one you choose. (Refer to pages 88–91 for a discussion of these real estate instruments.)

I want the seller to supply me with a (choose either an abstract of title or an owner's policy of title insurance) _____ _____

What Type of Deed Do You Want the Seller to Furnish, and Will the Property Be Transferred to You Free and Clear of All Liens and Encumbrances?

Review pages 80–83 concerning deeds and you will probably decide that you should specify in your offer to purchase that the seller furnish you with a general warranty deed.

On page 127 we discussed the advisability of including in your offer to purchase the provision that the seller furnish you with a full waiver of lien from each contractor or subcontractor who supplied services, labor, or materials for the improvement of the real estate within the time given him to file his lien.

Are there any easements on the property? Has the seller or a previous owner given another person the right to go upon the property for a particular purpose? Are you willing to allow the easement to exist or do you prefer that as a condition of the contract the seller have the easement removed? (Refer to pages 123–125 for easements.)

What uses you may make of the property will be influenced by municipal ordinances, zoning ordinances, building restrictions, and recorded easements for public utilities. Discuss these with the broker. Become familiar with them. Don't buy a property intending to make a certain use of it only to learn that the use is prohibited by building restrictions, recorded easements, or zoning ordinances.

Do any mortgages (liens) exist on the property that are not going to be removed before legal possession of the property is transferred to you?

If the seller has a mortgage on the property and you are going to assume and pay this mortgage, the mortgage shall exist as a lien against the property when the title to the property is transferred to you.

If the seller has a mortgage on the property and you are *not* going to assume and pay the mortgage, the mortgage should be removed as a lien against the property before title to the property is transferred to you. (Refer to pages 128–139 for mortgages.)

I want the property conveyed to me by a _____ deed.

I want the property conveyed to me free and clear of all liens and encumbrances excepting _____

The use I plan to make of the property is _____

Zoning ordinances, recorded easements for public utilities, and building restrictions will affect the use I want to make of the property in the following manner: _____

Has Any Government Agency Given the Seller Notice of Any Repairs That Are to Be Made on the Property?

For example, possibly a city fire inspector has given notice to the seller that he is to have his basement fireproofed within sixty days.

If this work is not done before legal possession of the property is transferred to you, who is to pay for the work? Even though the notice was given to the seller and not to you, the work will have to be done.

Often a buyer will put a provision into his offer that the broker is to hold the cost of the work in escrow to be returned to the seller only if the work is completed within the allotted time.

For example, the buyer asks in his offer that the broker hold in escrow $500 from the purchase price to assure that the basement is fireproofed within sixty days. If the seller has this work done and pays for it, the broker is to return the $500 to the seller. Otherwise the $500 is to be given to the buyer.

Answer the following questions before you submit your offer to purchase:

The seller has been notified by _____ that he is to make the following repairs or correct the following conditions:

_____

_____

This work is to be completed by _____
The cost of having this work done is to be paid by _____

_____

Do You Know What the Real Estate Taxes Have Been on the Property and What You Can Expect Future Taxes to Be?

When the seller accepts your offer to purchase and his acceptance has been delivered to you, you have entered into a contract to buy the property. Along with the property as described

in the contract, you acquire an obligation to pay the real estate taxes on the property.

Often a buyer is surprised when he receives his first tax bill on a newly purchased property. Before buying the property he asked the broker what the taxes had been on the property and the broker told him. But when he received his first tax bill, the taxes were much higher than anticipated.

What happened? He could have avoided this surprise if he had taken the time to make some inquiries. A prospective buyer should study the taxes on the property for at least the previous four years to learn what the trend has been. Have the taxes remained about the same, have they steadily increased, or has there been a sudden sharp rise in real estate taxes?

Can the taxes be expected to go up because of expanded or improved public services? What age and in what condition are the schools in the community? This is the age of new schools, which add to the tax bills.

Has the seller made any recent improvements in the property in an effort to attract a buyer? Will these improvements result in a higher property assessment and in higher real estate taxes next year?

Year   assessed   valuation×mill   rate=taxes
19——
19——
19——
19——

Recent improvements on the property that can result in increased taxes are _____

_____

What Will It Cost to Keep the Property Adequately Insured?

You learned from the broker what it cost the seller to insure the property. Will it cost you the same or more?

Has the seller insured the property *adequately?* Possibly not and possibly the amount and type of insurance you will want on the property will cost considerably more than the amount the seller has been paying for his coverage.

Ask your insurance agent to give you an opinion as to what type and amount of coverage you should have and get an estimate on the cost of this coverage. Possibly your insurance agent will decide that the coverage the seller has is fully adequate and at a very reasonable cost. You may wish to have his insurance coverage assigned to you. This involves your paying the seller for the unused portion of his coverage. (Refer to pages 118–119 for prorating of insurance.)

If you are buying the property on a land contract, the vendor (the seller) will probably reserve the right in the land contract to determine the type and amount of insurance you will be required to maintain on the property.

When financing with a mortgage, the mortgagee (the lender) often reserves the right to determine the kind and amount of insurance you will be required to maintain on the property. In every case it is a wise buyer who learns what his insurance will cost before he makes an offer to purchase a property.

The type and amount of insurance coverage I shall want or I shall be required to maintain on the property is _____
_____

This will cost $_____

Does the Property Conform to All Building Codes?

For example, possibly it is an old building and since it was built the requirements as to the type of electrical wiring required in a building have changed. Can you be ordered to have the building rewired? Possibly the seller was a home craftsman and made some repairs in the plumbing. Do these repairs conform to code?

Possibly you aren't unduly concerned because you consider everything about the house adequate for your own use. What about the day when you will want to sell the property? Will the next buyer demand that changes be made so that the property does conform to code?

Have a contractor check the property to learn if everything about it conforms to the local code.

The property conforms to all building codes except _____
_____

Cost of the changes necessary so that the property will conform to all building codes is $_____
The property was inspected by and the above estimate made by _____

WORKSHEET TO COMPLETE BEFORE MAKING YOUR OFFER TO PURCHASE

The price I am willing to pay for the property is $_____

The terms under which I am agreeable to paying for this property are
_____
_____

The conditions under which I am agreeable to going ahead with the provisions in this offer are _____
_____

The amount of earnest money payment I am willing to make is $_____

When the seller accepts the offer, I am agreeable to making an additional payment of $_____

My earnest money payment is to be retained in the _____
_____

I wish for my earnest money payment to be applied toward the purchase price only if the seller accepts the offer on or before _____
_____

If the seller does not accept this offer by the above date, I wish for my earnest money payment to be returned to me by _____
_____

I may withdraw this offer and get a full refund of my earnest money payment if I do so by _____

If I wish to withdraw my offer after the seller has accepted it and the acceptance has been delivered to me, my earnest money payment shall be __
_____

The following items are to be included in the purchase price (circle either "yes" or "no"):

Attached antennas	yes	no	Hot water heater	yes	no
Water conditioner	yes	no	Heating unit	yes	no
Draperies	yes	no	Linoleum	yes	no
Curtains and rods	yes	no	Lighting fixtures	yes	no
Venetian blinds	yes	no	Bathroom accessories	yes	no
Awnings	yes	no	Screen doors and windows	yes	no
Carpeting	yes	no	Storm doors and windows	yes	no

Others: _____ yes   no

_____ yes   no

_____ yes   no

The real estate I am offering to buy is (complete detailed description of the real estate) _____
_____

The prorating method I want used is _____

Planned public improvements that will result in special assessments against the property are _____

_____

Special assessments for work started prior to the date of this offer are to be paid by _____

Special assessments for work that is to be started after the date of this offer are to be paid by _____

The date by which I want physical occupancy of the property is _____

_____

I will allow the seller use of the property for _____ days after the day of closing in exchange for a use and occupancy charge of $_____ a day.

$_____ is to be withheld from the purchase price to be held in escrow by _____. If physical occupancy of the property is not delivered to me by _____, this money is to be awarded to me as liquidated damages. If physical occupancy of the property is delivered to me by the above date, the money is to be returned to the seller.

The closing is to take place on or before _____.

The closing is to take place at _____.

If the property is damaged before the time of closing, it will be handled in the following manner: _____

_____

I want the seller to supply me with a (choose either an abstract of title or an owner's policy of title insurance) _____

_____

I want the property conveyed to me by a _____ deed.

I want the property conveyed to me free and clear of all liens and encumbrances excepting _____

_____

The use I plan to make of the property is _____

_____

Zoning ordinances, recorded easements for public utilities, and building restrictions will affect the use I want to make of the property in the following manner: _____

_____

The seller has been notified by _____ that he is to make the following repairs or correct the following conditions: _____

_____

This work is to be completed by _____

The cost of having this work done is to be paid by _____

_____

Real estate taxes on the property for the last four years have been:

> *Year*   *assessed valuation × mill rate = taxes*
>
> 19____
>
> 19____
>
> 19____
>
> 19____

Recent improvements on the property that can result in increased taxes are _____

_____

The type and amount of insurance coverage I shall want or shall be required to maintain on the property is _____

_____

This insurance coverage will cost $_____

The property conforms to all building codes except _____

_____

Cost of the changes necessary so that the property will conform to all building codes is $_____

The property was inspected by and the above estimate made by _____

_____

Chapter Eleven

OTHER RESIDENTIAL HOUSING

BUYING INTO A COOPERATIVE OR CONDOMINIUM

"Own your own apartment! Live for less! Let your rent earn tax-free money for you!"

Sometimes these advantages are possible through ownership in cooperative or condominium housing projects, apartment buildings, or clusters of singe-family dwellings sharing the same grounds.

In a cooperative you own a prorated portion of the total project. If you are one of twenty stockholders you own $\frac{1}{20}$ of the entire project but not any one unit within the project although you have the right to live in one of the housing units.

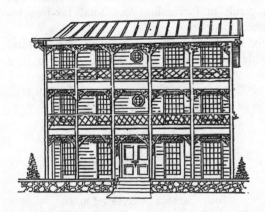

In a condominium you own a designated part of the project and share in joint ownership of the common elements. In an apartment building you own your unit, possibly six rooms, plus sharing with the other investors joint ownership of the common elements. In an apartment building ways, stairs, elevators, and roof.

Compared to investing in a single-family house, investing in cooperative or condominium housing sometimes yields a higher return on your housing dollars.

Better use is made of high-priced land. Possibly a hundred housing units, apartments, can

be established on an expensive piece of land that could accommodate only two or three single-family dwellings. Land that is too costly for private ownership becomes reasonably priced when the cost is spread among many owners.

As a private house owner, you are responsible for all maintenance. If you are an owner in a cooperative or condominium housing project, most of the maintenance is provided and at a lower cost than is possible with private house ownership. It costs less when a hundred families contribute to paying one man to care for the grounds than it does for one family to bear the entire expense.

Usually the cooperative or condominium owner provides most of the maintenance for the unit he occupies and shares in the cost of maintenance for the common areas—grounds, foundation, roof, etc.

As an owner of a single-family dwelling what would it cost you to have a swimming pool, a recreation center, a nursery? Probably the cost is prohibitive. But divide the cost among a hundred owners and it shows how cooperative and condominium housing can offer more elaborate services than usually are feasible with private house ownership.

As an owner in a cooperative or condominium housing project you are a part of the management. With your right to vote on the rules and regulations that control the conduct of the group you exercise more control over your neighborhood than is possible with single-family dwellings. All the tenant-owners living in the project, your neighborhood, follow rules and regulations established by the management, of which you are a part.

Most of the advantages, but not all, of cooperative or condominium housing, compared to those of owning a single-family dwelling, exist if you merely rent an apartment. Then why not rent an apartment instead of investing in a cooperative or condominium?

As a tenant-owner you have voting power. Should a new elevator be installed in the building? If you are only a tenant, your landlord will decide. If you are a tenant-owner, your vote will help decide.

Through their voting power, the tenant-owners can decide what services they want and by their decisions regulate their rent. If they vote to install a swimming pool, their rent will go up. If they vote to eliminate part of the services, their rent will go down.

As a tenant-owner your cost for maintenance should be less. You invest your money in the project and the final product is your housing. You are more careful and conscientious respecting maintenance costs when you own the property than if you are only a tenant.

The rent a landlord charges includes an allowance for vacancies. If through experience, the landlord learns that he averages four vacancies at all times, he adds onto your rent a portion of what the rent is on four units whether or not they are vacant. Someone has to pay the rent on his vacancies; it is paid by the other renters.

It is possible to have vacancies in a cooperative or condominium project; in this case, as with the landlord, expenses continue and somebody has to pay them. However, usually there are fewer vacancies because of the ownership characteristics of cooperative and condominium housing, so usually a smaller reserve is held for a vacancy allowance.

As a tenant-owner participating in the management of the project you eliminate part of the cost of management and proprietorship. You may employ a building manager but most of the decisions will be made by your elected board of directors. If at the end of the year there is a surplus of funds resulting from your monthly charges, these profits belong to the owner-tenants and not to a landlord.

When an apartment building owner puts a mortgage on a building he pays interest on the loan in addition to payments on the principal of his loan. These costs are passed on to each tenant in his rent. The landlord uses part of your rent to buy the project for himself. But when you are the owner-tenant your payments on mortgage principal increase your equity—your ownership—and not a landlord's equity or ownership.

For example, as an investor in a condominium or cooperative, $1,800 of your total yearly cost applies toward the reduction of your mortgage principal. Each year your ownership—not the landlord's ownership—increases by $1,800.

To determine your net cost of housing, deduct from your total annual cost that portion of your cost that increases your ownership.

For example, if your total cost for housing is $6,000, and of that amount $1,800 applies toward the reduction of your real estate mortgage, your total annual cost (net) for housing is $4,200.

Total annual cost for housing	$6,000
(less) portion of total cost that applies toward the reduction of the mortgage principal	$1,800
Total net cost for housing	$4,200

As a tenant-owner, you may deduct from your total taxable income payments for mortgage interest and real estate taxes. In some cases, this can result in increasing your total tax-free income.

For example, if you are a renter, if your total taxable income is $30,000 and if you are in a 34% income tax bracket, your income taxes are $10,200 and your tax-free income is $19,800. None of the costs of renting are deductible.

Total taxable income	$30,000
(×) income tax bracket	34%
Income taxes	$10,200
Total taxable income	$30,000
(less) income taxes	$10,200
Total tax-free income	$19,800

If you are a tenant-owner, the interest you pay on the financed portion of your investment and the real estate taxes you pay are both tax-deductible items. These tax deductions can result in preserving more of your taxable income for you.

For example, you invest $44,000 in cooperative or condominium housing, paying $20,000 down and financing $24,000 over ten years at 8% interest. Your real estate taxes are $1,200 yearly. As in the above example your average annual income is $30,000 and after all other deductions you are in the 34% income tax bracket.

Average annual interest you pay on the $24,000 you financed (plus)	$1,094.40
Annual real estate taxes	$1,200.00
Total tax-deductible costs	$2,294.40
Net taxable income	$30,000.00
(less) tax-deductible costs	$2,294.40
Net taxable income	$27,705.60
Net taxable income	$27,705.60
(×) income tax bracket	34%
Total income taxes	$9,419.90
Total taxable income	$30,000.00
(less) total income taxes	$9,419.90
Total tax-free income	$20,580.10

With an income of $30,000 in a 34% income tax bracket, as a renter your tax-free income is $19,800. If you are a tenant-owner, your tax-free income is $20,580.10. Because of the tax deductions allowed a tenant-owner, you save $780.10.

As a tenant-owner you have a tax-free income of	$20,580.10
As a renter, you have a tax-free income of	$19,800.00
Total savings	$780.10

To simplify the procedure for learning how much of a savings you can realize as a tenant-owner because of the tax-deductible features of real estate taxes and interest paid on the financed portion of an investment, use the following formula:

Total tax-deductible costs* $————
(×) income tax bracket ——$=$————
(your savings)

To determine your net housing cost, deduct this saving from your total housing cost.

For example, if your total annual cost for housing is $6,000 but through the tax-deductible features of real estate taxes and mortgage interest you save $780.10 in income taxes, your net cost for housing is only $5,219.90

* Include real estate taxes and your average annual interest on the financed portion of the purchase.

Total annual cost for housing	$6,000
(less) total saving on income taxes because of being allowed to deduct real estate taxes and mortgage interest	$780.10
Total net cost for housing	$5,219.90

In most instances, after making an adjustment for increased ownership and for savings through tax-deductible items, it appears that it costs less to invest in cooperative or condominium housing than it costs to rent similar facilities.

Unfortunately the typical advertisment showing the economical advantages of cooperative or condominium housing usually stops at this point. To get a completely accurate picture of the net cost of tenant-ownership, you must adjust the final cost figure by the potential tax-free income you lost by having your investment dollars tied up in housing rather than in securities, savings, etc.

For example, you invest $44,000 in housing, paying $20,000 down and financing $24,000 over ten years. During the ten-year period the annual average amount you have invested in housing is $34,800.

To determine the final cost of your housing, you should add to your yearly cost the tax-free income you could have received as investment income from the average annual amount you had invested in housing.

For example, if you are able to receive a 6% yield on your investments and are in the 34% income tax bracket, with an average annual investment in housing of $34,800, you forfeit annually a potential of $2,088.

Average annual investment in housing	$34,800
(×) possible yield if the money had been invested elsewhere	6%
Forfeited potential taxable investment income	$2,088

However, the potential return on your investment is taxable income, so your potentially forfeited taxable return must be adjusted by your income tax bracket to arrive at the tax-free income potential lost.

Potential investment income forfeited	$2,088.00
(×) income tax bracket	34%
Income tax on the return	$709.92
Total potential investment income	$2,088.00
(less) income tax on the return	$709.92
Potential tax-free income lost	$1,378.08

To determine the potential tax-free yield you forfeit when you invest in tenant-ownership, use the following formula:

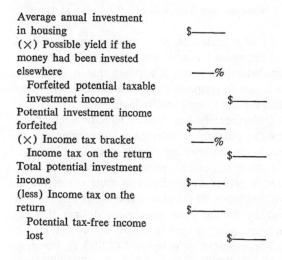

Average anual investment in housing	$————
(×) Possible yield if the money had been invested elsewhere	————%
Forfeited potential taxable investment income	$————
Potential investment income forfeited	$————
(×) Income tax bracket	————%
Income tax on the return	$————
Total potential investment income	$————
(less) Income tax on the return	$————
Potential tax-free income lost	$————

To determine your net cost of housing, add to your total cost the average potential tax-free yield you forfeited (from above formula) from having your money invested in housing.

For example, if your total annual cost for housing is $6,000 and it requires an annual average investment of $34,800, you forfeit $1,378.08 in tax-free dollars annually as a result of having your money tied up in housing. Hence your net cost for housing is $7,378.08.

Total annual cost of housing	$6,000
(plus) tax-free income you could have realized from your money if you hadn't had it invested in housing	$1,378.08
Total net cost for housing	$7,378.08

The savings through tax-deductible items, plus having a portion of your annual housing cost go toward increased ownership, plus a potential loss in income resulting from having your investment dollars planted in housing instead of elsewhere are all features of both cooperative and condominum housing. (Before making an investment in housing, be sure to complete the worksheet at the end of this chapter to determine your net cost of cooperative or condominium housing.)

Now let's explore some of the ways in which cooperative and condominium investments differ.

Title to the Property

In a cooperative the title to the property is held by the cooperative and as an investor you have shares of stock, a membership certificate, and a proprietary lease—the right to live in one of the units.

In a condominium you hold legal title to your particular unit just as you would hold title to a single-family house. In addition, you share with the other owners in joint ownership of the common elements of the project—grounds, foundations, roof, etc.

Real Estate Taxes

With a cooperative you are responsible for your proportionate share of the real estate taxes. If you own $\frac{1}{20}$ of the project you pay $\frac{1}{20}$ of the total taxes. If a shareholder does not pay his taxes the other shareholders have to pay them. If there are shares that aren't sold, held by the cooperative, the tax on them has to be paid by the other shareholders.

If the total real estate taxes are $16,000 a year and you are one of twenty shareholders, your share is $800 a year. If no tax revenue is received from two of the shareholders, their taxes will have to be paid by the other shareholders raising their taxes to $888.88 a year. Eighteen shareholders instead of twenty pay the $16,000 real estate tax load.

With a condominium you own a designated part of the project, hold title to that portion, and are taxed directly on your unit within the project. If your neighbor doesn't pay his real estate taxes you will not be assessed for them. You are individually and personally taxed on the assessed evaluation of your unit. However, you do join with the other owners of the project to pay the taxes on the common elements about the project. If a neighbor defaulted in paying his share of the taxes on the common elements, you possibly would have to pay a portion of these taxes.

Living in the Project

If a cooperative receives more than 20% of its income from outsiders (not stockholders) the real estate tax and mortgage interest deductions aren't allowed. As a stockholder in a cooperative you usually are required to live in the project.

In a condominium you hold legal title to your unit and are allowed real estate tax and mortgage interest deductions whether or not you live there. You may invest in a condominium, not live there, and still benefit from these deductions.

Mortgage Liability

The mortgage on a cooperative covers the entire project and the owners are all jointly liable for the debt. However, because the mortgage covers the entire project a mortgage foreclosure action cannot be brought against any one stockholder. If one stockholder defaults in his payments, the other stockholders have to make up his payments to prevent a foreclosure action on the cooperative.

As an owner in a condominium, you put a mortgage on your unit or hold title free and clear. If you place a mortgage on your unit, the payments are your responsibility. If you default in payments the foreclosure action is brought against you as an individual and not against the condominium.

Ease of Selling

In a cooperative the stockholder is restricted to the mortgage terms already put on the entire project. A prospective buyer has to accept the terms of the mortgage already on the project. The owner cannot remove the mortgage on his unit, as the mortgage covers the entire project.

With the first mortgage as a cloud on the cooperative title, the prospective buyer in need of financing has to look for a second mortgage, offering his cooperative shares as security for the loan.

With a condominium, because you own title to your unit, you may place mortgages against your unit or remove them as you wish, regardless of what your neighbors do. You may offer a prospective buyer title to your unit free and clear of any mortgages or you may offer him purchase money mortgage financing on any terms you wish.

Your Decision-making Privileges

As an owner in a cooperative, usually you have one vote no matter how many shares you own. If there are twenty shares representing ownership of the project and you own five of them, your voting privileges are no greater than your neighbor's, who owns only one share.

In a condominium, votes usually are acknowledged on the basis of the value of your ownership as compared with the value of the entire project. If your unit is valued at $60,000 and your neighbor's at $30,000, you have twice the voting power of your neighbor.

Insurance Costs

With a cooperative one insurance policy usually covers the entire project, and, as an owner, you pay your proportionate share of the total premium.

With a condominium, normally you are personally responsible for the coverage on your unit. Usually the "master deed" specifies minimum coverage to be held on each unit. You will share with the other owners the cost of insuring areas held in common.

Because condominium ownership requires a policy on each unit plus a policy covering the common areas, the cost is ordinarily higher than for cooperative ownership, where one large policy covers the entire project.

Mortgage Insurance

The function of mortgage insurance is to provide enough money to pay off any mortgages upon the death of the mortgagor. This leaves the property free of any mortgages for the survivor.

Mortgage insurance does not perform this function with cooperative ownership. The mortgage is against the cooperative title, and paying off your proportionate share does not remove the mortgage. If there is a $100,000 mortgage against the project and you are one of twenty owners, your share of the indebtedness is $5,000. If you pay off your $5,000, it reduces the mortgage to $95,000, which is still shared among the twenty owners. Your share is $4,750. You have not removed the mortgage against your share in the project.

With a condominium any mortgage is against your legal title to your unit. You may remove that mortgage at any time you wish regardless of any mortgage obligations your neighbors have put on their units. Mortgage insurance can perform its intended function for the investor in a condominium.

New state regulations controlling cooperative and condominium housing are constantly being introduced; it would be futile to recite any regulations now in force for any particular state. In some states investors are being asked to buy into projects even before the buildings are completed. Sound risky? It isn't. Most states regulate the types of offerings that may be made to cooperative or condominium buyers.

Before investing in a cooperative or condominium, talk to owners of similar projects, read the bylaws and purchase agreements for the project, and visit with your attorney and real estate broker. If then you still have questions, write to your state attorney general's office and ask for a copy of your state's cooperative or condominium housing regulations.

Cooperative or condominium housing is similar to renting in that you share the grounds and buildings with other occupants. Before investing in a cooperative or condominium ask the same type of questions you would ask before renting an apartment or house:

What areas are exclusively yours and what areas do you share with the other occupants?

_____

What are the restrictions on the uses you may make of the common areas? _____

What are the restrictions on the uses you may make of your individual unit? _____

What maintenance is furnished and what maintenance are you expected to furnish? What is the cost? _____

How is the cost of utilities handled? _____

Are there any restrictions on family size?

_____

As a tenant-owner in a cooperative or condominium you are part of the management and one of the owners. In addition to asking questions normally asked by a renter you should inquire about things that affect you as an owner:

What is your total cost compared to renting similar housing? (from worksheet at end of chapter) _____

What is the return on your investment compared to investing the same amount elsewhere and renting? _____

What are the total general operating expenses? What have they been for the last three years? What has been the charge per unit? Has there been an increase or a decrease? Why? _____

If there is a surplus or deficit at the end of the year how is it handled? _____

Are there any planned alterations or improvements that will raise monthly charges?

_____

How are the real estate taxes assessed? What have the assessments been each year for the last three years? _____

In the event of default in payments by an owner, how is this expense distributed among the other owners? _____

What are the provisions for damage or destruction of common areas and individual units? What are the requirements as to the insurance held on each unit? What is the cost? _____

In the event of partial or complete destruction of the project how will the insurance proceeds be distributed? _____

Are there any liens or mortgages on the project? What do they cover? _____

How can the units be financed and refinanced? _____

What are the restrictions on your right to sell, lease, or mortgage your investment? ___

_____

What have the units sold for? What will you be able to sell your unit for five years from now? _____

As a tenant-owner what are your voting rights? _____

What do other property owners in the neighborhood think of the project? _____

WORKSHEET TO DETERMINE YOUR NET COST OF HOUSING IN A COOPERATIVE OR CONDOMINIUM PROJECT

Total annual cost for housing $_____

LESS

    1. Portion of yearly cost that appplied

toward reduction of the mortgage principle $_____

        (refer to page 108 for example)

    2. Total tax-deductible costs $_____

   (×) Income tax bracket _____ % $_____

        (refer to pages 108–110 for example)

    To determine your net cost, deduct this

total from your total annual cost $==========

        Net housing cost after deductions $_____

PLUS

    Forfeited tax-free yield from average

annual amount invested in tenant-ownership

housing (refer to pages 108–109 for example)

    Average annual investment in housing

$_____ (×) possible yield if the money

had been invested elsewhere _____ % $_____

    Potential investment income forfeited

$_____ (×) income tax

bracket _____ % $_____

    Total potential investment income

$_____ (less) income tax on the

return $_____ $_____

    To determine your total net cost of housing, add to your net cost after deductions the average potential tax-free yield you forfeited (last answer in formula above) from having your money invested in housing $==========

        TOTAL NET COST OF HOUSING $_____

Following this worksheet is the third section of the book, which deals with various aspects of financial and legal practice in real estate transactions. Most of these procedures have been touched upon in preceding chapters, set within the context of specific examples. In Part III such subjects as proration, easements and liens, mortgage financing, land contracts, property owners' rights, and handling of taxation are explored more fully from a generalized background. There follows a brief look at the exciting possibilities of real estate as an investment.

PART III

Legal and Financial Aspects of Real Estate Transactions

Chapter Twelve

THE CLOSING

PRORATION—WHAT IT IS AND HOW IT WORKS

The closing is the transaction at which the buyer, the seller, and usually their wives and attorneys get together and the buyer transfers the purchase price of the property to the seller and the seller transfers ownership of the property to the buyer.

Also at the closing, normally part or all of the following items are prorated:

Real estate taxes for the current year.

Prepaid premiums on insurance policies when the buyer has the seller's coverage assigned to him.

Interest on any mortgages held by the seller but which mortgages the buyer is assuming and agreeing to pay.

Any possible rents.

Any special assessments against the property.

Water and utility bills.

Proration of Real Estate Taxes

Real estate taxes are assessed on the basis of the calendar year—from January 1 through December 31—even though they are not due until the first of the year following the year in which they are incurred.

For example, the property changes hands on June 21. The real estate taxes on the property the previous year were $1,080 and it is doubtful that they will be very different this year. The buyer and seller agree to use $1,080 as a base for prorating the current year's taxes.

The seller owns the property from January 1 through June 20, so he is expected to pay the taxes for that portion of the year. The buyer owns the property from June 21 through De-

cember 31, so he is expected to pay the taxes for that portion of the year.

Through prorating we learn the amount that each one—the buyer and the seller—owes toward the current year's real estate taxes.

If the taxes are $1,080 for the year, they are $90 a month.

		$90 taxes a month	
12 months	$1,080 taxes for the year		
January $90	February $90	March $90	April $90
May $90	June $90	July $90	August $90
September $90	October $90	November $90	December $90

($1,080 per year or $90 a month)

The seller owns the property from January 1 through June 20, so he pays taxes for that period —five whole months plus the amount for the first twenty days in June.

5 months × $90 a month = $450 in taxes the seller owes for the 5 whole months in the year that he owns the property

January (S)	February (S)	March (S)	April (S)
May (S)	June (S) (B)	July (B)	August (B)
September (B)	October (B)	November (B)	December (B)

(S) months seller owns the property
(B) months buyer owns the property

If the taxes are $90 a month, they are $3 a day, and the seller owes $60 in taxes for the twenty days in June during which he owns the property.

$3 a day for taxes

30 days in June $\overline{)\$90 \text{ a month taxes}}$

$3 a day for taxes×20 days=$60 owed by the seller for the 20 days in June he owns the property

June						
1 (S)	2 (S)	3 (S)	4 (S)	5 (S)	6 (S)	7 (S)
8 (S)	9 (S)	10 (S)	11 (S)	12 (S)	13 (S)	14 (S)
15 (S)	16 (S)	17 (S)	18 (S)	19 (S)	20 (S)	21 (B)
22 (B)	23 (B)	24 (B)	25 (B)	26 (B)	27 (B)	28 (B)
29 (B)	30 (B)					

(S) days seller owns the property
(B) days buyer owns the property

Next total the amounts. The seller owes the taxes for the period between January 1 and June 20, $510.

5 months×$90 a month	$450
20 days×$3 a day	$60
Total	$510

If the seller owes $510 as his portion of the year's real estate taxes, the buyer owes the balance of $570.

Total real estate taxes for the year	$1,080
Amount owed by the seller	$510
Total	$570

amount owed by the buyer for the portion of the year he owns the property

Normally, at the closing, the seller pays to the buyer the portion of the year's taxes he owes and then the buyer pays the entire tax bill when it is due.

The result is that each one—the buyer and the seller—pays his portion of the taxes for that part of the tax year during which he owns the property.

In some cases—usually because of rapidly escalating real estate taxes—a buyer and seller will not agree to prorate the current year's taxes on the basis of what the taxes were for the preceding year. Instead they choose to go ahead and prorate on the basis of the previous year's taxes but only with the agreement that when the current year's tax rates are published, they will make adjustments for any changes in the tax rates—either higher or lower than the previous year.

Or they may agree on a method to use and then agree to delay prorating the taxes until after the current year's tax rates are available. This is not particularly desirable, as it prolongs the closing.

Proration of Prepaid Insurance Premiums

For example, the seller has a three-year fire and extended coverage insurance policy on the property. The premium he paid on September 1 was $432 for three years. The buyer made arrangements to have this coverage assigned to him the day he becomes the new owner of the property, June 21.

Although the seller bought this insurance protection for three years, he will be using it only for that part of the three-year period during which he owns the property.

The buyer has the benefits of this coverage for that portion of the three-year period during which he owns the property. The buyer is expected to pay the seller for that portion of the coverage that he is giving to him when he becomes the new owner of the property.

The $432 premium paid by the seller bought insurance protection on the property for a three-year period starting September 1.

1st year

Sept.	Oct.	Nov.	Dec.

2nd year

Jan.	Feb.	March	April
May	June	July	Aug.
Sept.	Oct.	Nov.	Dec.

3rd year

Jan.	Feb.	March	April
May	June	July	Aug.
Sept.	Oct.	Nov.	Dec.

4th year

Jan.	Feb.	March	April
May	June	July	Aug.

Because the property changes ownership on June 21 of the second year that the policy is in force, the seller uses the coverage only for:

1 year	all of the 2nd year, and
9 months	4 months in the 1st year plus 5 months in the third year, and
20 days	the 1st 20 days in June of the 3rd year

The buyer has the benefits of the insurance during the remaining portion of the three-year period.

(S) portion of the three-year period the seller owns the property and uses the insurance.

(B) portion of the three-year period the buyer owns the property and uses the insurance.

Because the premium for the three-year period is $432, the premium for one year is $144.

3 years	$144 — cost of coverage for 1 year
	$432 premium for 3 years

Because the premium for one year is $144, the premium for one month is $12.

12 months in a year	$12 — premium for 1 month
	$144 premium for 1 year

Because the premium is $12 for one month, the premium for one day is 40¢.

30 days in June	40¢ — premium for 1 day
	$12 premium for 1 month

The seller uses $260 worth of insurance during the one year, nine months, and twenty days he has the coverage.

1 year (all of the second year)	$144
9 months (4 months in the first year and 5 months in the third year) (9 months ×$12 a month)	$108
20 days (the first 20 days in June) (20 days × 40¢ a day)	$8
Value of the coverage the seller uses during the portion of the 3-year period he owns the property	$260

To determine what the buyer owes the seller for the unused portion of the insurance coverage he has had assigned to him, subtract the portion used by the seller from the total coverage he originally bought.

Premium paid by the seller for 3-year coverage	$432
Value of the coverage the seller uses for the portion of the 3-year period he owns the property	$260
Amount the buyer owes the seller for the unused portion of the insurance coverage assigned to the buyer	$172

Many times the chore of prorating prepaid insurance premiums is handled by the insurance company that issues the policy. The insurance company simply makes a rebate to the seller for the unused portion of the policy and then enters into a new insurance contract with the new owner the buyer.

Proration of Mortgage Interest

For example, the seller has a mortgage on the property which mortgage the buyer will assume and agree to pay.

The seller wants $60,000 for the property and will sell for $28,800 if the buyer assumes and agrees to pay the seller's mortgage for $31,200.

Cash the buyer will pay toward the purchase price	$28,800
Mortgage against the property owed by the seller but the mortgage the buyer will assume and agree to pay	$31,200
Selling price	$60,000

Interest on the $31,200 mortgage is 8%, and it is adjusted semiannually. Interest paying dates are February 1 and August 1.

The buyer becomes the new owner and takes over the seller's mortgage on June 21. The seller last paid interest on the mortgage on February 1 and that payment represented interest due for the six-month period prior to February 1.

Interest is next due on August 1 and the payment will represent interest due on the mortgage for the period from February 1 through July 31.

	February	March	April
May	June	July	

6-month period for which interest
will be due on August 1.

Part of that six-month period the seller held the mortgage, until June 1, at which time the buyer took over the mortgage.

The seller pays the interest on the mortgage for that period during which he held the mortgage, for four months and twenty days of the six-month interest-paying period.

	February (S)	March (S)	April (S)
May (S)	June (S) (B)	July (B)	

(S) period for which seller owes
(B) period for which buyer owes

How much interest does the seller owe?

Amount of mortgage	$31,200
Annual interest (8%)	.08
Interest for 1 year	$2,496

Because the interest for one year is $2,496, the interest for one month is $208.

$$12 \text{ months in a year} \quad \frac{\$208 \text{ interest for 1 month}}{)\$2,496 \text{ interest for 1 year}}$$

Because the interest is $208 for one month, the interest for one day is $6.93.

$$30 \text{ days in June} \quad \frac{\$6.93 \text{ interest for 1 day}}{)\$208 \text{ interest for 1 month}}$$

Of the six-month interest-paying period—February 1 through July 31—the seller held the mortgage and is expected to pay interest for four months and twenty days.

4 months ($208 a month × 4 months)	$832
20 days ($6.93 a day × 20 days)	$138.60
Total interest the seller owes on the mortgage for the 4 months and 20 days he held the mortgage during the 6-month interest-paying period	$970.60

	February $208	March $208	April $208
May $208	June $138.60 for 20 days		

Usually the seller pays this amount to the buyer, and then the buyer pays the total amount of the interest due on the next interest-paying date.

In the example, the seller gives the buyer $970.60 to be used toward paying the interest, and then the buyer on the next interest-paying date, August 1, pays the entire amount of interest due for the six-month period ($208 interest for 1 month×6 months . . . $1,248).

Proration of Rents

For example, a tenant rents the upstairs bedroom and bath for $135 a month. He always pays his rent on the last day of each month and his monthly payments represent his rent for the following month. He always pays a month's rent in advance.

The buyer and tenant agree to continue this arrangement after the buyer becomes the new owner on June 21. On May 31 the tenant pays the seller $135, which represents his rent for all of June. However, the seller will be the owner of the property only during the first twenty days of June.

The buyer is entitled to that portion of the rent money represented by the part of the month he owns the property. Because the tenant pays $135 a month rent, his rent for one day is $4.50

$$30 \text{ days in June } \overline{)\begin{array}{c} \$4.50 \text{ a day rent} \\ \hline \$135 \text{ a month rent} \end{array}}$$

The seller owns the property for the first twenty days in June, so he is entitled to $90 of the rent money ($4.50 a day×20 . . . $90).

The buyer owns the property for the last ten days in June, so he is entitled to $45 of the rent money ($4.50 a day×20 days . . . $90).

June

1 (S)	2 (S)	3 (S)	4 (S)	5 (S)	6 (S)	7 (S)
8 (S)	9 (S)	10 (S)	11 (S)	12 (S)	13 (S)	14 (S)
15 (S)	16 (S)	17 (S)	18 (S)	19 (S)	20 (S)	21 (B)
22 (B)	23 (B)	24 (B)	25 (B)	26 (B)	27 (B)	28 (B)
29 (B)	30 (B)					

However, the tenant has already paid the seller $135 for all of June's rent.

The seller simply gives the buyer $45 of the rent money, the amount the buyer is entitled to because he owns the property during the last ten days of the month.

Several methods of prorating may be used. Often a more simple method than the one we demonstrated is used, which dictates that:

When the closing takes place after the 15th of the month, the seller (for proration purposes only) is considered the owner during that month.

When the closing takes place on the 15th of the month or prior to the 15th of the month, the buyer (for proration purposes only) is considered the owner during that month.

No matter what prorating method is used, both buyer and seller should understand the method and agree to it. Proration should be discussed prior to creating the sales contract. What items are to be prorated and what method is to be used should be part of that contract.

Do *not* wait until the day of closing to discuss proration. This can only create confusion, possibly hard feelings, and can even cause a delayed closing.

(Refer to pages 23–31 for information to have ready and decisions to be made before listing a property or making an offer to purchase a property.)

FIXTURES: WHAT THEY ARE AND WHO OWNS THEM

A fixture is an item that was at one time considered personal property but that is now real estate because it:

1. Is *attached* to the real estate in such a way that to remove it from the real estate will cause damage to the real estate, and

2. Is *adapted* to the use of the real estate to which it is attached, and

3. Was the *intention* of the person who attached it to the real estate that the item be a permanent part of the real estate.

For example, while shopping you find a very elaborate light fixture that you think will be perfect for your living room. You buy it. At this time and until you install it, it is personal property.

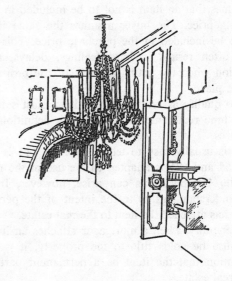

After you install the fixture, is it a part of the real estate and as such included in the selling price of the property? Or is it personal property that you will be allowed to take with you when you sell the property?

If it satisfies the three requirements—(1) it is attached, (2) it is adapted to the use of the real estate, and (3) it is your intention that it be a part of the real estate—the fixture probably will be considered a part of real estate and will be included in the selling price.

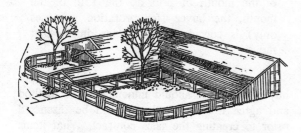

Another example is a fence you buy to enclose your yard. When you buy it and bring it home, it is personal property. After you cement in the posts and install the fence, it probably will be considered a part of the real estate.

A seller should make it clear in his listing contract which fixtures will be included and which excluded from his listing price. A buyer should make it clear in his offer to purchase what he expects to receive in exchange for paying the asking price for the property.

Items are often overlooked, not listed in the contracts, and not even mentioned. A seller assumes that an item is not to be included in the selling price. The buyer assumes the same item is to be included in the purchase price. This all too often results in hard feelings, delays, and friction when the actual transfer of the property takes place.

To qualify as real estate, an item must satisfy the three requirements given in the definition of fixtures.

It is usually easy to tell if the item (1) is attached and (2) is adapted to the use of the real estate. Complications can arise, however, from misunderstandings as to the intent of the person who has attached the item to the real estate.

Generally, when a mortgagor attaches an item, because he holds title to the property, it is his intention that the item be a permanent part of the real estate.

Generally, a seller attaches an item to enhance the value of the property and it is his intention that the item be a permanent part of the real estate.

Generally, if the item is attached by a tenant, the tenant does not intend for the item to be a part of the real estate but rather that the item retain its status as personal property that the tenant may take with him when he terminates his lease.

Trade Fixture

A trade fixture is an item that a tenant attaches to real estate for a temporary business use only. Although the item is attached to the real estate and is adapted to the use of the real estate, it is not the intention of the person who attaches it that it be considered a part of the real estate.

Trade fixtures retain their identity as personal property and tenants are allowed to remove them from the real estate when they terminate their leases.

For example, you rent a building, install a bar in it, and open a tavern. Although the bar is attached to the building—real estate—and is adapted to the use you are making of the building, it is not your intention that the bar be considered a part of the real estate. The court will probably decide that you installed the bar as a trade fixture only and will allow you to remove it as personal property when you terminate your lease.

However, the situation changes if there is already a bar in the building and you remove the old bar and replace it with a new bar. The new bar will probably be considered a substituted fixture.

Substituted Fixture

A substituted fixture is an item that a tenant substitutes for a similar fixture already on the property. Unless arrangements are made between landlord and tenant prior to the substitution, substituted fixtures normally become a part of the real estate.

In our example, the new bar you substituted for the old bar without first discussing it with your landlord will probably be considered a part of the real estate, so you will not be allowed to remove it when you terminate your lease.

Each case involving fixtures is weighed individually as to intent and local custom. Prevent misunderstandings. Have it clearly outlined in the listing and in the offer to purchase exactly what is to be included and what is to be excluded in the exchange of the property.

EASEMENTS: HOW THEY AFFECT YOUR PROPERTY RIGHTS

An easement is a right given by an owner of land to another person, permitting such person to enter upon the land for a particular purpose. Such right may be extended to one person only or to a person and his assigns and heirs.

The most common easements are the rights of service people to enter upon your property to service telephone and electrical facilities, and the right of utility companies to run lines across and erect poles on your property.

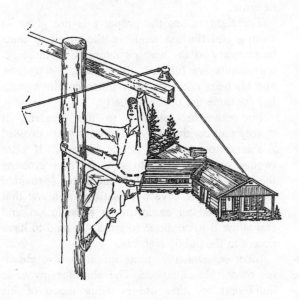

The seller should have it clearly outlined in his listing exactly what easements exist on the property. The buyer should in his written offer to purchase the property have it clearly outlined under exactly what conditions he is willing to buy the property. Is he willing to buy the property subject to the easements the seller has granted?

When the seller gives the buyer a general warranty deed to the property he guarantees him that there are no liens on or encumbrances against the property other than those stated in the deed.

Known easements, those not concealed but visible to the buyer, need not be mentioned in the warranty deed as easements against the property. For example, the telephone line running across the property, although it is an easement on the property, need not be listed in the general warranty deed.

Even though the sales contract makes no mention of known easements, if these easements are visible to the buyer he will not be able to back out of the sales contract on the basis that these easements were not mentioned in the contract.

No matter how firm and binding a sales contract is, when it does not mention known easements, or how valid a warranty deed is that does not mention known easements, both parties to a sale of real estate should be fully aware of what easements exist on the property and should be in complete agreement as to how these easements shall be handled.

Unfortunately this is not always the case, and as a result, hard feelings often arise from undisclosed and unmentioned easements. For example, you purchase a property and move onto it. Every morning and evening a neighbor walks across your lawn to reach his garage. It is a short cut for him but he *can* get to his garage without crossing your lawn.

You ask him to stop using your lawn for a short cut. A dispute arises when he insists that he was given the right to walk across your lawn by the person who sold you the property. You knew nothing about this right (easement) being given to your neighbor by the seller. This misunderstanding possibly could have been avoided if the seller had mentioned to you this right he had extended to the neighbor.

The parties to the different types of easements are the grantor, who gives the easement, and the grantee, who receives the benefits of the easement.

Express Grant

With an express grant, the grantor gives the grantee, his heirs, and his assigns the right to go upon his property for a particular purpose. The right is given in writing, is signed by the grantor, is delivered to the grantee, and is recorded.

Referring to the diagram, A gives B in writing the right to cross his land to get to the public highway.

Express Reservation

With an express reservation, the grantor reserves for himself, his heirs, and his assigns the right to make a particular use of another's property. The grantor transfers the property to another but reserves for himself, his heirs, and his assigns the right to make a particular use of the property.

For example, referring to the diagram, at one time B owned both parcels of land. He sold the parcel marked "A's Land" to A but reserved for himself, his heirs, and his assigns the right to cross over the land he sold to A in order to have access to the public highway.

There should be no misunderstandings with express grants and express reservations because both are in writing and should be recorded.

Easement by Implied Grant

Referring to the diagram, A owned both parcels of land. He then sold B the parcel marked "B's Land" but did not give B the privilege in writing (an express grant) of crossing over his land to reach the public highway.

Provided that there is no other way for B to reach the public highway, he probably will be entitled to an easement by implied grant to a right of way across A's land in order to have access to the public highway.

Easement by Prescription

Easement by prescription is a right awarded a person, his assigns, and his heirs because he or they have continuously and openly made a particular use of another's property for twenty years or more.

The right to use the property is not given in writing and the use made of the property must be contrary to the owner's interests. If these requirements are fulfilled, the person, his assigns, and his heirs can earn the right to continue making the same use of the property.

For example, referring to the diagram, B openly and continuously for twenty years crossed A's land to reach the public highway. If after twenty years, A tries to stop B from crossing the land, the court can, in some states (provided all requirements have been satisfied), allow that B has earned an easement by prescription and can allow B to continue to cross A's land to have access to the public highway.

Most easements by prescription involve absentee ownership situations. The absentee owner is indifferent to what use is being made of his property. He bought the property solely as an investment, hoping someday to sell it at a profit. Most absentee landowners would not be indifferent if they knew that they could possibly lose the exclusive rights to their land through an easement by prescription.

For example, an absentee owner's land has been used as a parking lot by the neighbors for twenty years. The absentee owner is aware of this but doesn't object. In some cases he can lose the right to make any use of that land other than allowing it to be used as a parking lot by the neighbors.

Easement by prescription isn't a simple way to acquire the use of another's land. Just because you can prove you have used the corner of your neighbor's lot for a parking lot for twenty years does not mean that you automatically have an easement by prescription to continue using it as a parking lot.

Requirements that must be met before a court will award an easement by prescription vary from state to state. Typical requirements are:

1. You muse use the land for one particular purpose for twenty years or more.
2. During the twenty years, the use must be continuous. For example, if for one year during the twenty-year period you did not park your car on the corner of the lot, you automatically lose any rights to an easement by prescription.
3. The adverse use you make of another's land must be open and visible to the owner of the land. You cannot earn an easement by prescription to cross your neighbor's land by sneaking across it at night every night for twenty years.

After fulfilling all these requirements, you will be awarded the easement by prescription only if you make a claim for it.

Removing Easements

The simplest way to remove an easement is for the grantee to discontinue making use of the easement. For example, referring to the diagram, if B creates another access route to the public highway and quits crossing A's land, the easement is automatically removed.

Another way to remove an easement is through the use of a quit claim deed. The grantee, who had the benefit of the easement, relinquishes to the grantor all his rights to enter upon the grantor's property.

The ethical seller is the one who tells the buyer all he knows about easements on the property. The wise buyer is the one who keeps his eyes open and asks questions about easements.

LIENS

Is the title to your house free and clear of all liens?

Perhaps you're sure it is because when you bought your house the seller declared in the sales contract that he was giving you a title free and clear of all liens and encumbrances.

But have you put any liens against your title since then? Have you mortgaged your house? Have you failed to pay any real estate taxes or special assessments? Has a creditor entered a money judgment against you? Do you still owe a contractor for work he did on your property? Any of these acts could cause a lien to be put on your property.

When you want to sell your house what will it cost you to have these liens removed?

As a buyer you should definitely require a clause in your sales contract in which the seller declares that the title is free and clear of all liens. If there are to be any exceptions, you will want them listed.

Lien laws vary from state to state; this discussion is offered only to acquaint you with acts that can cause liens to be put on your house and the possible consequences of having these liens as a cloud against your title.

Mortgage Liens

Depending upon the state in which your property is located, your mortgage may be considered simply a lien on your property or it may be considered a transference of title to your creditor. In some states the debtor retains his title and gives the creditor a mortgage and promissory note or bond as evidence of and security for the debt.

In other states the debtor actually turns over

his title to the property to the creditor. Regardless of which practice is followed, the creditor has security for the debt and is entitled to some form of recourse if the debtor doesn't make his payments on time.

Usually if the debtor doesn't make his mortgage payments he is given a limited time to catch up on his payments, his equity of redemption. If he doesn't get caught up on his payments the property is sold at public auction to raise enough money to pay the creditor. If not enough money is raised through the sale to pay the debt, the creditor, in some cases, is allowed a deficiency judgment and may attack the debtor's other assets.

Exceptions to this are found in Connecticut, Illinois, and Vermont, where if the mortgagor is not able to catch up on his payments during the period of redemption, legal title and legal possession of the property revert to the creditor. There is no public sale. The property is simply given back to the creditor.

For a further explanation of the consequences of putting a mortgage lien on your property, refer to page 101.

Tax Liens

Most states through their statutes provide that if your real estate taxes or special assessment taxes are not paid by a certain date, a tax lien may be put on your property and eventually your property may be sold to raise enough money to pay the tax.

The procedure varies from state to state, but usually, although delinquent, the real estate taxes may be paid at any time before the tax sale. Most states impose penalties in the form of interest and charges for delinquent payment of real estate taxes.

The tax sale may include the total property or, if the property can be divided, only as much of the property as is necessary to raise the money to pay the tax bill. Before the tax sale, the property owner must be given notice of the sale, usually in the newspaper, by a notice posted in a public place, or through a personal notice.

The sale must be public and must be held at the time and place specified in the notice. In some cities—New York, for example—the city takes a deed to the property and then the property owner is given the right to redeem his title by paying his taxes and costs. No public sale is held.

Usually the property owner, his spouse, or members of his family may not buy the property at the tax sale. This prevents the property owner from possibly buying back a clear title at the tax sale for less than the amount of the taxes and costs due. To recover his title, he must pay the taxes and costs.

After the tax sale, the property owner is given a period of time during which he has the right to pay the back taxes plus costs and redeem his title to the property.

Judgment Liens

In most states a creditor may put a lien on your real estate and perhaps eventually have your property sold to collect the amount due him even though you did not voluntarily give him any rights to your property as security for the debt.

For example, because of an unwise business decision you owe a creditor $10,000. Because you are unable to pay the debt, you are served a summons to appear in court and the court issues your creditor a judgment lien on your property. You are ordered to pay the judgment creditor the amount due him, and if you can't, after a period prescribed by the statutes he may have your property sold at public auction to recover the amount due him.

Usually after the sale you are given a limited time to pay the judgment and costs and thereby recover your property. If the judgment creditor does not exercise his right to have your property sold to satisfy the debt within a limited time, the lien automatically ends. The time varies from state to state. In New York and California it is ten years, in Pennsylvania only five years. Frequently the statutes allow the judgment creditor to renew his lien after these periods.

Because you do not voluntarily pledge your property as security for the debt, the judgment creditor is an "unsecured creditor," and even though the court awards him a judgment lien on your property, your property usually is exempt up to the amount of your homestead exemption. For example, in California your homestead is exempt up to $30,000 against the claims of unsecured creditors.

Mechanic's Liens

You arrange with a contractor for materials, services, and/or labor for the repair or improvement of your real estate. What assurance does the contractor have that he will be paid?

Most states provide that a contractor may put a lien on your local real estate for the cost of any materials, services, and labor he furnishes for the repair or improvement of your real estate. If he is not otherwise paid he may have a court order issued by which your property can be sold to raise enough money to pay the debt.

Perhaps while you were on a business trip your wife contracted to have the living room remodeled. You weren't consulted, you think the cost was entirely too high and darned if you'll pay for it.

Usually with spouses, joint tenants, and tenants in common, if one of the parties enters into a contract, it is considered that he is acting as the agent for the other party. The contractor may put a lien on the property and, if he isn't otherwise paid, may possibly have the property sold to collect the debt. With very few exceptions mechanic's liens have priority over any other lien put on a property after the actual commencement of the work on the property.

Usually the lien also has priority over any unrecorded mortgages when the contractor had no notice of the mortgages before he actually started work on the project. If the mortgage is recorded before the work was started, the mortgage lien usually has priority over the construction lien.

Possibly the contractor with whom you made arrangements for the improvement of your house delegated part of the work to another contractor, a subcontractor.

In some states, Pennsylvania, for example, if the subcontractor is not paid by the general contractor, the subcontractor may put a lien on the property for the amount owed him by the general contractor.

In other states, New York, for example, if the subcontractor is not paid by the general contractor, the subcontractor may not put a lien on the property for the amount the general contractor owes him.

The lien is against the property and not necessarily against the person who contracted for the work. For example, you ordered work done on your property but before paying the contractor, you sold the property. You still owe the debt but the real estate, now owned by the buyer, can be sold to pay the debt if you don't pay it otherwise.

On January 1 you purchased a house and in your sales contract the seller declared that there were no liens on the property. On March 1 a contractor files a notice of lien on the property. Unless you otherwise pay him, may the contractor have the property sold to collect the debt?

Possibly. In some states the lien attaches to the property when the work is begun, in other states when the contract is signed, and in still other states a contractor or subcontractor is given a limited time after the work is completed to file his lien. For example, in New York a contractor is given up to four months after the work is completed to file his notice of lien.

It is possible to buy a property free and clear of any contractor's or subcontractor's liens only to have a lien put on your property after you have received your title.

Even the abstract of title or owner's policy of title insurance ordinarily does not protect the title against attacks by lien claimants who file their liens after the deal is closed and within the time given them by their state's statutes.

A buyer should insist that the seller supply him with an affidavit listing all contractors or subcontractors who supplied materials, services, or labor for the repair or improvement of the real estate within the time period the state allows a contractor or subcontractor to file his lien.

For example, a buyer in New York should ask the seller to furnish him with a list of all contractors and subcontractors who furnished materials, services, or labor for the maintenance or improvement of the property within the previous four months. The buyer should then ask the seller to furnish him with a full waiver of lien from each contractor or subcontractor on the list.

In addition to satisfying a buyer that there will be no construction liens against the property, the list will supply the buyer with the names of contractors and subcontractors who have worked on the property. Possibly a buyer will want to approach these contractors in the future concerning discrepancies in their work, or to contract with them for additional repairs or improvements on the property.

Chapter Thirteen

MORTGAGES

MORTGAGE FINANCING

Depending upon what state your property is in, your mortgage may, in theory, be considered simply a lien on your property, or it may be considered a transference of the title to your property to your creditor. In "lien theory" states, a mortgage is considered a lien on the real estate as security for the debt. Title to the property stays with the debtor.

In "title theory" states, a mortgage is considered a deed that transfers title to the property to the creditor. The creditor has ownership rights and the debtor has only the right of redemption, the right to continue payments on the mortgage and so eventually earn a clear title to the property.

In theory the differences are significant but in every case the objective is to furnish the creditor with security for his loan. Depending upon whether the title is to rest with the creditor or the debtor, your state may allow one of the following, or a choice between them.

Trust Deeds (or) Trust Indentures

Where trust deeds or trust indentures are used, the legal title to the property is put in trust with a third party, the trustee. The trustee holds the title to the property until indebtedness is removed, and then the title passes on to the debtor, who originally surrendered his title as security for the debt. Usually the trustee is given the power of sale, by which he can have the property sold if the debtor doesn't make good his payments.

Some of the states that use trust deeds are California, Colorado, Idaho, and Texas.

Georgia uses a form of trust indenture called a security deed in which the debtor surrenders his title to the creditor instead of to a third party.

Mortgages

Where mortgages are used, the mortgage acts only as a lien on the real estate, given as security for the debt. The title to the property stays with the debtor. The two parties to the mortgage transaction are the mortgagor (debtor) and the mortgagee (creditor).

After the mortgage is executed, each party to the mortgage transaction has the following:

The mortgagor or debtor has:

1. Legal title and legal possession of the property, plus

2. The money or value that he exchanged for the mortgage and promissory note or bond, plus

3. Possibly a period of redemption, that is, the right to redeem the property if he gets behind in his payments and a foreclosure action is brought against the property.

The mortgagee or creditor has:

1. The mortgage instrument, which acts as a lien against the mortgagor's property for the amount due on the mortgage, plus

2. A promissory note or bond from the mortgagor in which the mortgagor declares the amount he owes and promises to pay that amount by a certain date, plus

3. The right to collect the amount due him as shown on the note or bond if the mortgagor doesn't otherwise make his payments.

Some states that use mortgages are Illinois, Massachusetts, New York, and Pennsylvania.

Even though the title is placed with a transferee (trust deed) or turned over to the creditor (security deed) most states agree that the debtor surrenders his title only as security for the debt —as is true with a mortgage—and does not actually give up his title and buy back the property.

In each case the creditor's interests are secured. States differ in the ways they allow a creditor to protect his interests in the property if the debtor fails to make his payments on time. In some states only one method is allowed; in other states a creditor has a choice of methods to protect his interests in the property.

Foreclosure by Sale
(through judicial proceedings)

When this method is used, the creditor enters a petition to foreclose on the mortgage. The court, after determining the amount of the debt and verifying that it is a valid debt, orders that public notice be given that the property is to be sold at public auction.

After the public auction, the proceeds are awarded to the creditor to satisfy the debt. If there is a surplus, it is awarded to the debtor. In some states the debtor is given a limited time to redeem his property after the public sale.

This method is commonly used in Illinois, New York, and Pennsylvania.

Foreclosure by Sale (through a power
of sale written into the mortgage)

In states where this procedure is used, the mortgage instrument must specifically outline what is to be considered a default and must give the creditor the right to sell the property at public sale to recover the amount due him. If there is a surplus, it is given to the debtor.

The big difference between this practice and a foreclosure through judicial proceedings is that the power of sale is written into the mortgage, eliminating the cost of a formal court foreclosure.

This practice is common in California, Massachusetts, and Texas.

Foreclosure Without Sale (or) Strict
Foreclosure

After giving the creditor the right to foreclose, the court ordinarily gives the debtor two to six months to catch up on his payments. If he doesn't make his payments within that period, the property goes to the creditor. There is no public sale, hence no possibility of there being any residue left over from the sale for the debtor.

Although strict foreclosure is allowed in other states, it is extensively used only in Connecticut and Vermont.

Foreclosure Without Sale (or)
Entry and Possession

Where this procedure is used, the court declares the amount the debtor owes the creditor and gives the debtor a limited time to make payments. If he doesn't get caught up on his payments, the creditor may enter and take possession of the debtor's property.

This is very similar to strict foreclosure except that in many cases the court allows the creditor to take possession only of an amount of property equal to the debt—not to take possession of all the property secured by the mortgage.

This recourse is available to mortgagees in Maine, Massachusetts, New Hampshire, and Rhode Island.

The foreclosure procedure that is selected or that is allowed in your state can make a big difference in the way you fare as creditor or debtor. For example, you originally bought the property for $60,000 with $20,000 down and gave the seller a mortgage for $40,000. Since then you have paid off $10,000 so that you now owe only $30,000 on the mortgage.

Because of some bad luck you are unable to make your mortgage payments and the seller brings a foreclosure by sale action against you. The property sells for $55,000—distress price.

	$60,000	original purchase price
(less)	$30,000	your $20,000 down payment plus the $10,000 you already paid off on the mortgage
	$30,000	still due on the mortgage
	$55,000	selling price
(less)	$30,000	amount that goes to the creditor as the balance due on the mortgage
	$25,000	balance left for the debtor (mortgagor)

With the foreclosure by sale action there is $25,000 left over after the sale for the mortgagor. But he originally made a down payment of $20,000 and, over the years, paid off another $10,000 on the mortgage. He paid $30,000 toward the purchase price and after the sale recovered only $25,000.

	$30,000	amount paid toward the purchase price
(less)	$25,000	amount recovered after the foreclosure sale
	$5,000	loss

The seller has—the total selling price.

The buyer has—a loss of $5,000 reduced by a value equal to what it would have cost to rent the property during the years he had possession.

With a foreclosure without sale action, the seller in some cases gets the entire mortgaged property and the buyer automatically forfeits all the payments he has made on the property.

In this example, the seller gets the property and the buyer forfeits the $30,000 he paid toward the purchase price.

The seller has—the property plus the money the buyer paid toward the purchase price ($30,000).

The buyer has—a value equal only to what it would have cost to rent the property over the years he had possession.

At first glance it appears that a foreclosure by sale action works in favor of the debtor or buyer. This is not necessarily so, since there is no guarantee that the property will sell for more than the amount due the creditor. Possibly the debtor has allowed the property to depreciate to an extent that it will sell for far less than the original cost.

When the debtor borrowed the money he signed a mortgage note or bond in which he declared the amount he owed and promised to repay it by a certain date. When the property sells at the foreclosure sale for less than the amount due the creditor, some states, and then only under certain conditions, allow a creditor to take a deficiency judgment against the debtor for the difference.

Deficiency Judgments

For example, if the amount owed on the mortgage is $30,000 and the property sells through the foreclosure action for only $25,000, the mortgagor still owes the mortgagee $5,000 on the mortgage.

Amount owed the mortgagee on the mortgage	$30,000
Amount the property sells for at the foreclosure sale	$25,000
Amount the mortgagor still owes on the mortgage	$5,000

The mortgagee may enter a deficiency judgment against the mortgagor in an effort to collect the $5,000 still due him.

As a result of the foreclosure action and deficiency judgment each party has the following:

The mortgagee or creditor has:

1. $25,000 resulting from the foreclosure sale, plus

2. A deficiency judgment against the mortgagor for the remaining $5,000 due him.

The mortgagor or debtor has:

1. Lost all future rights and interests in the property that was sold by the court at the foreclosure sale, plus

2. Lost all he has already paid toward the purchase price of the property, plus

3. A deficiency judgment against him for the $5,000 he still owes the mortgagee.

Unless there are extremely heavy mortgages in relation to the value of the property, there usually is enough money raised through a foreclosure by sale to satisfy the mortgagor's indebtedness.

To protect a mortgagor, the court usually reserves the right to refuse offered prices when the property is sold at public auction through a foreclosure sale. For example, a court would probably disallow a selling price of $25,000 on a property appraised at $60,000.

Alternatives to the Foreclosure Action

The easiest solution is for the mortgagor to refinance with a payment schedule more in line with his ability to make payments.

If this is not possible, he may transfer or sell his equity in the property to another party, who will have the right to catch up on the payments and save the property from a foreclosure action.

For example, if the mortgagor has already paid $30,000 toward the purchase price of $60,000 even though he is behind in his payments, he has a salable equity of the $30,000 he has already paid plus his equity of redemption, that is, his right to catch up on his payments.

The mortgagor may simply transfer or return his interest in the property to the mortgagee. In this case he will give a deed to the property to the mortgagee in exchange for a mortgage satisfaction.

This, of course, is not a very favorable arrangement for the mortgagor, as he forfeits all the payments he has made on the property to the mortgagee.

This type of solution is considered only in cases when very little has been paid in on the purchase price or debt. Generally a mortgagor, although behind in his payments, is given an equity of redemption, that is, the right to catch up on his payments and thereby not lose the property. The length of time given him is established by state statutes.

Period of Redemption

In some states after the mortgagor gets behind in his payments he is allowed a limited time to catch up before a foreclosure action is brought against him. States that follow this practice are Florida, Indiana, Nebraska, Oklahoma, and Wisconsin.

State	Period of redemption allowed by the statutes
Florida	two months
Indiana	one year
Nebraska	nine months
Oklahoma	six months
Wisconsin	one year

For example, in Florida, even though the mortgagor is behind with his payments, he is given two months to catch up before he loses all rights to the property through a foreclosure action.

Other states allow a foreclosure to be brought against the mortgagor when he gets behind in his payments, but then allow him a period after the foreclosure proceedings to redeem his rights to the property.

Although the foreclosure has taken place, the mortgagee ordinarily receives only a certificate of entitlement to the deed. The mortgagor does not give up his title until after his period of redemption has expired.

Note how the period of redemption varies from state to state.

State	Period of redemption allowed by the statutes
New York	none
Illinois	one year
Pennsylvania	none
Maine	one year
Alabama	two years

For example, in Illinois, even though the foreclosure action has been brought against the mortgagor, he has one year—his period of redemption—in which to make payments and preserve his rights to the property.

In addition to the mortgage or trust deed, usually the mortgagor gives the mortgagee a promissory note or bond in which he declares the amount he owes the mortgagee and promises to pay that amount by a certain date.

Promissory Notes

A promissory note is an absolute, unconditional promise in writing that one person will pay a certain amount to another person at a specific date. This can be as simple as—

"I _____ promise to pay to Jens Nielsen of Dodgeville, Wisconsin, the sum of _____ dollars with interest payable _____ annually at the rate of _____ per cent per annum with the whole amount due and payable on _____
_____"

_____ (seal)

However, usually promissory notes that accompany mortgages are in the more complicated form of cognovit notes.

Cognovit Notes

A cognovit note, when this is used, is a form of a promissory note in which the person who signs the note:

    1. Admits that he owes the amount stated in the note, and

    2. Authorizes the person to whom he owes the money to enter a money judgment against him to collect the amount owed in the event he defaults on any payment, and

    3. Agrees to pay all interest and any court costs accrued in the collection of the money as stated in the note, and

    4. Agrees to allow the person to whom he owes the money to enter a money judgment against him without first serving a summons or complaint against him.

The form of promissory note—it may be a simple promissory note or a cognovit note—that accompanies a mortgage is called a mortgage note.

Mortgage Note

A mortgage note is a form of a promissory note signed by the mortgagor in which he promises to pay a certain amount by a certain date to the mortgagee. In addition, the mortgagor states in the note that when he signed the note, he also gave to the mortgagee a mortgage as security for the debt.

Negotiable Promissory Note

It is possible for a mortgagor to end up owing a person other than the original mortgagee when the mortgagor signs a negotiable promissory note.

A negotiable promissory note is like a check in that once it is endorsed it is payable to the person who possesses it.

A negotiable promissory note may be as simple as:

    "_____ promise to pay to the order of Jens Nielsen, the sum of _____ etc."

Note that your checks probably contain some of the same wording.

    "pay to the order of _____"

If you write a check for $100 to your wife and she endorses it, she can sell that check for $100.

Non-negotiable Promissory Note

A non-negotiable promissory note states specifically to whom the amount is owed and to whom payment is to be made.

    "_____ promise to pay Jens Nielsen the sum of _____ etc."

Note the absence in the non-negotiable note of the words "to the order of" or equivalent wording.

Payment on a non-negotiable promissory note may be made only to the person named in the note.

In some cases, the type of mortgage note you sign makes a difference when the mortgagee assigns or sells the note to a third person. A situation may arise then in which you should not be required to pay the amount due on the note.

For example, you purchase a property for $60,000, you pay $37,500 in cash, and you give the seller a purchase money mortgage and mortgage note for the balance of $22,500.

After moving onto the property you learn that the area is being rezoned from residential to commercial. Also, in checking your sales contract, you learn that the seller declared that he knew of no anticipated changes in the zoning ordinances when he sold you the property. However, you learn that actually the seller was notified of the anticipated zoning change six months before he signed the sales contract.

You feel very strongly that the property, because of the anticipated change in zoning, is not worth more than $50,000. Because the seller was not entirely honest with you, you refuse to pay the $22,500 pledged by your promissory note.

If you signed a negotiable note ("pay to the order of" or equivalent wording), you could not ordinarily use this situation as your defense in refusing to pay the $22,500 to the third party. In refusing to pay the third party, you can use the same defense as you could use against the original mortgagee, the seller. Because of this difference, negotiable notes are usually popular with lenders just as non-negotiable notes are popular with borrowers.

In some states a mortgage "bond" is used in place of the mortgage promissory note. The bond is a formal IOU in which the borrower declares his debt and promises to repay it. It may contain the same provisions as the mortgage note and has the same legal effects.

Also in some cases, rather than have one instrument act as security for the debt (mortgage or trust deed) and a separate instrument act as evidence of the debt (note or bond), the provisions of both are incorporated into one instrument. Instead of using a mortgage and a separate note, the provisions of both are incorporated into one form.

Mortgage Assignments

A mortgage assignment is a written instrument by which the mortgagee transfers his interest in the mortgage and note to a third party and declares that the mortgagor is to make his payments to such third party.

For example, you borrow $40,000 from XX bank and give them a mortgage on your property plus a mortgage note as security. They assign your indebtedness—your mortgage and note —through a mortgage assignment to YY bank. Now instead of owing $40,000 to XX bank you owe it to YY bank.

To protect the parties to the transaction, all mortgage assignments should be recorded. For example, the mortgagee assigns his interest in the mortgage and note to a third party.

The mortgage assignment is not recorded.

The mortgagee then gets together with the mortgagor and gives him a mortgage satisfaction, which is recorded. According to the records in the office of the county recorder the mortgage has been satisfied and the property is now free and clear of this lien.

The mortgagor then sells and deeds the property to another buyer. The deed is recorded. The records now show a new owner for the property. The innocent purchaser who bought the property thinking the mortgage had been satisfied becomes the record owner and the mortgage assignment is worthless to the third party.

Mortgages may or may not include an assignability clause.

Mortgage Satisfaction (or mortgage release)

A mortgage satisfaction is a document executed by the mortgagee in which he declares that the mortgage has been paid in full. If the mortgage is assigned to a third party, the mortgage satisfaction should be signed by the party to whom the mortgage was assigned.

When the person named in the mortgage as the mortgagee is deceased, the mortgage satisfaction should be signed by the executor or administrator of the deceased mortgagee's estate.

The mortgage satisfaction should be recorded in the office of the county recorder in the county where the property is located. This recording is usually done by the mortgagor. Unless the mortgage satisfaction is recorded, according to the public records, the mortgage lives on as a lien against the property.

Assuming and Agreeing to Pay Mortgages

Often the situation exists in which the seller has a mortgage against the property and the buyer does not have enough cash to buy the property outright and therefore needs financing.

If the seller and his mortgagee agree, they may allow the buyer to assume and to pay the existing mortgage. Then instead of the seller's owing the mortgage, the buyer will have assumed and agreed to pay the debt.

For example, the selling price is $60,000 and the seller has a $30,000 mortgage against the property. The buyer can buy the property by paying only $30,000 in cash and by assuming and agreeing to pay the $30,000 mortgage.

Amount paid in cash by the buyer	$30,000
Amount of the seller's mortgage, which mortgage the buyer assumes and agrees to pay	$30,000
Total asking price received by the seller	$60,000

When this arrangement is made the buyer is liable to the mortgagee for the payment of the mortgage.

If the buyer doesn't pay the mortgage, the original mortgagor—in our example, the seller— can be sued for the amount owing on the mortgage. If the buyer fails to make his payments, and this results in the public sale of the property through a foreclosure action, the action can be brought against both the buyer and the seller to collect the amount due.

If the public auction of the property fails to yield enough to pay the mortgage, in some cases the mortgagee may enter a deficiency judgment against both the seller, who originally signed the mortgage, and against the buyer, who assumed and agreed to pay the mortgage.

Under certain conditions both the buyer's and the seller's property can be seized and sold to satisfy any deficiency judgment. For example, the property sells for $28,500 at the foreclosure sale. The amount still owed on the mortgage is $37,500.

The mortgagee can bring a deficiency judgment against both the original holder of the mortgage and against the party who assumed and agreed to pay the mortgage for the difference of $9,000.

Amount still owed on the mortgage	$37,500
Amount the property sold for at the foreclosure sale	$28,500
A deficiency judgment for this amount can be brought against both buyer and seller	$9,000

Buying Subject to the Mortgage

Instead of the buyer's agreeing to assume and pay the seller's mortgage, the buyer can buy the property with the seller's mortgage existing as a lien against his title to the property. The seller will not have the mortgage removed prior to transferring the title to the property to the buyer.

When this arrangement is made, the seller remains responsible for the mortgage. If there is a deficiency judgment as a result of a foreclosure action, only the original mortgagor—the seller—is liable under the deficiency judgment.

With this arrangement, however, if the seller fails to make his mortgage payments, the buyer can lose the equities he has built up in the property through a foreclosure by sale action brought against the seller. The seller may choose to pay off the mortgage and remove it as a lien against the property before selling or the buyer may request that the mortgage be removed before title to the property is transferred to him.

When this arrangement is followed, the buyer should specify in his offer to purchase that upon his paying the purchase price, the seller is to convey the property to him free and clear of all liens and encumbrances.

This makes the seller responsible for having the mortgage removed as a lien against the property before their deal is closed. A mortgage satisfaction recorded in the office of the county recorder acts as proof that the mortgage has been removed.

TWO BASIC TYPES OF MORTGAGES

Mortgages fall into two groups, depending upon what is done with the money received in exchange for the mortgage.

Regular Mortgages

A regular mortgage is a lien on real estate given as security for a debt. The mortgagor may do as he wishes with the money he receives in exchange for the mortgage.

For example, you own your property outright and wish to borrow some money. You are willing to give a mortgage against your property as security for the debt. You make your request at the bank and they lend you the money in exchange for a mortgage on your property plus a promissory note in which you declare how much you owe them and promise to repay that amount by a certain date.

You may do as you wish with the money you borrow. You may buy a boat with it, you may take a vacation with it, or you may buy a new car with it.

Purchase Money Mortgages

A purchase money mortgage is a lien on real estate given as security for a debt. The mortgagor may use the money resulting from the mortgage only toward payment of the purchase price of the property described in the mortgage.

This type of mortgage may result from borrowing money from a third party—for example, a bank—to be used toward the purchase of a property or it can act as security for the seller for an unpaid balance on the purchase price of the property.

For example, you wish to buy a $60,000 property but only have $15,000 in cash. In exchange for a purchase money mortgage against the property, the bank lends you $45,000 to be used only toward payment on the purchase price of the property.

Cash you already had	$15,000
Amount lent to you by the bank on a purchase money mortgage	$45,000
Total price of the property	$60,000

Or the seller may agree to sell the property to you for $15,000 cash and a purchase money mortgage for the balance of $45,000.

Cash you already had	$15,000
Amount of the purchase money mortgage held by the seller as security for the amount you still owe on the property	$45,000
Total price of the property	$60,000

So far the one big difference is that with a regular mortgage, the money may be used as the borrower wishes. With a purchase money mortgage, the money is to be used only toward payment of the purchase price of the property described in the mortgage. Other differences arise when claims crop up against the mortgaged property.

In some states—for example, California, Montana, and North Carolina—a mortgagee is not allowed a deficiency judgment when insufficient money is raised through a purchase money mortgage foreclosure action to satisfy the debt.

For example, the property sells at a foreclosure by sale proceedings and after all liens and judgments that have priority are satisfied, there is only $6,000 left. You owe the mortgagee $10,000. The $6,000 is awarded to the mortgagee and you still owe him $4,000.

In some states, if it had been a purchase money mortgage, the mortgagee would not have been allowed a deficiency judgment for the $4,000 you still owe him. If it had been a regular mortgage the mortgagee would have been allowed a deficiency judgment.

The question is how to arrange financing to buy a property other than through a purchase money mortgage. If you pledge property other than the property you are buying as security for the amount you borrow, the mortgage will be the more desirable regular mortgage.

For example, you wish to buy a $60,000 property but have only $15,000 in cash. Rather than give a mortgage against the property you are buying to raise the $45,000, give a mortgage against a different property. When this is possible, it is well worth considering.

Special provisions can appear in any type of mortgage. One that often comes as a surprise to a borrower is the acceleration clause.

Acceleration Clause

The acceleration clause provides that if you miss one payment, the entire balance owed on the mortgage becomes due immediately. Don't let an acceleration clause in your mortgage come as a surprise to you. Have your attorney check your mortgage.

Prepayment Penalty Clause

This clause requires that you pay a penalty if you make your mortgage payments in advance. Possibly the mortgagee's income is such that he will be thrown into a higher income tax bracket if he receives more than a prearranged number of mortgage payments each year.

To protect himself, the mortgagee puts a prepayment penalty clause in the mortgage and you will have to pay a penalty if you make any mortgage payments in advance.

Prepayment Without Penalty Clause

This clause allows the mortgagor to make mortgage payments in advance and requires the mortgagee to accept these payments without imposing a penalty upon the mortgagor.

The advantage is to the mortgagor, as this clause allows him to reduce his debt more quickly and hence reduce the amount of the total interest he will pay. If the mortgage contains the prepayment without penalty clause, the mortgagor can make payments for two years in one year. He saves the interest for the second year.

For example, with a $10,000 mortgage at 8% interest per annum with the mortgage to be repaid in five years with five annual payments of interest and principal:

Payment number	Net interest	Payment for principal	Balance of loan
1	$800	$2,000	$8,000
2	$640	$2,000	$6,000
3	$480	$2,000	$4,000
4	$320	$2,000	$2,000
5	$160	$2,000	$0

If in the fourth year the mortgagor pays the entire unpaid balance on the mortgage ($4,000), he escapes the interest payment of $160 for the fifth year.

Who knows—tomorrow you may be rich and wish to pay off the entire mortgage. Will your mortgage allow you to do this without paying a penalty?

Open-end Clause

An open-end clause in a mortgage allows the mortgagor to borrow against the mortgage, at the original interest rate, an amount equal to the amount he has paid off on the mortgage.

For example, the mortgage was originally for $25,000 at 8% interest to be paid off in yearly installments of $5,000 each plus interest. The mortgagor made two yearly payments of $5,000 each for a total of $10,000 plus interest

If the mortgage contains an open-end clause, he can reborrow the $10,000 he has already paid off on the mortgage. His interest will be at the original rate of 8% and the mortgage will be extended for two years. He is to repay the $10,000 with two $5,000 yearly payments plus interest.

The advantage to the mortgagor of an open-end clause in a mortgage is that he can reborrow against the mortgage at the original interest rate. Usually this interest rate is lower than he would pay on a short-term loan.

For example, possibly the mortgagor will need to borrow money to finance a new car or to pay a hospital bill. It is to his advantage to be able to borrow against his real estate mortgage rather than to pay a higher interest rate on a short-term loan. Discuss with your mortgagee the possibility of including an open-end clause in your mortgage.

Sources of Mortgage Money

Don't miss a chance to save a little on your mortgage just because you are too quick to accept an offer of mortgage money. Check many sources: banks, savings and loan associations, life insurance companies, and mortgage companies. Study what the use of the money—interest plus charges for extras—will cost. Ask questions

No matter where you get your mortgage money, the mortgage will be a conventional mortgage, an FHA-insured mortgage, or a VA-guaranteed mortgage.

A conventional mortgage is a mortgage not insured by the FHA (Federal Housing Administration) or guaranteed by the VA (Veterans Administration).

An FHA-insured mortgage is a mortgage you acquire from another lender that is insured and regulated by the FHA. A VA-guaranteed mortgage you acquire from another lender that is guaranteed and regulated by the VA. In special cases, the VA will make a direct loan to a borrower.

	Conventional mortgage	FHA-insured mortgage	VA-guaranteed mortgage
Who can use it?	Anyone who can find an agreeable lender.	Anyone found acceptable by the FHA (special features for veterans).	Veterans and anyone who takes over a VA mortgage from a veteran.
Amount you may borrow is based upon	Your net worth, earning power, and the inclination of the lender.	Will not insure loans for more than the appraised value of the property.	Will not insure loans for more than the appraised value of the property.
Amount you may borrow	Depends upon you and the lender, usually from 70% to 90% of the property value.	Will insure not more than 97% of 1st $15,000, 90% of next $5,000, 80% of remainder, based on FHA appraisal.	Will guarantee the lender against loss up to 60% of the VA-appraised value. Will guarantee up to $17,500 only.

	Conventional mortgage	FHA-insured mortgage	VA-guaranteed mortgage
Down payment required	Usually about 25% but depends upon you and the lender.	In some cases may be as low as 3% of the cost of the property.	Up to the lending agency, but usually low.
Time for repayment of the loan	Usually 20 years or less but depends upon the lender and you.	May be up to 30 years.	May be up to 30 years.
Interest rate	Varies according to the demands for the lender's money.	8½% plus ½% for FHA insurance, but it fluctuates.	8½%, but it fluctuates.
Costs other than interest	Sometimes an orgination fee; amount varies with different lenders.	Appraisal fee $75	For post-Korean veterans a funding fee of ½ of 1% of the amount of the loan.
	Closing costs.	Closing costs. May be points.	Closing costs. May be points.
Prepayment clause allowances	Usually allowed but up to the lender.	Allow prepayment without restrictions	Allow prepayment without restrictions.

FHA-insured and VA-guaranteed loans:
1. Generally require less down payment, and
2. Generally allow the borrower more time to repay the loan, and
3. Generally offer lower interest rates, and
4. May or may not cost more than conventional loans.

If the interest on an FHA or VA loan is less, why should a would-be borrower, if he qualifies for an FHA-insured or a VA-guaranteed mortgage, be interested in a conventional mortgage?

The answer is tied into the mechanics of FHA-insured and VA-guaranteed loans.

The FHA and VA may only insure and guarantee mortgage loans when the loans are made by lenders at the interest rates established by the government for FHA and VA treatment.

Banks and other lending institutions set their interest rates according to the demand for their money and their interest rates on conventional mortgages may be equal to or higher than the rates allowed on FHA and VA mortgages.

For example (these rates change; those used here are for the purpose of example only):

FHA and VA mortgages:
Interest rate (includes ½% for insurance for FHA) as set by the government   9%
Conventional mortgages:
Interest rate set by the demand for money   9½%

The FHA may only insure the loan and the VA may only guarantee the loan when the interest charged by the lender is not more than the amount allowed by the government, which in the example is 9%.

If a lender can get 9½% interest on conventional mortgages, why should he lend money on FHA-insured or VA-guaranteed mortgages at 9% interest? He would forfeit possible earnings.

For example (on a $15,000 mortgage for 20 years):

Total interest on a conventional mortgage at 9½% interest	$18,556.80
Total interest on an FHA or VA mortgage at 9% interest	$17,390.40
Difference in total interest received by the lender	$1,166.40

Can you expect a lender, in business to make a profit, to take $1,166.40 less in interest just because the loan is FHA-insured or VA-guaranteed?

Lenders do lend mortgage money at the lower interest rates required for FHA and VA mortgages but they do it in such a manner that their total earnings on these loans are equal to what their total earnings would have been at the higher conventional mortgage interest rates. They do not forfeit any earnings by lending at the lower interest rates.

Referring to the previous example, somehow the lender has to get an extra $1,166.40 if he lends the mortgage money at the 9% FHA or VA interest rate so that his total earnings will equal what he would have received if he had lent the money on a conventional mortgage at 9½% interest.

He does this by charging for "extras."

For example:

Total interest on a conventional mortgage at 9½%	$18,556.80
Total earnings on an FHA-insured or VA-guaranteed loan	
Interest at 9%	$17,390.40
"Extras"	$ 1,166.40
Total earnings received by the lender	$18,556.80

The lender satisfied the requirement that the interest on the FHA or VA mortgage loan is not in excess of the rate set by the government (9%) and the lender realizes earnings equal to those he would have received for the use of his money at the higher conventional mortgage interest rate of 9½%. The borrower or mortgagor receives his mortgage money at the lower FHA or VA interest rate.

The extras that enter into the transaction so that the lender receives an amount equal to the amount he would receive if he made the loan at the higher conventional mortgage interest rate are represented by the paying of points.

Points or the "points premium" is the amount charged by the lender with an FHA or VA loan so that his total earnings are equal to what they would be at the higher interest rate on a conventional mortgage.

For example:

Total interest that could be earned on the loan at conventional mortgage interest rates equals Total interest at the lower FHA or VA interest rates plus points

The government requires as a provision for approving an FHA-insured or VA-guaranteed loan that the buyer not be required to pay the charge for points.

The seller is expected to pay the points charge.

For example:

Sale price of $60,000 with a $15,000 mortgage and to qualify for FHA or VA handling at the 9% interest rate, 8 points, each being 1% of the amount of the mortgage, are charged by the lender.

The lender actually lends:

Total amount of the mortgage	$15,000

Because he can receive 9½% on conventional mortgages for the use of his money, he charges 8 points, so he actually receives 9% interest plus 8 points, which is an additional $1,200.00 (8%×$15,000).

The borrower or mortgagor receives:

Debt represented by the $15,000 mortgage	$15,000 debt

The borrower receives his mortgage money at the lower FHA or VA interest rate and by the provisions to qualify for the FHA or VA mortgage, the borrower does not pay the amount of the points.

The seller actually receives:

Sale price of the property	$60,000
(less) Cost of 8 points that he had to pay the lender so his buyer would qualify for FHA or VA financing. 8 points×$15,000 mortgage	$ 1,200
Amount the seller actually receives after paying the 8 points	$61,200

The lender and borrower should be happy. They received what they wanted. The seller received less than he probably expected from the sale of his property because he was required to pay the lender the points charge as a provision in acquiring financing for the buyer.

Will the seller always be required to pay points when his buyer wants FHA or VA financing?

Not necessarily. The government controls the maximum interest a lender may charge on an FHA-insured or VA-guaranteed loan.

One lender may charge no points because of the value to him of having the loan insured by the FHA or guaranteed by the VA.

Another lender on the same day, and only a block away, may charge 6 or even 8 points on FHA-insured or VA-guaranteed mortgage loans.

The total cost of borrowing money with the FHA-insured or VA-guaranteed loan may be more or less than the cost of borrowing the same amount with a conventional mortgage.

When you need mortgage money, ask questions and go shopping!

Since the kind of mortgage instruments and how they are used vary from state to state, a general discussion is all that has been possible here. Before entering into a mortgage-financing arrangement, talk to your attorney. Get the answers to the questions asked on the worksheet that follows this chapter.

WORKSHEET OF QUESTIONS TO ANSWER BEFORE ENTERING INTO ANY MORTGAGE-FINANCING ARRANGEMENT

What will be the total interest if all payments are made as agreed?

_____

Will there be any additional charges for extras, points, or orientation fees? _____

What will be the total cost, interest plus extras, of borrowing the money?

_____

Who is to pay for having the financing instruments drawn up? _____

_____

Will a trust deed or mortgage be used? _____

If a trust deed is used, does the trustee have the power to sell the property if the debtor gets behind in his payments? _____

    Under what conditions? _____

    Who will act as trustee? _____

    What are his qualifications? _____

If payments aren't made and a foreclosure by sale is used, will it be through judicial proceedings or through a power of sale? _____

_____

If payments aren't made and a foreclosure without sale is used, does the creditor receive all the mortgagor's property or just an amount equal in value to the unpaid balance on the debt? _____

_____

If through a foreclosure by sale action the property sells for less than the unpaid balance on the mortgage, may the mortgagee take a deficiency judgment? _____

Is a period of redemption allowed if the debtor gets behind on his payments? _____

    Is this before or after the foreclosure proceedings? _____

    How long is the period of redemption? _____

Will the note be a regular note or a cognovit note? _____

Will it be a negotiable or non-negotiable note or bond? _____

May the creditor assign his interests in the mortgage instrument and note? _____

May the debtor assign his interests in the mortgage instrument and note?

_____

If the buyer agrees to assume and pay an existing mortgage, who is liable under a foreclosure action? _____

    Who is liable under a deficiency judgment? _____

Will a regular money or purchase money mortgage be used? _____

_____

If a purchase money mortgage is used, who can be held liable under a deficiency judgment? _____

Will the mortgage instrument contain an acceleration clause? _____

_____

Will the mortgage instrument contain a prepayment penalty clause? _____

What will the penalty be? _____

Will the mortgage instrument contain a prepayment without penalty clause? _____

Will the mortgage instrument contain an open-end clause? _____

What are the restrictions on borrowing at the original rate? _____

_____

If an FHA or VA mortgage is used, what will be the charge for points?

_____

Who will pay the points charge? _____

Who will be responsible for keeping the property insured? _____

_____

What amount and kind of insurance will be carried on the property?

_____

Who will be required to pay the real estate taxes and special assessments?

_____

Will the creditor have the right to pay these taxes if the debtor doesn't and to add the amount of the taxes to the debt? _____

_____

Will the mortgagor be required to pay a mortgage tax on the mortgage principal? (For example, in New York a tax of ½ of 1% is levied on the principal of new mortgages. On a $20,000 mortgage, the tax would be $100.) _____

Chapter Fourteen

LAND CONTRACT FINANCING

LAND CONTRACT FINANCING USED INCREASINGLY

In states where they are accepted, land contracts are steadily gaining in popularity as a means of financing the purchase price of real estate. Some of the reasons for the increased popularity of land contracts are:

1. The amount required for a down payment when financing with a land contract is usually less than the amount required when financing with a mortgage.

2. When the deal is closed—possession of the property given to the buyer and down payment and promise of future payments given to the seller—there may be less in costs when land contracts are used than when mortgages are used.

For example, the buyer using a land contract does not receive title and a deed to the property until he has paid for the property. The seller can defer these costs until he has been paid for the property.

3. Land contracts usually result in quicker sales because they eliminate the time and effort involved in establishing financing through a third party.

A land contract is a written contract between vendor (seller) and vendee (buyer) in which the vendor agrees to transfer legal possession of the real estate to the vendee along with the promise that he, the vendor, will transfer legal title to the property to the vendee when the vendee has completely fulfilled the provisions of the contract.

For simplicity's sake, we'll continue to refer to the parties to the land contract as seller and buyer rather than use "vendor" and "vendee."

What happens when you buy or sell using land contract financing?

For example, you enter into a land contract to sell your house for $60,000. The buyer is to pay $20,000 down and an additional $4,000, plus interest, each year for ten years.

The buyer pays the $20,000 down and moves into the house. The seller retains title to the property, giving the buyer only legal possession of the property plus his promise that he will transfer legal title to him after all payments are made.

The buyer makes all the agreed-upon payments, $4,000 plus interest each year for ten years. At the end of ten years the seller transfers legal title to the property to the buyer.

Let's review:

When the land contract was executed, each received:

The seller received:

1. $20,000 down payment toward the $60,000 selling price.

2. The promise of payments of $4,000 a year plus interest for ten years.

3. Legal title to the property.

4. The right to a foreclosure action if the buyer fails to make his payments on time.

The buyer received:

1. Legal possession of the property.

2. The promise that after he makes all payments the seller will give him a legal title to the property.

3. An equitable interest and an equitable title to the property that imposes certain obligations upon him.

If the seller had financed the sale by transferring title to the buyer and holding a mortgage for the unpaid balance, he would have forfeited all rights to the property other than the right to foreclose on his mortgage if the buyer defaulted in his payments.

With land contract financing the seller, although he retains legal title to the property, does bar some of his rights to the property.

These things usually are true of *the seller:*

1. He may not sell his interests in the property to another.

2. He may not encumber the property by putting another lien against it. The legal title held as security for the unpaid balance acts as a primary lien against the property. The seller may not mortgage the property. He may make no further transfer of his interest in the property.

3. He forfeits the right to give title to the property to a third person through his will. When the land contract was formed, the seller transferred legal possession to the buyer along with the promise that he would deliver legal title to him after he fulfills the terms of the contract. The title must be preserved for the buyer.

The seller does have an equity represented by the money paid in on the contract and the buyer's promise of future payments. He may direct in his will how these are to be distributed.

4. When the seller's wife joins in signing the land contract, she relinquishes all possible dower and homestead rights in the property. She does, however, retain any joint tenancy, tenancy in common, or community property rights in her husband's equities resulting from the sale of the property, that is, all money paid in plus the promise of future payments. (Refer to pages 151–156 for who will inherit your property.) (Refer to pages 76–79 for joint tenancy.)

The seller is in somewhat the same position he would have been in if he had transferred legal title to the buyer and held a mortgage for any unpaid balance. The buyer, although he has only an equitable title—the right to make his payments and eventually earn the legal title—has somewhat the rights he would have if he had received legal title to the property and given a mortgage for any unpaid balance.

These things usually are true of *the buyer:*

1. He may sell or assign the equitable interest he has in the property he buys on a land contract.

For example, if he pays $20,000 down and makes one yearly payment of $4,000, he has an equitable interest in the property of $24,000.

Down payment	$20,000
One yearly payment	$4,000
His equitable interest in the property	$24,000

In addition to the $24,000, his equitable interest includes the promise of legal title to the property after he makes the rest of his payments.

2. He may encumber the equitable interest he has in property he buys on a land contract.

He may put a mortgage or lien against his equitable interest.

The primary encumbrance against his interest is the legal title held by the seller. Any mortgage or lien he puts against his equitable interest is second to the legal title held by the seller.

However, if he buys under a mortgage held by the seller, any additional mortgages or liens he puts on the property are second to the mortgage held by the seller.

Usually his ability to borrow against his equitable interest is the same, regardless of whether he finances with a land contract or with a mortgage.

3. He may transfer his equitable interest in the property to his heirs through a provision in his will. If he has paid in $24,000 toward the purchase price, he may direct in his will who is to receive this share plus his right to continue payments and eventually earn legal title to the property.

4. He may have a lien placed against his equitable interest in the property.

For example, the buyer owes money to another party, other than the seller. This person enters a money judgment against him for the amount he owes. This is a court order that states that the buyer owes him a certain amount, plus court costs.

When this money judgment is filed, it becomes a lien against the buyer's equitable interest. This can result in his interest's being sold and the proceeds used to repay the debt.

5. In states where dower is recognized, the buyer's wife has dower rights in his equitable interest. Regardless of any provisions he may make to the contrary in his will, his wife has dower rights—a right to a percentage of the estate—or other property rights as given to her through the state's laws of descent.

6. Normally the buyer has homestead rights granted to him through the equitable title he has to the property.

In the event there is a forced sale of his equitable interest by a judgment creditor, the proceeds are exempt up to and including the amount of the homestead exemption above any liens or mortgages against the property. (Refer to pages 151–153 for homestead rights.)

So far it appears that a buyer's and seller's rights under a land contract financing arrangement are very similar to those they would have under a mortgage financing arrangement. Depending upon your state's laws, a big difference can crop up when the buyer is unable to make his payments and a foreclosure action is brought against him.

The most common remedy used when a buyer defaults in payments is a strict foreclosure action. The buyer loses all rights and claims to the property if he fails to make his payments within the period of redemption (time given him to get caught up on his payments) and the property is returned to the seller.

For example, you enter into a land contract to purchase a property for $60,000 with a $15,000 down payment and the balance to be paid in nine yearly installments of $5,000 each plus 8% interest. After making your down payment of $15,000 and your first yearly payment of $5,000 plus interest, you are unable to make your second $5,000 yearly payment.

The seller brings a court action of "strict foreclosure" against you. The court orders you to pay the entire balance owing on the land contract and gives you a time period (period of redemption) in which this payment must be made. In this example, you are required to pay $40,000.

Purchase price	$60,000
(less) down payment	$15,000
	$45,000
(less) one yearly payment	$5,000
Amount the court orders you to pay the seller—the entire unpaid balance	$40,000

If you are able to pay this amount within the time period set by the court, the seller will transfer legal title to you as promised in the land contract. However, if you are unable to make this $40,000 payment, you lose all equities and rights to the property and legal possession of the property is returned to the seller.

In this example, not only do you give up legal possession and the right to continue payments and eventually earn legal title, but you suffer a loss of $20,000.

Down payment	$15,000
First yearly payment	$5,000
Total you paid toward the purchase price	$20,000

Your loss:

1. The $20,000 you already paid on the contract
2. Legal possession of the property
3. The right to continue payments and earn legal title to the property

Sound severe? Remember that in some states the same recourse is available to a creditor when a buyer gets behind in his mortgage payments. The creditor keeps all the payments and has the property returned to him.

In other states, with mortgage financing, a foreclosure by sale action is used when the debtor gets behind in his payments. (Refer to pages 128–139 for mortgage financing.)

For example, you agree to buy the $60,000 property with a $15,000 down payment plus nine yearly payments of $5,000 each plus 8% interest. The unpaid balance is secured with a mortgage. After making the down payment and your first yearly $5,000 payment you are unable to make the second payment.

The seller brings a foreclosure by sale action against you. The court orders you to get your payments caught up and gives you a limited time in which to do this. If you are able to catch up on your payments, the contract lives on as agreed.

However, if you are not able to catch up on your payments within the time allowed by the court, the property is sold at public auction to raise enough money to pay the seller the balance you owe him.

Purchase price	$60,000
(less) down payment	$15,000
	$45,000
(less) one yearly payment	$5,000
Amount you still owe the seller	$40,000

The first $40,000 from the sale of the property is used to pay the seller the balance due him. Any money in excess of this $40,000 is yours. However, if the property sells for less than $40,000, possibly the seller can file a deficiency judgment against you in an effort to collect the difference. If the property sells at public auction under the foreclosure by sale action for $50,000, what is your loss?

Amount you have paid on the property:	
Down payment	$15,000
One payment	$5,000
Total paid toward the purchase price	$20,000
Amount you still owe:	
Purchase price	$60,000
Already paid in	$20,000
Balance you owe the seller	$40,000
Amount left from the sale after the seller is paid the amount owed him:	
Price at which the property sold	$50,000
Amount you owe the seller	$40,000
Amount left over	$10,000
Amount of your total loss:	
Amount you've paid on the contract	$20,000
Amount left for you after the sale and the seller is paid in full	$10,000
Total loss	$10,000

Your loss:
1. $10,000
2. Legal possession and legal title to the property
3. The right to continue payments and earn a clear title to the property

In both examples you lose possession and title to the property. But you lose $10,000 less through the foreclosure by sale action used with a mortgage than you do with a strict foreclosure action used with a land contract.

Your losses (compared):	
Financing with a mortgage (through a foreclosure by sale action)	$10,000
Financing with a land contract (through a strict foreclosure action)	$20,000

This example gives you the extremes and is offered in the hope that it will make you curious enough to inquire into what foreclosure actions are used in your state. Possibly, as a creditor, you would fare better through a land contract foreclosure than through a mortgage foreclosure.

With a land contract the seller retains title and the buyer has possession of the property. Who is the owner, and therefore responsible for the property? Some of the subjects that should be covered in the land contract are:

Payment of Real Estate Taxes and Special Assessments

Usually the contract will read that the buyer is to pay all real estate taxes and special assessments put on the property after he takes possession. The taxes for the year in which the buyer took possession are usually prorated between the buyer and seller. (Refer to pages 117–118 for prorating taxes.)

Keeping the Property Insured

Usually the buyer is obligated to keep the property insured and usually the land contract outlines the type and amount of insurance he is required to carry on the property. If the buyer does not keep the property insured, usually the seller has the right to insure the property and charge the cost to the buyer.

The land contract usually specifies to what degree the seller is allowed to dictate the amount of insurance the buyer is required to carry on the property.

Keeping the Property in Good Repair

The buyer is required to keep the property in good repair. What the seller expects him to do should be clearly understood and spelled out in the land contract. Just as the buyer can lose his rights to the property through his failure to make payments on time, he can also lose his rights to the property by failing to keep the property in good repair.

Loss of Additions

Normally, after the buyer takes possession, if any additions he makes to the property are lost or destroyed, he cannot expect the seller to be held responsible and share in the loss. Often, if the loss takes place before the buyer takes possession, the buyer may back out of the contract.

Loss by Eminent Domain

If the property is seized through an eminent domain proceedings after the buyer has taken possession, he is generally held to the terms of the land contract and must continue to make payments. If the property is taken before he is given possession, as a rule the buyer may back out of the contract.

Title to the Property

The land contract should specify in what form the seller will give title to the buyer after all payments are made. Will the seller furnish a general warranty deed or a special warranty deed? Will the seller furnish an abstract of title or an owner's policy of title insurance?

Foreclosure Action

If the buyer defaults in making his payments, what type of foreclosure action will be brought against him? If this is not clearly outlined in the contract, at least both parties to the contract should be familiar with the state statutes covering the subject.

Tax Advantages of Land Contract Financing

There are possible tax advantages to land contract financing as compared to selling for all cash or selling for a down payment and holding a note and mortgage as security for the unpaid balance.

Even though you hold a note and mortgage as security for an unpaid balance on the sale of your property, you do give the buyer title to the property. On this basis it is generally presumed that the entire profit from the sale is realized in the year of the sale and you are taxed on the total amount. An exception to this is when the buyer assumes and agrees to pay an existing mortgage.

For example, when the adjusted base is $50,000, selling expenses are $4,700, and the property sells for $65,000, you have a gross profit of $10,300 and in some cases can be taxed on the total in the year you sell the property. (The "adjusted base" is what you pay for your property plus the cost of additions and improvements.)

When you finance with a land contract, because the title is retained by the seller until the entire purchase price is paid, the seller is required to pay income tax only on the profit he actually receives. This spreads his profit out over the years during which the buyer is making his payments.

When this method is used, the procedure followed will depend upon whether the seller receives more or less than 30% of the sale price the first year.

INSTALLMENT SALES METHOD
(used when the payment in the year of the sale is *not over* 30% of the sale price)

With this practice a fixed percentage of the yearly payments is handled as profits on the sale. This results in the profits' being spread out over several years and can in some cases reduce the total tax you pay on the profits.

For example, the property sells on a land contract for $65,000 with the buyer paying $20,000 down and agreeing to pay $5,000 a year for nine years with 8% interest per annum.

Selling price	$65,000
(less) adjusted base	$50,000
	$15,000
(less) selling expenses	
Broker's commission $3,900	
Attorney's fees $800	
	$4,700
Gross profit	$10,300

You have a gross profit of $10,300, but you still retain title to the property. As the buyer makes his payments over the years, only a fixed percentage of each payment is considered profit. The percentage that is considered profit is determined by dividing the selling price into the gross profit (after deducting interest from each payment).

$$\frac{gross\ profit}{selling\ price} \ (or)\ \frac{\$10,300}{\$65,000} = 16\%$$

Each year you report only 16% of the payments as profits. If the buyer had assumed a $10,000 mortgage, the formula would be this:

$$\frac{gross\ profit}{selling\ price\ (-)\ mortgage\ assumed} \ (or)\ \frac{\$10,300}{\$55,000\ (\$65,000-\$10,000)} = 18.73\%$$

With the buyer assuming the $10,000 mortgage, each year the seller would report only 18.73% of the payments as profits.

Depending upon how you sell, there can be big differences in the amount of profits on which you have to pay taxes in any one year. In each case the property sells for $65,000 with $20,000 down and with payments of $5,000 a year for nine years.

AMOUNT THAT IS TREATED AS PROFIT AND ON WHICH YOU PAY TAX

	Buyer get his mortgage from the bank	Buyer assumes your $10,000 mortgage	You sell on a land contract
First year	Taxed on entire gross profit of $10,300	Taxed on 18.73% of $20,000 down payment or on $3,746	Taxed on 16% of $20,000 down payment or on $3,200
Second year through Ninth year	Entire tax was paid first year	Each year taxed on 18.73% of the $5,000 yearly payment	Each year taxed on 16% of the $5,000 yearly payment

Through using the installment sales method of reporting your profits through the sale with a land contract, you can possibly defer your taxable income to years when your tax bracket is lower and hence pay less total tax on the sale.

DEFERRED PAYMENT METHOD
(used when the payment in the year of the sale is *more than* 30% of the sale price)

With this method no gain is taxed until the payments the seller has received are in excess of the adjusted base of the property plus the cost of selling.

For example, the property sells on a land contract for $65,000 with the buyer paying $30,000 down and agreeing to payments of $5,000 a year for seven years with 8% interest per annum.

Selling price		$65,000
Adjusted base	$50,000	
(plus) selling expenses		
Broker's commission	$3,900	
Attorney's fees	$800	
	$54,700	

No tax is imposed on the profits from the sale until the total of the payments received exceeds $54,700.

Payments

First year—$30,000 down payment—not interpreted as profit so not a taxable gain.

Second year—$5,000 yearly payment. Total paid in is $35,000 so no profit and no taxable gain.

Third through fifth year—$5,000 yearly payment. Total paid in to date is four yearly payments of $5,000 each and the $30,000 down payment for a total of $50,000. Still no profit so no taxable gain.

Sixth year—$5,000 yearly payment. Of this $5,000, $4,700 shall not be interpreted as profit and not taxed. The remaining $300 of this $5,000 payment will be considered profit and taxed.

(None of the payments are considered a profit until after the amount of the adjusted base plus selling costs has been paid, in this example, $54,700)

Sixth through ninth years—$5,000 yearly payments, all interpreted as profit and a taxable gain.

In every case the tax advantage from selling with a land contract varies with your income structure, but usually there is an advantage in spreading out the profits over a number of years or in delaying payment on the profits until years when you have less taxable income or offsetting losses.

Statutes governing land contracts vary from state to state, so get acquainted with an attorney. Have him help you answer, for your state, the questions asked at the end of this chapter before you enter into any land contract financing arrangement.

WORKSHEET OF QUESTIONS TO ANSWER BEFORE ENTERING INTO ANY LAND CONTRACT FINANCING ARRANGEMENT

When will the buyer receive legal possession of the property? _____
_____

After the buyer has made all payments, what will he receive as proof of ownership? _____
(Refer to pages 88–91 for abstract of title or owner's policy of title insurance.)

What type of title will the buyer receive? _____
(Refer to pages 88–91 for the title to your property.)

Prior to transferring legal title, may the seller encumber his interests in the property? _____

Prior to transferring legal title, may the seller put any liens on his interests in the property? _____

Has the seller's spouse barred any rights to dower and homestead in the property? _____

May the buyer sell or assign his equitable interest in the property? _____
_____

May the buyer encumber—for example, mortgage—his interest in the property? _____

May the buyer put liens on his equitable interest in the property? _____
_____

If the buyer gets behind in his payments, what remedies are available to the seller? _____
_____

If a foreclosure action is used, will it be a foreclosure with sale or without sale? _____

What is the buyer's period of redemption if he gets behind in his payments? (This is the time allowed a buyer to catch up on his payments before he loses his property.) _____
_____

Does the land contract contain a liquidated damages clause? Such a clause provides that when a buyer defaults, the seller may keep all the payments the buyer has made toward the purchase price of the property. _____

Does the contract contain an acceleration clause, which provides that if the buyer misses one payment, the entire unpaid balance is due? _____

Does the contract contain a prepayment and coasting clause, which allows a buyer to make payments in advance and then to coast without making additional payments as long as he is not behind the agreed-upon payment schedule? _____

_____

Does the contract contain a prepayment penalty clause, which provides that the buyer pay a penalty if he makes any payments in advance of due dates? _____

Who is to pay the real estate taxes and special assessments? _____

_____

If the taxes are to be prorated for the year of the sale, what prorating method will be used? (Refer to pages 117–118 for prorating.) _____

_____

What type and amount of insurance is to be maintained on the property and who is to pay for it? _____

What is meant by keeping the property "in good repair" and what are the penalties for failing to do so? _____

_____

If the property is taken by eminent domain after the contract is signed, but before the buyer takes possession, is the buyer tied to the terms of the contract? _____

If the property is taken by eminent domain after the buyer takes possession, may the buyer back out of the contract? _____

If any additions to the property are lost or destroyed after the buyer takes possession, does the seller share in the loss? _____

_____

Will the payment schedule allow the seller to take advantage of reporting his profits on the installment sales method? _____

_____

Will the payment schedule allow the seller to take advantage of reporting his profits by the use of the deferred payment method? _____

Chapter Fifteen

PROPERTY OWNERS' RIGHTS: INHERITANCE LAWS

HOMESTEAD RIGHTS

Homestead rights are the rights that some states grant property owners to help protect the family dwelling against the claims of unsecured creditors.

Perhaps because of an unwise business decision you owe a creditor $30,000. He has entered a money judgment against you to recover the $30,000. The judgment acts as a lien on your house, and unless your creditor is paid he may apply for an order of execution to have your house sold to raise enough money to pay the debt.

Can your house be seized and sold to raise the $30,000, leaving you without a home for your family and possibly without enough money to re-establish one?

The objective of homestead rights is to preserve the house for the family. How much protection is granted the house varies from state to state; for example, in California your homestead exemption as head of a family is $30,000 in excess of secured liens and encumbrances.

If your equity in your house is
$40,000:

Equity in your house	$40,000
California homestead exemption	$30,000
Equity in excess of the exemption	$10,000

When your equity in your house is more than the homestead exemption, your house can be seized and sold. Provided the house sells for $55,000, although you owe $30,000, your judgment creditor will receive $25,000 and you will receive $30,000 from the sale to re-establish a home for your family.

$25,000	value in excess of your homestead exemption that goes to your judgment creditor
$30,000	your homestead exemption as head of a household in California
$55,000	sale price

You still owe your judgment creditor $5,000. Can he collect? In most states the homestead exemption lives with the family. Even upon the death of the head of the household the widow is entitled to the homestead exemption until the youngest child is twenty-one. Only when the youngest child reaches twenty-one is the house no longer exempt from the claims of unsecured creditors.

Although you live in a state that grants a homestead exemption, don't assume that you are automatically entitled to it. Some states—for example, California—require that you declare your homestead and file a declaration of homestead in the county clerk's office before your property is protected by the homestead exemption.

Most states stipulate that homestead rights extend only to land and dwellings owned and occupied by a resident owner. If you sell your house must you use the proceeds from the sale to pay off any unsecured debts?

The objective of homestead rights is to preserve the home for the family and not to force a family to live in any one particular house.

Usually your homestead rights provide that the proceeds from the sale of your house are protected up to the amount of your homestead exemption provided you use that money to establish another homestead for your family within a limited time.

In California, for example, if you are the head of a household your homestead exemption is $30,000; you may sell your house, and $30,000 from the proceeds is protected from creditors provided you establish another homestead within six months. If your house sells for $55,000, $30,-000 is yours to use in establishing another homestead provided you do so within six months. The $25,000 can be used to pay unsecured debts.

If you contracted with a carpenter to build an addition on your house and then found that you didn't have quite enough money to pay him, could he put a mechanic's lien on your house and have it sold to collect, or must he wait for his money because of your homestead rights? You voluntarily ordered the work done and it was for the improvement of your homestead.

The states are not uniform on what is not protected through the homestead exemption, but, for example, in California the homestead exemption does not protect the property against:

1. Mechanic's liens (refer to pages 125–127 for liens).
2. Judgments executed before the declaration of homestead was recorded.
3. Any liens and encumbrances put on the property and recorded before the declaration of homestead was recorded.
4. Secured debts. Liens and encumbrances executed and acknowledged by you after the declaration of homestead was recorded.

The homestead exemption is protection only against unsecured debts. If you place a mortgage on the property, the mortgage is a secured debt and it can diminish or destroy your exemption.

For example, you place a mortgage on your homestead property for $30,000. Also a money judgment (unsecured debt) is entered against you by a judgment creditor for $20,000. Because you aren't able to make your mortgage payments, there is a forced sale of your property. It sells for $70,000.

Price the property sells for at the forced sale	$70,000
Amount used to pay off the mortgage—a secured debt	$30,000
Amount left over	$40,000
Amount awarded to you through your homestead exemption (for example, in California)	$30,000
Balance left over to pay the the $20,000 money judgment	$10,000

The secured debt (mortgage) is deducted before you are allowed your $30,000 homestead exemption. In this example the selling price is high enough so that you receive the $30,000 exemption even though the money judgment (unsecured debt) is not paid.

If the homestead property sells for only $50,-000, your $30,000 homestead exemption is reduced to only $20,000.

Price the property sells for at the forced sale	$50,000
Amount used to pay off the mortgage—a secured debt	$30,000
Amount awarded to you through your homestead exemption	$20,000

Instead of $30,000 you have only $20,000 to re-establish a home for your family.

If the homestead property sells for only $30,-000, your $30,000 homestead exemption is completely wiped out.

Price the property sells for at the forced sale	$30,000
Amount used to pay off the mortgage—a secured debt	$30,000
Amount awarded to you through your homestead exemption	$0

You had the right to a homestead exemption but you destroyed it with the secured debt—the mortgage you voluntarily placed on your property.

A forced sale of the entire property is not always necessary because of a mortgagor's inability to make payments. In some cases an owner may set aside that part of his homestead property he thinks has the same value as his homestead exemption and allow the remainder of his property to be sold to satisfy his secured debts. Usually he may do this only with the consent of his creditors.

For example, the owner's homestead property

consists of his house, a connected garage and six acres of land. He claims the house, garage, and one fifth of an acre are worth $30,000. The creditors agree with this and only the remaining acres (six acres less the one fifth of an acre) are sold to raise funds to pay the owner's secured debts.

If the creditors do not agree with the owner as to the value of the property the owner wishes to set aside from the sale to preserve his homestead, they can ask the court to establish what parts of the property should be exempt from the sale.

Or the creditors can ask that the entire property be sold and agree to setting aside from the sale the amount the owner is entitled to through his homestead exemption. The owner is then entitled to this money only if his intention is to use it to establish another homestead within a limited time.

Homestead rights are given to you by the state and cannot be taken from you, but you can destroy them. Usually any one of the following will destroy your homestead exemption:

1. Mortgages you put against your homestead property can diminish and even destroy your homestead exemption. The payment of mortgages—secured debts—has priority over your homestead exemption.

2. Provided husband and wife both enter into the sale, selling homestead property terminates any homestead rights unless the homestead is re-established within a limited time. Some states allow a spouse to establish a homestead separate from that of the family unit.

3. When a widow moves out of the state she relinquishes her homestead rights. The law is designed to preserve a homestead for the family and it is considered that a widow who doesn't even live in the state has so little interest in her family unit that she doesn't deserve the benefits of the homestead.

4. Usually a widow who remarries loses the benefits of the homestead and, upon her remarriage, these benefits pass on to the child or children who survive as the heir or heirs of her deceased husband. The widow's new husband has the moral obligation to establish a new home for her and the law provides for the children of the deceased husband by transferring the benefits of the homestead to them.

5. A married man may abandon his homestead, forfeiting his homestead rights in the property. When a person ceases to occupy the property, the property is no longer considered his homestead. After abandoning the property, a man may convey or encumber his rights to the property without his wife's consent.

Homestead laws vary from state to state; all that is possible here is a general discussion hoping to arouse your curiosity enough so that you will ask questions about the homestead rights in your state. Do you have to record your homestead to establish it? How can you destroy your homestead rights?

	Amount of homestead exemption	Time given after sale of house to establish another homestead	Recording or filing necessary to establish your rights
California	Head of family—$30,000 Anybody else—$15,000	six months	yes
Illinois	$10,000	one year	no
Massachusetts	$30,000	none	no
Pennsylvania	—no homestead exemption law—		

WHO WILL INHERIT YOUR REAL ESTATE?

Finally, after a lifetime of budgeting to make your house mortgage payments, you own your house free and clear of all liens and encumbrances. You have even had a mortgage-burning party.

You are comforted in the assumption that upon

your death your widow will inherit your family house and other real estate investments.

If your state recognizes it and you hold title to your real estate in joint tenancy with your wife, or as tenants by the entireties, upon your death your interests go to your wife. (See pages 76–79 for joint tenancy.) But if you hold title to your real estate as tenants in common, usually your interests will go to your heirs. Is this what you wanted?

Perhaps you hold title to your real estate in your name only but have provided for your wife in your will. In most states a surviving spouse is given the "right of election," that is, the right to inherit according to the terms of the will and the right to reject the terms of the will and inherit as though there had been no will.

For example, in New York, if the deceased leaves no children or parents the surviving spouse is entitled to the entire estate regardless of any provisions made otherwise in the will. Even though the deceased asked that $10,000 from his estate be given to a friend, the surviving spouse could "elect," under New York's laws of descent, that the entire estate be turned over to her.

Even with a will the laws in your state will affect the distribution of your real estate. Does your state recognize community property, common-law dower and curtesy, or are other state laws of descent in force? Let's explore the differences.

Community Property

The community property concept is based on the assumption that both members to the marriage make an equal contribution to the family unit; the husband, who goes to work and brings home the paycheck, contributes no more than the wife, who stays home and cares for the house and the children.

Inasmuch as both of their contributions to the family unit during their marriage are considered equal, any property they acquire during their marriage belongs to both of them and is considered community property.

Income from community property belongs to both husband and wife. For example, with money earned during their marriage, a couple bought an apartment building as an investment. The apartment building is community property and the income from it belongs to both of them.

Any property the husband and wife owned before the marriage or acquired during the marriage by gift or inheritance is "separate property" and belongs to the one who received it. Unlike community property, the owner of separate property may generally dispose of it as he wishes regardless of his spouse's wishes.

Depending upon the state's laws, income from separate property—for example, rents—may be a part of the community property or belong to the separate property holder.

States recognizing community property laws have modified these laws so that today there is a large variance from state to state as to how community property is handled upon the death of one of the owners.

In some states, upon the death of either spouse, the surviving spouse becomes the sole owner of all the community property. A spouse may not dispose of any interests in the community property through a will.

In other states, upon the death of either spouse, the surviving spouse receives only one half the value of the community property and the other half is divided or distributed according to the terms of the will.

Some states—California, for example—in addition to recognizing community property and separate property also recognize property held in joint tenancy or tenancy in common by a husband and wife.

Just because you live in a community property state do not think that you are automatically entitled to one half of the property acquired by your family during your marriage. All or part of your community property rights can be destroyed. (The following notations are general and vary from state to state.)

1. Usually earnings of the husband who has been abandoned by his wife are his separate property.

2. As a rule, upon a divorce or legal separation, the community property is divided equally between the spouses. This destroys any future interests one may have in the other's property.

3. A spouse may not convey, encumber, or lease his interest in community property for more than one year unless the other spouse bars any rights to the community property by signing the deed or other instrument.

Note that where community property laws are in effect a surviving spouse is always entitled to a minimum of one half interest in the property jointly accumulated during the marriage. Dower, curtesy, and other laws of descent that offer less do not apply in states that extend community property rights.

States that recognize community property are Arizona, California, Idaho, Louisiana, Nevada, New Mexico, Texas, and Washington.

Dower and Curtesy

Dower is the common-law concept that a widow is entitled to a life interest in one third of her husband's real estate.

Curtesy is the common-law concept that a widower is entitled to a life interest in one third of his wife's real estate if there has been a child born of the marriage.

By a strict interpretation of these concepts, only a "life interest" is awarded—the right to the use of, and income from, the real estate.

A hundred years ago a successful businessman might have invested his surplus funds in farms or other real estate. His widow through her dower rights would inherit a life interest in one third of all the real estate he owned during their marriage. Perhaps she would consider this an ample reward for their years of marriage.

Today it is more likely that the successful businessman will invest his surplus funds in insurance and securities. Probably less of his estate will consist of real estate and as a result a widow's one third interest in her husband's real estate will

consist of a smaller part of his total estate than it would have a hundred years ago.

Because of the changes in the ways we handle our investment dollars, most states offering dower and curtesy have modified the original common-law concepts. For example, in some states a surviving spouse is entitled to an amount of money from the estate of the deceased equal to one half the value of the real estate owned during the marriage. Note that this modification allows the survivor an actual outlay of cash as compared to the original concept of only a life interest.

Although the original concept referred to all real estate owned during the marriage, most states today do not grant dower and curtesy in the following type of real estate:

1. Real estate that a husband and wife own in joint tenancy with a third party.

2. Real estate that a husband or wife owns in a partnership or corporation with others when the title to the property is held in the name of the partnership or corporation.

3. Real estate that the husband and wife declare as their homestead. Recall that through a widow or widower's right to homestead, the family home is preserved for the family unit until the youngest child is twenty-one.

Just as you can transfer the title to your real estate or encumber it with mortgages, you can destroy your dower and curtesy rights. In most dower and curtesy states any of the following reasons will destroy your rights:

1. Divorce or an invalid marriage destroys your rights. The usual exception is when the divorce is based on the husband's or wife's misconduct.

2. In some states a wife may destroy her dower rights through misconduct even though a divorce is not involved. For example, a wife or husband guilty of adultery or abandonment usually forfeits dower and curtesy rights.

3. In some states a wife may release her dower rights and a husband his curtesy rights by an agreement either before or during the marriage.

4. A husband or wife may release the right to dower or curtesy by signing away the right.

For example, during the marriage you held fee simple title to an apartment building. Although it is not your home, your wife may have dower rights to your interests in it. If you sell the building and your wife signs the deed she automatically releases her dower rights. If she refuses to sign the deed she retains dower rights to a third of your interests in the building.

The objective of dower and curtesy is to provide a surviving spouse a fair share or an amount of money equal to a fair share of the deceased's real estate. Most states protect these rights against attacks by third persons:

1. Usually dower and curtesy rights will be honored before mechanic's liens against the property are allowed, provided the work was done or material furnished sometime during the marriage. (Refer to pages 125–127 for liens.)

2. A creditor with an unsecured debt may place a judgment lien against your property to collect amounts due him. But in most states your dower and curtesy rights will be honored before the lien will be recognized.

3. Regardless of what provisions you make in your will, in most states dower and curtesy rights have precedence over any prohibitive provisions in your will. You may not deny your wife her dower rights through your will.

States that recognize dower and curtesy in some form are Alabama, Arkansas, Hawaii, Kentucky, Massachusetts, New Jersey, Ohio, Rhode Island, Virginia, West Virginia.

State Laws of Descent

If your state does not recognize community property rights and has abolished dower and curtesy rights or passed statutes in lieu of them, upon your death your real estate will be distributed in accordance with your state's laws of descent.

You may direct in your will how you want your estate handled but remember that your survivor probably has the "right of election"—the right to inherit according to the terms of your will or to have your will set aside and inherit according to the laws of the state.

States' laws of descent vary greatly and usually are based upon the relationship of the survivors. For example:

Survivors	New York	Pennsylvania	Illinois
Spouse and two or more children	Spouse gets 1st $2,000 and ⅓ of residue. Balance divided among the children.	Spouse gets ⅓. Balance to the children.	Spouse gets ⅓. Balance to the children.
Spouse and one child	Spouse gets 1st $2,000 and ½ of residue. Balance to child.	Spouse gets ½. Balance to child.	Spouse gets ⅓. Balance to child.
Spouse and no children but parents	Spouse gets 1st $25,000 and ½ of residue. Balance goes to parents.	Spouse gets 1st $25,000 and ½ of remainder. Balance goes to parents.	Spouse gets ⅓. Balance goes to parents.
Spouse with no children or parents	Spouse receives all.	Spouse receives all.	Spouse receives all.

When you buy or sell real estate you are involved in more than the transfer of the tangible property alone, the things you can see and touch. You acquire or relinquish future rights, the rights of a widow or widower in the property.

Become familiar with the future rights granted to you by your state. Learn how these rights can be destroyed or diminished.

Chapter Sixteen

HANDLING TAXATION IN REAL ESTATE TRANSACTIONS

DEFERRING TAXES ON THE PROFITABLE SALE OF A RESIDENCE (SELLER UNDER SIXTY-FIVE)

When you pay $40,000 for a house and sell it for $40,000, there is no loss or gain and no tax. When you invest $40,000 in a house and sell it for $35,000, you suffer a loss of $5,000, but you are not allowed a deduction for losses on the sale of a residence.

When you invest $40,000 in a house and sell it for $45,000, you realize a profit of $5,000. You cannot escape outright from paying a tax on the profit, but you can defer paying the tax if you can prove that:

1. You bought and occupied the second house within eighteen months either before or after you sold the first house ("first house" refers to the house you sell; "second house" refers to the house you buy after selling the first house). If the second house is newly constructed, you must prove that the construction was completed and that you occupied the second house within eighteen months before or within two years after you sold the first house, and

2. You used the first house as your principal residence and are using or intend to use the second house as your principal residence, and

3. The price you are paying for the second house is equal to or greater than the adjusted sale price of the first house.

Providing that the first two provisions are met, compare the cost of the second house with the adjusted sale price of the first house to learn if there is a taxable gain. To arrive at the adjusted sale price of the first house, deduct selling expenses and fix-up costs from the actual selling price.

Adjusted sale price of first house:

Selling price of first house		$40,000
(less) selling expenses of		
Legal fees*	$500	
Broker's commission	$2,400	
Advertising	$200	
Total selling expenses	$3,100	$3,100
Amount received from the sale of the first house		$36,900
(less) fix-up costs of		
Painting†	$400	
Work on lawn	$150	
Domestic help	$200	
Total fix-up costs	$750	$750
Adjusted sale price of the first house		$36,150

To arrive at the cost of the second house, deduct expenses involved in the purchase of the second house from the amount paid for the second house.

Cost of the second house:

Amount actually paid for the second house (less) expenses‡		$40,000
Attorney fees	$400	
Recording fees	$4	
Total expenses	$404	$404
Cost of the second house		$39,596

* Have records to prove legal fees, broker's commission, and cost of advertising.

† Have records to prove that this work was done only to make the house more salable and that it was done within ninety days prior to the selling date and paid for within thirty days after the property was sold.

‡ Have records to prove these expenses.

In our example there is no taxable gain because the cost of the second house is greater than the adjusted sale price of the first house.

Cost of the second house	$39,596
Adjusted sale price of the first house	$36,150

If the amount you invest in your first house is only $31,150 but has an adjusted sale price of $36,150, you realize a profit of $5,000 on the sale of the first house.

Adjusted sale price of the first house	$36,150
Amount actually invested in the first house	$31,150
Your gain	$5,000

Provided that the three requirements are satisfied, regardless of how much greater the adjusted sale price is than your total investment, you may defer the tax on the gain when the cost of the second house is greater than the adjusted sale price of the first house.

If the second house costs less than the adjusted sale price of the first house, but the difference in the selling and buying price is less than the difference between what you invested in the first house and what you received from the sale of it, the taxable gain is based only on the difference between the cost of the second house and the adjusted sale price of the first house.

For example:

Total invested in the first house*	$36,000
Adjusted selling price of the first house	$48,000
Cost of the second house	$44,000

You receive a profit of $12,000 on the sale of the first house.

Adjusted selling price of the first house	$48,000
Total invested in the first house	$36,000
Total gain on sale of first house	$12,000

However, when all the requirements are satisfied, the taxable gain is based on the difference between the cost of the second house and the adjusted selling price of the first house when this amount is less than the actual gain.

* Original cost of the house plus or minus improvements or losses.

Adjusted sale price of the first house	$48,000
Cost of the second house	$44,000
Taxable gain is based on	$4,000

When the second house costs less than the adjusted sale price of the first house, but the difference in the buying and selling price is greater than the actual gain, the tax is based on the actual gain.

For example:

Total invested in the first house	$36,000
Adjusted sale price of the first house	$38,000
Cost of the second house	$34,000

You receive $2,000 more from the sale of the first house than you actually invested in it.

Adjusted selling price of the first house	$38,000
Cost of the second house	$34,000
Difference	$4,000

You will not be taxed on more than the actual gain. In this example, you are taxed only on the $2,000 actual gain.

Fill in the following to determine on what basis the gains you realize through the sale of your house will be taxed:

Cost of the second house	$_____
(subtract) Adjusted sale price of first house	$_____
Answer	$_____

(If the answer is "plus" and all requirements are satisfied, you probably will be allowed to defer any tax on the gain from the sale of the first house.)

When the adjusted sale price of the first house is greater than the cost of the second house, use the following formula:

Adjusted sale price of the first house	$_____
(subtract) Total invested in the first house	$_____
Gain on sale of the first house	$_____
and	
Adjusted sale price of the first house	$_____
(subtract) Cost of the second house	$_____
Decrease in amount invested in a house	$_____

When the "gain on the sale of the first house" is greater than the "decrease in amount invested in a house" the taxable gain is based on the "decrease in amount invested in a house."

When the "decrease in amount invested in a house" is greater than the "gain on the sale of the first house" the taxable gain is based on the "gain on the sale of the first house."

Note that when you sell a house and then buy another, you only defer the payment of the tax on your gain until you sell your house at a profit and then do not buy another house.

Whether you will be taxed on any gains at that time depends upon whether you sell the house for more than the cost basis of the house.

For example:

Adjusted sale price of the first house	$44,000
Total amount invested in the first house	$38,000
Cost of the second house	$40,000

You realize an actual gain of $6,000 through the sale of the first house.

Adjusted sale price of the first house	$44,000
(subtract) amount invested in the first house	$38,000
Gain from the sale of the first house	$6,000

When you satisfy the requirements as to buying a second house, the tax gain is based on the difference between the adjusted sale price of the first house and the cost of the second house if this amount is less than the gain you realize on the sale of the first house.

Adjusted sale price of the first house	$44,000
(subtract) cost of the second house	$40,000
Taxable gain is based on	$4,000

To learn the cost basis of the second house, use the following formula:

Cost of the second house	$40,000
(subtract) nontaxable gain, which is total gain ($6,000) less taxable gain ($4,000)	$2,000
Cost basis of the second house	$38,000

If now you wish to sell the second house and not buy another house—for example, move into an apartment—the cost basis of the second house is $38,000.

If you sell it for $38,000 or less, you realize no profit and probably won't have to pay any tax. Losses on the sale of a residence are not deductible. However, if you sell it for more than $38,000—your cost basis—you have a taxable gain on the amount in excess of $38,000.

AVOIDING TAX ON THE PROFITABLE SALE OF A RESIDENCE (SELLER OVER SIXTY-FIVE)

Unlike a seller under sixty-five, who may defer the payment of tax only when he sells his house at a profit, a person over sixty-five may completely escape paying a tax on profits realized through the sale of his residence.

The following requirements must be met:

1. The seller must have used the house as his principal residence for at least five eighths of the eight-year period preceding the date of the sale. The seller must prove that the house was his principal residence for 1825 days during the preceding eight years. The days do not have to be consecutive and the periods the seller is absent for vacation, within reason, are considered periods the seller used the property.

2. The seller must be over sixty-five when he transfers title or ownership of the property to another. If the seller owns the property jointly with another and they file a joint tax return, this requirement is satisfied when only one of the two owners is over sixty-five on the date the property is sold.

3. The seller must elect to use this tax exclusion in a signed statement that he attaches to his tax return the year the property is sold.

4. The adjusted sale price of the property must not be over $35,000.

The adjusted sale price is different from the actual selling price. Use the following formula to determine the adjusted sale price:

Actual selling price $_____
  Selling expenses
    Legal fees $_____
    Broker's commission $_____
    Advertising $==========
    Total $_____
  Fix-up costs
    (Work done within ninety days prior to the sale date to make the property more salable and paid for within thirty days after the sale date)

item	cost
_____	$_____
_____	$_____
_____	$==========
Total	$_____

Subtract total selling expenses
($_____) and total fix-up costs
($_____) from the actual selling
price $==========
Adjusted sale price $_____

Provided the first three requirements are satisfied, when the adjusted sale price is not greater than $35,000, no matter how great the seller's actual gain is, there is no taxable gain.

For example:

Adjusted sale price	$35,000
Actual amount invested in the property	$27,000
Gain realized on the sale	$8,000

Although the seller realizes an $8,000 gain, if all the requirements are met there is no taxable gain. No deductions are allowed when a residence is sold at a loss, so by all means sell at a profit!

When the adjusted selling price is more than $35,000, the portion of the gain that is taxed is computed using the following formula:

$$\frac{\$35,000}{\$\_\_\_\_} \times \$_____ = \$_____$$

           (gain realized   (tax-free yield)
(adjusted sale   on the sale of
price)   the property)
             AND

Gain realized on the sale of $_____
property
(subtract) tax-free gain $==========
  Taxable gain $_____
For example:
Adjusted sale price $40,000
Total amount invested in the property $32,000
Actual gain from the sale of the property $8,000

$$\frac{\$35,000}{\$40,000} \times \$8,000 = \$7,000 \text{ tax-free gain}$$

Gain realized on the sale of the property	$8,000
(subtract) tax-free gain (see formula)	$7,000
Taxable gain	$1,000

Although you realize an actual gain of $8,000 on the sale of the property, as a senior citizen you are allowed to calculate your taxable gain according to this formula, resulting in a taxable gain of only $1,000.

If you qualify for a tax deferral and elect to use the tax advantage awarded to those over sixty-five you can, according to our example, buy another residence and completely escape any immediate taxable gain.

For example:

Adjusted sale price	$40,000
(subtract) tax-free gain	$7,000
Base figure	$33,000

If the residence you buy from the proceeds from the sale of the first house costs $33,000 or more, you have no taxable gain.

If the second residence costs less than $33,000, the taxable gain is based on the difference between the cost of the second residence and $33,000. But it will not be based on more than the amount of your taxable gain of $1,000.

For example:

Base figure	$33,000
(subtract) cost of second property	$33,000
No taxable gain	$0
Base figure	$33,000
(subtract) cost of second property	$32,500
Taxable gain	$500
Base figure	$33,000
(subtract) cost of second property	$30,000
Gain	$3,000

In the last example, although the second property cost $3,000 less than the base figure, the taxable gain is based on $1,000.

No matter what the difference is between the cost of the second property and the base figure, the taxable gain is not more than the gain realized on the sale of the property less the tax-free gain.

Gain realized on the sale of the property	$8,000
(subtract) tax-free gain (see formula)	$7,000
Taxable gain	$1,000

If you are approaching sixty-five, or are over sixty-five, and are contemplating the sale of your house, whether or not you plan to buy another house, it is time to talk to your attorney. A little careful planning at this stage can save you thousands of dollars.

WHEN A LOSS ON THE SALE OF A HOUSE MAY BE DEDUCTED

Remember that we said a loss resulting from the sale of a residence is not deductible. However, if certain conditions are met that result in changing the property from a residence to a profit-making property, sometimes a loss resulting from the sale of the property can be deducted.

The most common method of converting a residence into a profit-making property is by renting the property.

Rental Property

Before a loss is allowed on the sale of a property that is converted into rental property, the following requirements must be met:

1. Renting the property must produce a profit for the lessor.

This disallows renting a property at a very nominal rate just to satisfy the requirements that the property is rental property.

Actual amount received as rent $_____
(subtract) Charges for interest, repairs, insurance, and other costs   ======
Must show a PROFIT   _____

2. When renting the property the lessor must actually turn over possession of the property to the lessee during the lease period.

You must actually give up physical occupancy of the property during the lease period. You may not put the property up for rent but actually not rent it and declare a loss when the property is sold on the basis that it is rental property.

In some cases when you try to rent a property but are unable to rent it, you may be allowed to deduct maintenance expenses. When you rent only a part of the property, you are allowed to declare a loss only on that portion of the property you converted to rental—profit-making—property.

3. The lessor must prove that he definitely established the property as rental—income-producing—property.

Merely an occasional rental, possibly while you are on vacation, is not enough to establish that the property is used for a profit-making purchase.

When you buy or build a house intending to sell it at a profit but eventually sell it at a loss, in some cases you are allowed deductions.

Investment Real Estate

You are allowed a deduction for your loss only when you can prove that you actually bought or built the house as an investment, planning to resell it at a profit. You must prove that your intent was not to establish the house as your residence.

If you never lived in the house—it remained vacant from the time you acquired it until you offered it for sale—there will be little question as to your intent. You bought it as an investment hoping to make a profit by reselling it. Under these conditions you will be allowed a deduction for any loss you suffer from the sale of the property.

In some cases you may be allowed a deduction on a loss even though you actually lived in the house. But be prepared to prove that your intent was actually to sell the house at a profit. Be prepared to prove that you lived in the house solely:

1. To keep the house in good repair, to provide necessary maintenance.

2. To protect the house from damage by natural or unnatural causes, to protect your investment.

3. To make the house more appealing to prospective purchasers.

Provided you established the property as rental property or as investment property your loss is based on the difference between the selling price and whichever is lower—your original investment or the fair market value of the property when you converted it.

For example, you originally invested $48,000 in your house. When you converted it to rental property an appraiser declared that it had a fair market value of $60,000. After renting the property for two years you sold it for $52,000.

Selling price	$52,000
Original cost	$48,000
Taxable gain	$4,000

Gains are based on the difference between selling price and original costs. (Usually there is an adjustment for depreciation on investment property.) In this example, even though the fair market value was $60,000 and the property sold for only $52,000, there is a taxable gain because the original cost was less than the selling price.

You can declare a loss only when the selling price is less than whichever is lower—your original investment or the fair market value of the property when you converted it.

Original cost	$48,000
Selling price	$44,000
Deductible loss	$4,000

If the fair market value had been $46,000 (less than the original cost of $48,000), it would be used to calculate the loss.

Fair market value	$46,000
Selling price	$44,000
Deductible loss	$2,000

If you anticipate selling rental or investment property at a loss, check with your attorney to be sure that you establish a clear and acceptable basis on which you can be allowed to deduct this loss.

TAX SAVINGS WHEN YOU TRADE RESIDENCES

When you trade residences, taxable gains on any profits are calculated on the same basis as they would be if you sold the first house outright and then bought a second house.

When the exchange value of the second house is greater than the exchange value of the first house and you satisfy the requirements for deferring taxes on the gain, you have no taxable gain until you sell the second house at a profit. (Refer to pages 157–159 for how taxes are handled when you sell a house and then buy another.)

For example:

Exchange value of the second house	$40,000
Amount invested in the first house	$32,000
Gain	$8,000

You realize a gain of $8,000 but because the exchange value of the second house ($40,000) is greater than the amount you invested in the first house ($32,000) you are not required at this time to pay a tax on the $8,000 gain. When the exchange value of the second house is less than the amount you invested in the first house, you have a loss.

For example:

Amount invested in the first house	$40,000
Exchange value of the second house	$32,000
Loss	$8,000

You have no taxable gain since you suffered a loss. Losses on the sale or exchange of a residence are not deductible. It is unlikely, however, that houses with different exchange values will trade evenly. Usually, additional money changes hands to represent the difference in values.

When money in addition to real estate changes hands in a trade, the same rules as used above apply:

For example (when you receive extra cash):

Amount invested in the first house	$32,000
Value of the second house	$40,000
Amount you receive in cash	$4,000

Total you receive in exchange for the first house is

Value of the second house	$40,000
Additional cash you receive	$4,000
Total	$44,000

Your actual gain is $12,000

Exchange value of second house plus $4,000 cash	$44,000
Amount invested in the first house	$32,000
Actual gain	$12,000

This is handled as though you sold your first house for $44,000 and then bought the second house for $40,000.

Total received in exchange for the first house	$44,000
Value of the second house	$40,000
Basis for taxable gain	$4,000

Although you realize an actual gain of $12,000 on the trade, your taxable gain is based on $4,000—the difference between the value of the second house and the total you receive in exchange for the first house.

In our example, if the difference between the exchange value of the second house and the amount you invested in the first house is less than $4,000, you are not taxed on more than the actual gain. When you pay extra cash, the taxable gain is computed by the same method as is used when you receive extra cash in the trade.

For example (when you pay extra cash):

Amount invested in the first house	$32,000
Value of the second house	$40,000
Amount you pay in cash	$4,000

Cost to you of the second house:

Amount you invested in the first house	$32,000
Additional cash you pay	$4,000
Total	$36,000
Value given in the exchange for the second house	$36,000
Value of the second house	$40,000

If all requirements are met, you have no taxable gain at this time. The value of the second house is greater than the exchange value of the first house and your additional cash payment.

POSTPONING TAXES WHEN YOU TRADE REAL ESTATE (OTHER THAN A RESIDENCE)

To be allowed to postpone payment of taxes on gains realized through the trade of real estate other than a residence, you must meet the following three requirements:

1. The real estate traded must be used in a trade, for a business, or held for an invest-

ment, and must be traded for other real estate used in a trade, for a business, or held for an investment.

Real estate used as a residence does not qualify when it is traded for property used in a trade, for a business, or held for an investment.

2. The real estate must be traded for real estate of a "like kind" but not necessarily for real estate used for the same purpose.

For example, a farm may be traded for city property. Uncleared land may be traded for land already developed.

3. The pieces of real estate traded must be of equal market value.

It must be an "even swap" with no additional property of value (for example, cash or mortgages) included in the exchange. If additional property of value is included there may be a taxable gain up to the amount of the value of the "extras" thrown into the trade.

When the "traded for" property is offered for sale immediately after the trade, the exchange of properties does not qualify for special tax treatment.

Before you plunge into a real estate trade, weigh the advantages and disadvantages.

Advantages

You do not escape any tax but you do postpone the tax on your gain until you sell the traded-for property. At that time you will be taxed on the selling price of the property in excess of the tax base on the property. Postponing the payment of the tax enables you to keep your capital intact for investment rather than using it for payment of taxes on your gains.

Disadvantages

By trading you may end up with a lower tax basis for depreciation than if you sell the property outright and then buy the second property.

You are required on a trade deal to carry the same depreciation basis on the traded-for property as you carry on the property you traded. If your trade results in a loss, you may not be able to deduct this loss.

In some cases, if you sell the property outright at a loss and then buy a second property, you can deduct the loss.

It is difficult to find two investment or business properties identical in value so that an "even swap" can be made. Usually one or both of the properties carry mortgages and often there has to be extra cash included in the swap because of a difference in the value of the properties.

Even if additional values, cash or mortgages, are included in the trade, provided the first two requirements are met, it is possible to enjoy a partially tax-free trade.

No matter how great the actual gain, you are not taxed on more than the value of the additional values thrown into the deal. If the actual gain is less than the value of the extras thrown into the deal, you are taxed only on the basis of the actual gain.

When cash is included in the trade as an extra the taxes are handled in the following manner. For example:

Value of the property you trade	$40,000
Value of the property you receive	$45,000
Cash you receive as an extra in the trade	$5,000
You receive the following in the trade:	
Value of the property you receive	$45,000
Cash you receive as an extra	$5,000
Total	$50,000
(less) value of the property you trade	$40,000
Actual gain	$10,000

Although you have an actual gain of $10,000, you are taxed only on the value of the extras thrown into the deal, taxed only on the extra $5,000 cash you received in the trade.

A mortgage is considered an extra whether or not the second party agrees to assume and to pay the mortgage or whether he takes the property subject to the mortgage.

When both a mortgage and cash are included as extras in a trade, the taxes are handled in the following manner. For example:

Value of the property you trade	$40,000
Cash you receive as an extra in the trade	$5,000
Amount of the mortgage on the property you trade	$7,000
Value of the property you receive	$45,000
You receive the following in the trade:	
Value of the property you receive	$45,000
Cash you receive as an extra	$5,000
Amount of the mortgage on the property you trade	$7,000
Total value you receive in exchange for the property you trade	$57,000
(less) value of the property you trade	$40,000
Actual gain	$17,000

Even though your actual gain is $17,000 you are taxed on the lesser amount, on the amount of gain represented by the extras thrown into the trade. For example:

Extra cash in the trade	$5,000
Mortgage	$7,000
Basis for taxable gain	$12,000

When you have a situation in which the value of the extras is greater than the actual gain, the tax is only on the amount of the actual gain.

For example:

Value of the property you trade	$43,000
Value of the property you receive	$40,000
Cash you receive as an extra	$5,000

You receive the following in the trade:

Value of the property you receive	$40,000
Extra cash you receive	$5,000
Total	$45,000
(less) value of the property you trade	$43,000
Actual gain	$2,000

The value of the extras, the cash, is $5,000, but you are taxed only on the actual gain of $2,000. When the value of the extras is greater than the actual gain, you are taxed only on the amount of the actual gain.

TAX TREATMENT OF PROFITS AND LOSSES RESULTING FROM THE SALE OF REAL ESTATE

After the taxable gain on the profitable sale of real estate is established, the amount of taxes is influenced by whether the gain is treated as a capital gain or an ordinary gain.

Capital Gains

Before a profit realized through the sale of real estate is given capital gains treatment, the following requirements must be met:

1. You must have owned the property for more than 1 year and

2. You must own the property as (a) your residence, or (b) an investment, or (c) depreciable trade or business property, and

3. You must prove that the transaction which results in the profit is the kind which is considered a sale or trade.

When these requirements are met, the gain is handled in the following manner:

If you are in the over 50% tax bracket, you are taxed on the capital gain at the 25% tax rate. You will not be taxed at more than the 25% rate on the gain regardless of your other income.

If you are in the under 50% tax bracket, add only one half the amount of your capital gain to the amount of your ordinary taxable income. The result is that you are taxed on your capital gains at only one half the ordinary rate.

For example:

A single person, not head of a household, has $18,500 income from his employment plus a $6,500 profit from the sale of some real estate.

Taxable income for the year, exclusive of the gain realized from the real estate transaction	$18,500
(add) Profit from the sale of the real estate which profit qualifies for capital gains tax treatment and so is taxed at only one half the ordinary rate (50% of $6,500)	$3,250
Total taxable income	$21,750
The tax is (federal income tax only considered)	
Tax on the 1st $20,000	$6,070
Tax on the next $1,750 (48% of the amount over $20,000)	$840
Total tax	$6,910

ORDINARY INCOME

A gain realized through the sale of real estate is treated as ordinary income when:

1. The profit results from the sale of real estate used in a trade or business and which is not held for more than 1 year or

2. The profit results from the sale of real estate acquired primarily for resale, realty which is put into an inventory, and realty which a person buys and sells as a dealer.

When the profit results from the sale of the above type of real estate, the profit is handled as ordinary income and is taxed on the same basis as other ordinary income.

For example: (use the same situation and figures as were used in the example of a capital gain).

Taxable income for the year exclusive of the
gain realized from the real estate transaction $18,500
(add) Profit from the sale of the real estate $6,500

Total taxable income $25,000
The tax is (federal income tax only considered)
Tax on the first $22,000 $7,030
Tax on the next $3,000 (50% of the total
over $22,000) $1,500

Total tax $8,530

When the gain is treated as ordinary income instead of as a capital gain, you pay $1,620 more in taxes.

	Total income	Total taxable income	Total tax
When the gain is treated as ordinary income	$25,000	$25,000	$8,530
When the gain receives capital gains treatment	$25,000	$21,750	$6,910
Difference in taxes			$1,620

In the example, $1,620 is saved (by paying less tax) when the gain resulting from the sale receives capital gains treatment. The amount saved depends upon the total taxable income but there is a savings in tax dollars to be had when the gain qualifies for capital gains treatment.

Will the profits you realize from the sale of your real estate qualify for capital gains tax treatment? When the sale of real estate results in a loss, the amount you may deduct from your income tax depends upon whether the loss is an ordinary loss, a capital loss, or a nondeductible loss.

ORDINARY LOSS

Before a loss resulting from the sale of real estate is treated as an ordinary loss, you must prove that:

1. The real estate is depreciable property which is used in your trade or business and that you held the real estate for more than 1 year, or

2. The loss resulted from the sale of real estate you owned primarily for resale, realty which you put into an inventory, and realty which you buy and sell as a dealer.

When the loss results from the sale of the above type of real estate, when computing the net taxable income, the total amount of the loss is deducted from the income.

For example:

A single person has an income of $18,500 and suffers a $6,500 loss from the sale of real estate.
Total income $18,500
(subtract) Total loss resulting from the
sale of the real estate $6,500

Total taxable income $12,000
The tax is (federal income tax only considered)
Tax on the first $10,000 $2,190
Tax on the remainder (32% of the
amount in excess of $10,000—$2,000
×32%) $640

Total tax $2,830

CAPITAL LOSS

Before a loss resulting from the sale of real estate is considered a capital loss, you must prove that:

1. You held the real estate for more than six months as investment property and that it is not real estate used in your trade or business.

When the loss results from the sale of this type of real estate and your loss is in excess of your capital gains—possibly earned through the sale of other investment property—the first $2,000 of the loss is deducted from your income during the year in which you suffer the loss. Any loss in excess of $2,000 can be deducted in the following years.

For example (based on the same situation as described under ordinary loss):

Total income $18,500
(subtract) With a capital loss you deduct
the first $2,000 loss the first year and the balance
during later years $2,000

Total taxable income $16,500
The tax is (federal income tax only considered)
Tax on the first $16,000 $4,330
Tax on the remainder (42% of the amount
in excess of $16,000—$500×42%) $210

Total tax $4,540

NONDEDUCTIBLE LOSSES

Losses on the sale of real estate used for personal uses such as a house—residential real estate—are not deductible.

If residential property is converted into rental or income-producing property, any loss on it is handled in the same way as for trade or business property and a loss may be taken as an ordinary loss.

When determining your taxable income, you are not allowed to deduct a nondeductible loss from your income.

For example (based on the same situation as described under ordinary loss):

Total income	$18,500
(subtract) You may deduct nothing with a nondeductible loss	$0
Total taxable income	$18,500

The tax is (federal income tax only considered)

Tax on the first $18,000	$5,170
Tax on the remainder (45% of the amount in excess of $18,000—$500×45%)	$225
Total taxes	$5,395

In these examples, if you qualify for a loss for ordinary loss treatment, instead of for treatment as a nondeductible loss, you save $2,565 on your federal income tax.

When the loss is treated as:	Total income	Amount of loss	Total taxable income	Total tax on income	Take-home money
Nondeductible	$18,500	$6,500	$18,500	$5,395	$13,105
Capital loss*	$18,500	$6,500	$16,500	$4,540	$13,960
Ordinary loss	$18,500	$6,500	$12,000	$2,830	$15,670

* You are only allowed to deduct $1,000 of the loss the first year as we did in the example. The total advantage of the capital loss to the seller is not reflected in this table.

If you are anticipating a loss through the sale of real estate, check with your attorney or tax consultant to learn whether you can qualify for the loss to be handled as an ordinary loss or even as a capital loss.

And check before you close the deal! Possibly waiting another month before your closing—thereby satisfying the one year holding requirement for an ordinary loss—can save you thousands of tax dollars.

Chapter Seventeen

REAL ESTATE AS AN INVESTMENT

Real estate as an investment offers no guarantees but it does provide exciting possibilities for those who are informed and who move cautiously.

The selling price of single dwelling residences has gone up three times faster than the cost of living in the last four years. It seems to be the height of wisdom to at least own your own house. Property ownership is one of the best buffers available today against the declining buying power of the dollar.

Owning real estate as an investment—for example, rental property—isn't always rosy. You have no guarantee that the property will be rented all the time or even part of the time. Your overhead continues whether or not you have tenants. Even though real estate investments offer no

guarantees, many people do invest in real estate and make fortunes through their investments.

One of the things which make investing in real estate attractive is that often real estate can be bought without paying the full purchase price. Ordinarily up to one half the purchase price can be financed. You can spread your investment dollars over a wider area and create greater possibilities for dollar growth.

For example, when you are able to finance half of the purchase price, with $40,000 you are able to acquire property worth $80,000. This gives you the profit potential from an $80,000 investment although you only invest $40,000 of your money.

Another attraction is that depreciation on investment property is based on the full cost of the property regardless of what portion of the purchase price is financed. For example, if the property cost $80,000 and it is bought with $40,-000 cash and a $40,000 mortgage, the depreciation schedule is based on the $80,000 cost.

This allows you to take depreciation charges on a mortgagee's investment which enables you to build an equity in property through tax-free dollars. These tax-free dollars are produced through the interplay between deductions for depreciation and mortgage payments.

Deductions for depreciation do not require a cash outlay in the year the deduction is taken but they do reduce taxable income in that year.

Taxable income		*Cash income*	
Rental income	$80,000	Rental income	$80,000
(less) Operating expenses which include mortgage interest	$32,000	(less) Operating expenses which include mortgage interest	$32,000
	$48,000		$48,000
(less) Depreciation	$8,000	(less) Mortgage payment	$4,800
Taxable income	$40,000	Cash income	$43,200

Amortization payments (mortgage payments) do require a cash outlay in the year they are paid. When the depreciation deductions are greater than the amortization payments, tax-free income is produced.

For example:

Depreciation	$8,000
Mortgage payments	$4,800

As long as the amount taken for depreciation is greater than the payments on the mortgage, tax-free income is produced.

In this example, although you have a cash income of $43,200, because of the allowance for a depreciation deduction, the taxable income is only $40,000. You earn $3,200 tax free.

Cash income	$43,200
Taxable income	$40,000
Tax-free income	$3,200

When the situation is reversed—when the mortgage payments are greater than the depreciation deduction—the taxable income exceeds the actual cash income.

When this occurs it is time either to refinance to reduce the mortgage payments to a level at which they are below the depreciation deduction; or it is time to sell and take a capital gain on the profit.

The tax-free dollars, gained when the depreciation deduction is greater than the mortgage payments, are tax free only until you sell the property. When you sell, the amount taken for de-preciation is subtracted from the cost of the property to compute the gain made on the sale of the property.

For example:

Selling price		$180,000
Base:		
Original cost	$200,000	
Cost of improvements	$20,000	
	$220,000	
(less) depreciation:		
$10,000 a year for		
eight years	$80,000	
	$140,000	$140,000
Taxable gain on the sale of the property		$40,000

You escape some taxes during the years because the depreciation is greater than the mortgage payments but you have a profit due to the depreciation's being deducted when you compute the cost basis of the property.

If all the requirements are met, the gain when you sell will be taxed at the capital gains rate only, which is half the normal rate and never more than 25%. (For your gains to qualify as capital gains you must hold the property more than one year and use straight-line depreciation. If you use other than straight-line depreciation, any gain for 1964 and later years, in excess of what your gain would be if you had used straight-line depreciations, is treated as ordinary gains and you are taxed on the total gain.)

The savings come from the tax-free dollars gained over the years through the straight-line depreciation deductions taken on the property

	Your income tax bracket				
Your gain	20%	30%	40%	50%	70%
Tax-free dollars earned over the ten years	$32,000	$32,000	$32,000	$32,000	$32,000
Your cost Tax paid on the gain of $40,000 from the sale. Capital gains rates apply which are 50% of normal rates and not more than 25%	$400	$600	$800	$1,000	$1,000
Net gain Net tax-free dollars earned	$31,600	$31,400	$31,200	$31,000	$31,000

compared to the amount of tax paid at capital gains rates on the sale of the property.

For example (considering only federal income taxes):

Taxable gain on the sale of the property	$40,000
Tax-free dollars earned during the years you own the property ($3,200 a year for ten years)	$32,000

When the property is sold at a profit and the tax on the gain is allowed at the capital gains rate, the tax is much less than the amount of the tax-free dollars saved over the years.

Amount of tax-free dollars earned as a result of the straight-line depreciation deduction's being greater than the mortgage payments	$_____
(less) Tax paid at capital gains rates as a result of the property's being sold at a profit	$_____
Net tax-free dollars earned	$_____

This alone results in savings on income taxes but, in addition to this allowance, there are methods by which the tax resulting from a profitable sale of real estate can be even further reduced.

Taking payment for the property over a number of years instead of all in one year makes it possible for you to reduce the amount of your taxable gain each year. To qualify, the payments must be spread over two years or more and your initial payment may not be more than 30% of the total value.

Spreading the gains over a number of years, by treating a fixed percentage of each payment as the gain, results in a reduction in the amount of yearly gain and yearly total taxable income.

Another opportunity available to the investor in real estate is a method by which he can defer his capital gains to years when he has offsetting losses. This can reduce or completely eliminate any tax on the gains. In some cases a person may defer his gain to years when his tax bracket is less than 50%. Remember that when gains qualify for capital gains treatment, they are taxed at one half the normal rate but never at more than 25%.

Other tax advantages are available to the investor in real estate. Are you interested? Move cautiously.

Many fortunes have been made and still are being made through real estate investments but the road to these riches can be a perilous and even a disastrous one for the uninformed.

If you are contemplating real estate as an investment, get acquainted with a local real estate broker. Property values are rapidly changing and your local real estate broker is your best source for an astute evaluation of current real estate opportunities in your area.

Get acquainted with an attorney too. Laws as to the buying and selling of real estate are constantly changing. And get acquainted with a tax consultant. Visit him frequently, especially before you make a purchase or a sale. Plan your maneuvers in advance and figure out what the tax consequences will be.

Finally, words of sound encouragement to investors in real estate from the great New Dealer, sounding here rather more like Benjamin Franklin than Franklin Delano Roosevelt: "Real estate cannot be lost or stolen, nor can it be carried away. Purchased with common sense, paid for in full, and managed with reasonable care, it is about the safest investment in the world."

APPENDIX

FORMS ORDINARILY USED IN REAL ESTATE TRANSACTIONS
(All or part of these may be used)

Listing contract An employment contract between seller and broker in which the seller agrees to pay the broker commission when the broker produces a buyer at a price and on terms agreeable to the seller. The person who signs the listing and agrees to pay commission should receive a copy of the listing.

Offer to purchase Lists the price and conditions under which the buyer agrees to purchase the property. The buyer should receive a copy of his offer to purchase.

Offer to purchase with acceptance or sales contract Contract, signed by buyer and seller, which outlines what each agrees to in the exchange of property. Buyer and seller each receive a copy.

Closing At this transaction the buyer receives ownership of the property and the seller receives his selling price. Depending upon local practices, there may or may not be a formal form used.

Broker's statement to seller Usually if the broker makes expenditures on behalf of the seller—for example, pays to have an abstract brought up to date or for attorney's fees—the broker will submit an itemized statement to the seller.

Mortgage (or) trust deed The instrument by which a borrower pledges his real estate as security for debt. Whoever borrows the money should have a copy of this instrument.

Note (or) bond An unconditional promise in writing by the borrower that he will repay the amount he borrowed by a certain date. The borrower should have a copy of the note or bond.

Land contract A contract by which an owner transfers legal possession of his property to a buyer with the promise that he will also give him legal title when the buyer fulfills all the terms of the agreement. When contract is used, buyer and seller should each have a copy of the land contract.

Earnest money receipt The buyer ordinarily makes an earnest money payment when he makes his offer to purchase a property. He should receive a receipt for this payment.

Deed The deed is evidence that a previous owner has transferred legal title of a property to another person. The deed should be recorded in the office of the county recorder in the county where the property is located. The buyer should receive the deed or a copy of it.

Owner's policy of title insurance An agreement in which a title insurance company guarantees to defend the person named in the policy from attacks against his title to the property. If this is used, the buyer should have it or a copy of it.

Abstract of title A history of the recorded documents pertaining to a piece of land, starting with the patent and extending to the certificate issued by the abstract company. If this is used, the buyer should have it or a copy of it.

Attorney's opinion of title A commitment by an attorney in which he declares that the title to the property in his opinion is marketable; or, if it is not marketable, what should be done to make it a marketable title. The buyer should have his attorney's opinion before he accepts title to the property.

Certificate of title When this is used, instead of an abstract and attorney's opinion of title, the buyer receives a certificate from an attorney declaring that he has examined the records and states that there are no liens or encumbrances against the title. The buyer should have the certificate or a copy of it.

Torrens certificate When used, this is a certificate issued by the court declaring that the title has been recorded in the new owner's name. Prior to issuing it, the court invited lien claimants to sue and then dismissed or settled all known liens against the title.

Survey This is a diagram of the property showing all encroachments. It is made by a surveyor; its purpose is to establish boundary lines. Usually the buyer requests that the seller furnish him with a survey as part of the contract. The buyer should have a copy.

Certificate of occupancy When used, this is a certificate from the local building inspector certifying that the building conforms with local housing codes. The buyer should have a copy.

Insurance policy on the property Depending upon the type of policy, this insures the property owner against damage to the property. Whoever paid for the protection should have the policy.

Bills for utilities and taxes At the closing, costs of water, electricity, sewage, and rents will be prorated for the current month. Also real estate taxes and charges for special assessments can be prorated at the closing. The seller should have these bills available at the closing.

Escrow agreement Possibly as a condition of the sale, the seller was to have the house repainted. To assure that this be done, the buyer asks that his attorney hold $500 in escrow until the job is finished. Both parties to the agreement should have a copy of any escrow agreements.

INDEX